WITHDRAWN

HARVARD LIBRARY

WITHDRAWN

Fighting the Antichrist

Fighting the Antichrist

A CULTURAL HISTORY OF
ANTI-CATHOLICISM IN TUDOR ENGLAND

Leticia Álvarez-Recio

Translated from the Spanish by Bradley L. Drew

sussex
ACADEMIC
PRESS
Brighton • Portland • Toronto

Copyright © Leticia Álvarez-Recio, 2011 (original Spanish copyright © 2006).

Rameras de Babilonia. Historia cultural del anticatolicismo en la Inglaterra Tudor was originally published in Spanish in 2006. This translation is published by agreement with Ediciones Universidad de Salamanca.

Rameras de Babilonia. Historia cultural del anticatolicismo en la Inglaterra Tudor se publicó originalmente en español en 2006. Esta traducción se publica con el permiso de Ediciones Universidad de Salamanca.

The right of Leticia Álvarez-Recio to be identified as Author of this work has been asserted in accordance with the Copyright, Designs and Patents Act 1988.

2 4 6 8 10 9 7 5 3 1

First published in 2011 by
SUSSEX ACADEMIC PRESS
PO Box 139
Eastbourne BN24 9BP

and in the United States of America by
SUSSEX ACADEMIC PRESS
920 NE 58th Ave   Suite 300
Portland, Oregon 97213-3786

and in Canada by
SUSSEX ACADEMIC PRESS (CANADA)
90 Arnold Avenue, Thornhill, Ontario L4J 1B5

All rights reserved. Except for the quotation of short passages for the purposes of criticism and review, no part of this publication may be reproduced, stored in a retrieval system or transmitted in any form or by any means, electronic, mechanical, photocopying, recording or otherwise, without the prior permission of the publisher.

The English translation of this work from the Spanish original has been subsidised by the Andalusian regional government (Junta de Andalucía).

British Library Cataloguing in Publication Data
A CIP catalogue record for this book is available from the British Library.

Library of Congress Cataloging-in-Publication Data
Alvarez Recio, Leticia.
[Rameras de Babilonia. English]
Fighting the Antichrist : a cultural history of anti-Catholicism in Tudor England / Leticia Álvarez-Recio.
  p cm.
Includes bibliographical references (p.   ) and index.
ISBN 978-1-84519-427-7 (h/c)
  1. Anti-Catholicism—England—History—16th century. 2. Catholic Church—Controversial literature—History and criticism. 3. England—Church history—16th century. I. Title.
BX1775.G7A3813 2011
282'.4209031—dc22

2010022923

Typeset and designed by Sussex Academic Press, Brighton & Eastbourne.
Printed by TJ International, Padstow, Cornwall on papers certified in accordance with the rules of the Forest Stewardship Council. This book is printed on acid-free paper.

Contents

List of Illustrations — vii
Acknowledgements — viii

PROLOGUE — 1

CHAPTER ONE
Anti-Catholic Discourse during the Reigns of Henry VIII (1509–1547) and Edward VI (1547–1553) — 7
Crisis of Succession and the Reason of State — 7
From Anticlericalism to Anti-Catholicism: Origins of the Catholic Stereotype — 18

CHAPTER TWO
Mary I (1553–1558) and the Discourse of Victimhood — 38
The Return to Catholicism and the Spanish Threat — 38
Anti-Catholic Pamphlets: An Admonitory Discourse — 45
Dramatic Literature: The Dark Side of the Reformation — 55

CHAPTER THREE
Elizabeth I (1558–1579): A Failed Attempt at Reconciliation — 62
The Iconographic Construction of Elizabeth I and its Anti-Catholic Implications — 62
The Quest for Internal Religious Conformity and the European Political Crisis — 68
Responses to the *Status Quo*: Propaganda and Representation: The Pope's Renewed Role as Protagonist in Pamphlet Literature — 73
Anti-Catholic Theatre and Doctrinal Problems — 77

CHAPTER FOUR
Elizabeth I (1580–1603): Gloriana and the Victory of Protestantism — 100
The Apogee of the Elizabethan *Status Quo* — 100
Reformist and Catholic Discourse in the Face of Accusations of Disloyalty — 101
Elizabeth I as Head of European Protestantism — 106
The Triumph of Gloriana — 113

v

Pamphlet Literature in the Second Phase of Elizabeth's Reign: The Multiple "Other"	114
The Society of Jesus	115
The Spanish Stereotype and the Black Legend	119
The Imperial Image of Elizabeth I	123
Anti-Catholic Discourse and the New Theatre	127
Anti-Catholic Discourse at Court	127
Anti-Catholic Discourse in Public Theatres	134
An Example of Anti-Catholic Discourse in the Private Theatre	152
EPILOGUE: Nostalgia for Elizabeth and Anti-Catholic Discourse	157
Notes	170
Recommended Reading	216
Index	220

List of Illustrations

The cover illustration is reproduced with permission of the British Library: "The Pope as Antichrist riding the Beast of the Apocalypse." Artist unknown. From *Fierie Tryall of God's Saints* (1611). The Folger Shakespeare Library. Copyright © The British Library Board (1125.b.26).

The plate section is placed after page 98.

1 *Edward VI and the Pope*, ca. 1570. Portrait number 4165, Portrait number 4165, copyright © National Portrait Gallery, London.

2 George Gower, *The Armada Portrait*, 1588. Reproduced by kind permission of His Grace the Duke of Bedford and the Trustees of the Bedford Estates.

3 "Elizabeth as a Second Constantine." Engraving from the first edition (1563) of *Actes and Monuments* by John Foxe. Reproduced by permission of The Huntington Library, San Marino, California.

4 Crispin van de Pass, *The Jacket Portrait*, 1596. Reproduced by kind permission of the Parham Foundation, Parham House, West Sussex.

Acknowledgements

I would like to thank Professors Manuel J. Gómez-Lara, Rafael Portillo and M. José Mora for their useful comments on an earlier draft of this work.

Thanks also to Mr. Bradley L. Drew for his translation from the Spanish original.

Finally, I am very grateful to Ediciones Universidad de Salamanca for their permission to reproduce this English edition, and to Mr. Antonio Sánchez Sacristán for his kind and valuable help in the process.

Fighting the Antichrist

A CULTURAL HISTORY OF
ANTI-CATHOLICISM IN TUDOR ENGLAND

Prologue

Anti-Catholicism has formed part of the political and religious thought of a broad sector of English society from the sixteenth century to the present day. At critical moments, the image of Catholics, or of the Spanish, have provided a source of cohesion for Protestant England, satisfying certain historiographic parameters that exalted the English people's autonomous and liberal character (the *whig* concept of English history) as compared to the absolutist and obscurantist tendencies associated with the Catholic powers. The complexity of this process raises a great many questions that critics and historians continue to ask: "When and why did anti-Catholicism become such a powerful element in English national identity? When and why did it begin the trajectory that established it as an ever more ensconced hallmark of English, and then British, nationalism through the seventeenth and eighteenth centuries?"[1]

Since the middle of the 1970s several attempts have been made to answer these questions, efforts that have brought into focus many of the principles upon which this cultural construct was based.[2] The most significant result of these studies has been the introduction of the Catholic perspective, by means of the use of numerous theological, political and autobiographical texts that challenge the monolithic conclusions of the Protestant tradition. The comparison of the texts produced by both tendencies has opened up new inroads to historical and literary research, demonstrating many paradoxes and contradictions.

This book analyses the mechanisms that the state and certain Protestant groups employed to exclude the Catholic community, to a greater or lesser degree, and thus guarantee the stability of the English Protestant regime. I have chosen the Tudor age as a historical point of reference from which to observe the evolution of anti-Catholic discourse, from its origins in the 1530s up until the time of its greatest expansion, the last twenty years of the sixteenth century, when religious and nationalistic motives united to bring about collective action against Rome and its followers. The original aspects of the study lie both in the specificity of the time period (in general, the writings cited analyse fewer texts, and usually cover shorter time periods), and in the primary sources chosen to undertake it (plays and political and doctrinal pamphlets). A reading of these sources reveals numerous incongruities in the anti-Catholic discourse, in addition to other implicit messages that might pass unnoticed by scholars of our century, but not by their Renaissance audiences.

These two genres were not chosen by mere chance. In the case of the pamphlets, their authors[3] could freely express their support of or disagreement with the regime, thanks to the anonymity of the genre and the fact that printing and distribution were carried out either in foreign countries or clandestinely.[4] Their reduced format and easy, cheap and, above all, quick method of production also worked in favour of such freedom of expression. Even so, the increased public readership was also a cause of restlessness, because it became more difficult to control the responses of a growing number of readers.[5]

The influence of pamphlet literature on public opinion is undeniable, and its rise coincided with that of the printing press and the increase in literacy rates. Nevertheless, the illiteracy of much of the public barely posed an obstacle, since anti-Catholic discourse also cultivated a full visual vocabulary – texts often appeared with detailed illustrations – that made up for it. Thanks to the repeated use of the same images, the public were able to associate different texts to the stories they told.[6] Added to this was the oral transmission of all sorts of news and rumours that had been circulated by means of printed texts.

The price of the pamphlets – especially as the sixteenth century went on – was generally lower than that of attending plays, which aided the proliferation of the former, as well as their assimilation within the literate circles of English society.[7] Also, the majority of the texts printed were of a religious nature, underscoring the close alliance between the printing press and the doctrinal discourses of Protestants and Catholics.[8] The people's growing preoccupation with political and religious conflicts both justified and fuelled such efforts. Pamphlets could educate or even entertain, but above all they attempted to promote certain attitudes in their readers and to move them to act, in one direction or another.[9] It should come as no surprise, then, that many of these writings were organized according to the rhetorical principles of Cicero (very popular during the Renaissance), according to which one should seek to avoid the possibility of any discordant interpretation:

> [It was necessary to include] A preamble with which to attract the listener, or to incite him to become informed; expose the matter briefly, in a plausible and clear manner, so that its subject can be understood; demonstrate the pertinent arguments, destroy those of the adversary, and do this not in a disorderly fashion, but concluding each of the argumentations in such a way that the conclusions follow the supposed premises in demonstration of each point; finally finish off with a peroration that either inflames or appeases.[10] (Translation by BD)

The pamphleteers made use of these rhetorical precepts to delimit the responses of the growing number of readers. The words of Umberto Eco on medieval allegories could easily be applied in this case:

The reader of the text knows that every phrase, every letter, is open to a multiform series of meanings that he must uncover; he will even, depending on his frame of mind, elect the key point of the reading that he finds most exemplary and will "use" the work according to such meaning . . . But, in this case, "openness" does not at all mean an "absence of clarity" in what is communicated, "infinite" possibilities of form, or a freedom to enjoy the text at will; there is but a single kernel of outcomes of the reader's enjoyment, prearranged and conditioned in such a way that the reader's interpretative reaction never escapes the author's control.[11] (Translation by BD)

The relationship between dramatic literature and political pamphlets was readily apparent: the same authors who wrote the pamphlets also wrote plays, dramatic texts were published in pamphlet form, and in many cases they shared common sources and material in their arguments. But there were substantial differences: while dramatic performances were limited to the space of the stage, the pamphlet was a material object that could occupy multiple spaces successively and simultaneously.[12] Despite that, drama could be more effective in presenting both sides of a conflict onstage, since, as Professor John King explains, Protestant theatre dramatized the complexity of human behaviour, as compared to the unidirectional view of pamphlet literature.[13] Although the conclusion of these plays almost inevitably imagines a restoration of governmental order and doctrine, the dramatic portrayal of conflicting points of view gave room for more objective considerations, since the attractive, seductive nature of the characters opposed to the established order sometimes reveals errors within the system itself, and in particular illuminates the complexity that was involved in the process of portraying the Catholic "other".

John Gillis, in his book *Shakespeare and the Geography of Difference*, analyses the construction of the "other" by means of a very specific paradigm: that of geographical borders. Thus he goes back to Greece to explain how the concept of the barbarian was assimilated by way of the discourse of Greek tragedy and of the Athenian *polis*, and was then transmitted to Rome and, later, into the varieties of imperial discourse that appeared in Renaissance Europe. The idea of the barbarian not only implied mere geographical difference, but was inevitably tied to moral transgression and, above all, confusion, on both a biological and social level (incest and racial mixing).[14] During this same period, also, the concept of citizenship was intimately linked to the creed of each city. Fustel de Coulanges explains that the citizen was recognized as such insofar as he participated in the city's religious life, through which he would acquire any civil and political rights. Thus, religion established a deep dividing line between citizens and outsiders, which affirmed the identity and centralized locus of the former in the face of foreign enemies.[15]

The present study focuses on a different paradigm to that of geography, and on another historical period, but the ideas outlined above are just as relevant to the texts considered here. When we speak of geographical borders, it is possible to determine both those who are within such limits and those who are outsiders. However, the paradigm of English anti-Catholicism poses a serious problem: that of clearly identifying an enemy operating from within. In a society that up until 1533 had officially been part of the Church of Rome and that continued to preserve Catholic traditions and rituals even after the schism, the process of discriminating between a "true" Englishman and another who was not was not an easy task, and the fear of a faceless adversary grew among broad sectors of the public.

In a period when the permutations of politics and diplomacy were most clearly intermixed with ecclesiastical matters, religious intolerance increased, and with it the use of strategies to escape the penalties that were imposed by the law without renouncing the Catholic faith. Within this context, anti-Catholic discourse created a stereotype that attempted to establish a differentiating paradigm, and so set the boundaries of the new Protestant orthodoxy. The conflict lay in the difficulty of defining an internal "other", an "other" who had been born and lived in England and who was probably still a neighbour.

The rhetorical mechanism that sought to transform the internal into the external and the domestic into the foreign was often contradictory. Analysing this process, K. U. Syndram has shown how the mutual dependency between the images of oneself and of the "other" transcends the limits of a text and predetermines individuals' real experience of the world. When they are elaborated in a literary or artistic medium, these images become conventions that escape any critical examination as to their veracity.[16] Sigmund Freud alluded to this very idea when he described how the masses

> think by means of images that are evoked associatively with each other, such that they appear to the individual in a state of free imagination . . . Inclined in every direction, the masses are only excited by excessive stimuli. Whosoever would influence them need not present logical arguments but should paint them the most vivid images, exaggerate, and repeat this endlessly.[17] (Translation by BD)

This would explain the obsessive re-elaboration of certain characters that one sees in the Protestant literature of the Tudor period, since they are the result of the accumulation of a great many metaphors, intended to portray as an unimpeachable reality the vicious and corrupt character of Spain and the Church of Rome in contrast to the purity of England. It is interesting to note, however, the way in which such a body of images was also used by Catholics to assert their Church's authority in the face of the innovators of the day. The discourse was the same, only the positions and objectives to be defended changed.

The purpose of this study is to analyse the origins and evolution of this process, which would give rise to the principal elements of English Protestant identity in the Tudor reform period. To this end, we will study here the interaction between the various texts, official and clandestine, that shaped the framework of anti-Catholic discourse. The analysis of the selected texts takes clear account of concepts such as intertextuality and intersubjectivity,[18] while being aware of the constant dialogue between them, independent of the genre or historical period to which they are assigned.

The selection of materials varies with the genre being discussed: theatre or pamphlets. As to the former, I have tried to be exhaustive, and only those works which, in my view, are relevant to the research topic are considered; the pamphlet texts dealing with anti-Catholic polemics are, however, quite numerous, so I have attempted to make a broad and representative selection. I have also included the testimony of individual Catholics as well as fragments of royal decrees, chronicles and private letters, with the intention of offering the greatest number of possible perspectives that can enrich and illuminate the understanding of anti-Catholic writings. Also analysed, therefore, are descriptions of royal entries and coronation ceremonies, in order to delve more deeply into the role that anti-Catholic discourse played in the production of the monarchical image. The study of these texts clarifies the apparent incongruities of many of the dramatic works and reveals the contradictions and implicit messages found in them, aside from mere questions of doctrine and denunciations of Rome. Additionally, attempts have been made to situate the various rhetorical components of this discourse – emblems[19] as well as biblical, mythological, and geographical references – focusing particularly on their potential ambiguity. Finally, I examine how, when and why the Catholic and Spanish stereotypes and their various political implications came together, as well as the differences that arose according to the particular medium – pamphlets or dramatic works – that are under examination.

With regard to the structure of this book, it is interesting to note that the historical image of these hostilities that has come down to the present day is the result of the negotiation and confrontation of various different Catholic and anti-Catholic discourse(s), and that the pamphlet and drama literatures had already articulated this same reality for their contemporaries. There is no historicist intent in this work other than to clearly demonstrate this construct's ideological nature, and the way it conditioned individual perceptions. The study is divided into four chapters, which correspond to the reigns of the different Tudor monarchs under whom anti-Catholicism emerged and evolved. These were the reigns of Henry VIII and Edward VI (CHAPTER ONE), the reign of Mary I (CHAPTER

Prologue

TWO) and that of Elizabeth I, which, because of its length, and especially its relevance in the formation of anti-Catholic discourse, occupies CHAPTERS THREE AND FOUR. Given the difficulty of providing a definitive analysis of a cultural process that continues to unfold even today, the conclusions deal briefly with anti-Catholicism in the first years of the reign of James I, not in the form of a new chapter but as a summary of the basic elements of the discourse that, by that time, were already fully assimilated.

CHAPTER ONE

Anti-Catholic Discourse during the Reigns of Henry VIII (1509–1547) and Edward VI (1547–1553)

CRISIS OF SUCCESSION AND THE REASON OF STATE

The Act of Supremacy of 1534, by which Henry VIII was proclaimed head of the English Church, became – or at least so it was presented – the dividing line that separated medieval England, beholden to the power of the papacy, from the England that, influenced by the new reforming currents and European humanism, was to place itself at the vanguard of the Protestant cause. Nevertheless, and in spite of an intensive campaign of propaganda in support of the new system, this change was too extreme to be universally accepted. A large segment of the English people continued not to understand the reasons for the schism, as the numerous revolts that arose in the years 1534 to 1537 demonstrate;[1] Catherine of Aragon continued to enjoy great popularity among what were still her subjects, and the king himself appeared to be ambivalent in certain matters of doctrine.

Until 1525, the approximate date of the appearance of the first problems in the king's marriage, England had been involved, to a greater or lesser degree, on the European political stage. With the accession of Henry VIII to the throne in 1509, an era of constant wars and alliances with France, different German states, Spain and the papacy was inaugurated. The presence of Cardinal Wolsey at the beginning of Henry's reign seemed to moderate the aggressive tendencies of the young monarch, who delegated part of his power to him between 1520 and 1530. At that time the sovereign offered absolute military and economic support to the popes in Rome, and even argued that he himself should be placed at the head of a crusade in support of Christianity.

The appearance of Martin Luther significantly influenced this process. Following his excommunication in 1521, Luther's creed spread throughout large parts of Europe and England. Henry, who had already received various appeals from Rome to put a stop to this offense against the Catholic world, responded with the *Assertio Septem Sacramentorum* (1521), a treatise that the English monarch himself wrote in response to

Luther's work *De Captivate Babylonica* (1520). In his document Henry reaffirmed papal supremacy, condemned the schism, and defended the indissolubility of marriage – three ideas that evoke a certain irony when considered from the vantage point of only one decade later. There is in fact relevant testimony from the king himself, who, years later, denied writing the book and laid responsibility for it with Wolsey.[2] The *Assertio* went through more than twenty editions and translations in many of Europe's capitals – Rome, Frankfurt, Paris, Antwerp, Cologne, and London, among others – and gave rise to a lengthy polemic.[3] Six weeks after the book's publication, the pope granted the English monarch the title of *Defensor Fidei*. Even in 1525, the year that the disputes surrounding his marriage began, the king stood firm in the face of the Protestant offensive.

The sovereign had other matters with which to concern himself. After sixteen years of marriage, he had not provided England with a male heir, and the problem of succession was gaining prominence as a factor that could jeopardize the regime's stability. The possibility of a civil war or of the union of England with some continental power did nothing to calm the monarch, who began to consider the lack of a successor as a form of divine punishment. Catherine's attempts at childbearing had indeed been unlucky; three of her children died within hours of birth, and two more did so within weeks; Princess Mary, who was ten years old in 1526, was the only surviving child. The failure of his marriage – if not in moral terms, then in the light of political demands – was a reality. On another front, relations with Emperor Charles V, Catherine's nephew, were deteriorating seriously as a result of the emperor's reluctance to collaborate in the military plans of Henry VIII.

By 1527, divorcing Catherine had become an urgent matter, as much on a diplomatic as on a dynastic level. In May, an extraordinary tribunal was convened in which the validity of the monarchs' union was discussed. Three weeks earlier, Spanish imperial troops had sacked Rome and taken Pope Clement VII prisoner. If Catherine appealed to this tribunal, she could count on the support of the pontiff, as he was in the hands of the queen's nephew.[4] In spite of Wolsey's diligence in attempting to prevent news of the proposed divorce from reaching him, Charles V was informed almost immediately, and did not hesitate to show firm support for his aunt. Catherine, then, could rely on the backing of the greatest power on the continent, of the most distinguished figures within the cultural and religious panorama of Europe[5] and, most of all, of the Holy See. The fight for his divorce was not going to be easy for Henry VIII, who, despite the support of universities and religious schools, was consistently in a clear position of disadvantage compared to his wife.

Henry VIII employed two main arguments to question the validity of his marriage. The first of them was based on the position that the union of a man with his brother's wife is incestuous and therefore contrary to the Law of God. Secondly, it was argued that as a consequence of the first argument, the dispensation offered by Pope Julius II in 1503, thanks to which the English monarchs had been allowed to wed, was invalid. The first argument was based on two biblical passages from Leviticus that condemned this type of relationship: "Thou shalt not uncover the nakedness of thy brother's wife: it is thy brother's nakedness" and "If a man shall take his brother's wife, it is an unclean thing; he hath uncovered his brother's nakedness, they shall be childless" (Lev. 18:16; 20:21). A strict interpretation of these passages made it possible for the monarchs' illicit union to be blamed for England's problems of succession. It was, therefore, the king's obligation to dissolve this marriage, a union that could lead the country to ruin.

Continuous delays by Rome, which did not seem able to make a decision in favour of divorce, made Henry and his advisors restless. These delays were presented as attacks on the English people in *A Glasse of the Truthe* (1532), a political and theological treatise – possibly written by Henry himself – in which the reasons for the king's divorce were explained and justified. Laid out as a dialogue between a theologian and a lawyer, it emphasized the invalidity of the royal marriage, Catherine's disingenuousness, and the rejection of papal authority. The text has great relevance within the process of creation of English anti-Catholic discourse, since it constituted the monarchy's first attempt to justify its disobedience to the Holy See by vilifying the pope:

> For the cause why I speke hit, is for the great weightie cause of christendome: concernynge the kynges separation from the quene. [?]it is tossyd and turned over the hye mountaynes, laboured and vexed at Rome, from iudge to iudge, without certayne ende or effecte: beynge very perillous for his hyghnesse, and moche more dangerous (if God helpe nat) for ys his poore and lovinge subjectes.[6]

However, Catherine's popularity among the people posed a serious obstacle to the king's wishes, and as rumours circulated that he was going to repudiate her, public consternation increased. Aware of this, the king felt obliged to frame his actions not as an offense against the queen, but rather as an unavoidable obligation that he was bound to fulfil as a king and a Christian. According to Henry, Catherine's qualities were so evident that if he had to remarry, and if such a marriage was admissible, there was no doubt that he would choose her again as his wife.[7] But if Cardinal Campeggio[8] considered the union between the monarchs to be contrary to the Law of God, the king, even at the cost of great pain to himself, had to abandon his wife and recognize that he had been living in sin for twenty years.[9]

Henry VIII insisted on his blamelessness and cultivated his image as the victim of Rome's intolerance: he presented himself as a new Christ, who, by this divorce, would atone for the sins that had been imputed to his people due to the accursed marriage. The stage was set for the confrontation with the papacy, and all that remained was to legitimize it, as is seen in *A Glasse of the Truthe*:

> Alas, is hit nat great pitie, the prince having so manifest and playne groundes for hym, he beynge also so lovyng to us as he is, so glad and so harty to take paynes for this his comune welth: that we, whiche that be his subjectes, shuld be to hym so unnatural, that other for other considerations worldly, or for reportes of sinistre persons, shulde lette to do our very duetie to him? Ye and leavynge the playne truth, rather to beleve maligners agaynst his cause, whiche soweth more division than obedience: [and] not according to our very duties to stycke fastly and surely unto hym, whiche is in the very right. (sigs C3v-C4r)

The passages from Leviticus stood in contrast to another biblical text that supported the opposing argument: "If brethren dwell together, and one of them die, and have no child, the wife of the dead shall not marry without unto a stranger: her husband's brother shall go in unto her, and take her to him to wife, and perform the duty of an husband's brother unto her" (Deut. 25:5).[10] Henry tried to reconcile the two texts by suggesting the mystical or spiritual character of the verses from Deuteronomy:[11]

> For in the begynnynge that lawe semeth to propoune and lymytte certayne poyntes and circumstaunces, without the whiche that lawe ware no lawe: as playnely by the texte hit selfe hit dothe manifestly appere. That is to saye, fyrst as whanne they dwelled together: the seconde, whanne he dyed without yssue: the thyrde, to suscytate the brothers sede: the iiii that his fyrste sonne shuld be called by his brothers name: the fyrst cause and grounde of that lawe was that the name within the tryebe shulde not be forgotten nor abrogate in Israel: mooste specially the trybe of Judas, whereof it was prophecyed that our lorde shulde come of. Neverthelesse to the intent that ye myghte well perceyve that this lawe was trulyer to be observed in the mysticall sense, than in the litterall, and that most specially nowe by us christen men: the smalnes of the payne whiche foloweth it, declareth it full well. (sigs B4v, B5r)

For the monarch the conclusive proof is the Word of God, which, according to Henry, is stated only in the verses from Leviticus, in which the Deity speaks to Moses so that he may communicate His wishes to the people. This is an early appearance, therefore, of the contraposition so often repeated in anti-Catholic discourse between the Sacred Word and human laws, although in this case the debate is formulated on the basis of different biblical passages, a potentially perilous practice since it could appear to cast doubt on the divine inspiration of some of them.

The Reigns of Henry VIII (1509–47) and Edward VI (1547–53)

Theological discussion between supporters and detractors of the divorce seemed endless, and in no way guaranteed the sovereign the outcome he desired. It was necessary, therefore, to seek a second pretext that would ensure him the possibility of victory. The dispensation of 1503 became the prime target of the king and his sympathizers, since its invalidation would implicitly annul the royal marriage. After several fruitless petitions,[12] the king's advisors centred on a statement Catherine herself had made following the death of her first husband, Prince Arthur. At that time she had given assurances that she was still a virgin, and therefore saw as unnecessary a papal bull to permit her to remarry. She was unaware of how dangerous this statement could become, and in fact the Spanish ambassador at the time, Dr. Puebla, had ignored her statement and supported the decision of the English to ask for the dispensation from Rome. The Royal Council, determined to exploit all possible irregularities in their efforts to render the papal decision illegitimate, made out of Catherine's affirmations one of their primary weapons. In addition, Pope Julius II himself had not seemed very convinced of the document's legality at the time, since he had included in his wording the term *forsan* – "perhaps" – when referring to Catherine's virginity. The queen's supposed virginity implied the possibility that her first marriage could have been invalid; and this would bring with it the annulment of whatever dispensation may have been granted for a second wedding, since this would have arisen from an erroneous premise, as is stated in *A Glasse of the Truthe*:

> Our soveraynes counsell founde fautes in the bulle, which ware sufficient in lawe (as lawyers doth affirme) tho the pope mighte dispense (as he may nat indede) to annihilate and fordo the mariage bitwene the king and her. For where one of the fautes whiche the kinges counsell founde was that after the dethe of prince Arthur in suynge for dispensation she atteyned a bull, wher of the suggestion was nat true. Beynge in one place (as it was said) in the bull *Forsan cognitam . . . Whiche maketh a doubte of that thynge whiche she knew well ynoughe byfore. And thereby hit may well be coniectured that she feared to tell the truethe, lest that the pope perceyvinge that she had bene knowen by prynce Arthoure, wolde never have dispensed with this lattre maryage.* (Sigs E5v, E6r) (My emphasis)

In 1528, a second dispensation had appeared, the original of which had probably been discovered in Spain, and of which Catherine possessed a copy.[13] The new document required to be treated differently and separately from the 1503 bull, and at no point was it examined by the Commission charged with the matter of the divorce. *A Glasse of the Truthe* also attempted to demonstrate the illegitimacy of this document: "She [Catherine] thanne fearynge that by this faulte and other, whiche ware founde in the sayde Bulle, she shulde fayle of her purpose: dyd accordynge as tofore is sayde, in her defence exhibyte this *brieffe*: thynkynge thereby to take away al these doughtis which were founde in the Bull, and specially that of *Forsan cognitam*" (sigs E6r-v).

The king and the members of his Council protested in 1532 that it was too late to prove the queen's virginity, though Henry insisted that his brother Arthur had always asserted to the contrary and that he, Henry, had no doubt that if the marriage had not been consummated, Catherine's parents would have raised an objection, which had never happened. Consequently, Catherine's word was discredited, and with it, all of her actions and those of her supporters (sigs E5v, E6r-v, E8r-v).

The situation was critical. The king and his followers had exhausted practically all their options, and the problem had become steadily worse since 1527. In 1528, Wolsey and Henry VIII had tried to convince Catherine to renounce her marriage and retire to a convent. The queen ignored such proposals, and when the court convened in 1529, she rejected its authority and legitimacy and appealed directly to Rome. Shortly afterwards, in the summer of 1530, Henry was summoned to appear in public audience before the Holy See, which ignited a long debate and was the immediate cause of the schism. In August of the same year, the monarch laid claim to his own authority before the papacy[14] and threatened, for the first time, a separation from the Church of Rome. The pontiff refused to address the question of the divorce any further until Henry appeared for the appointed audience, something that he was not disposed to do. That October, the king considered the possibility of ignoring the conditions set by the Holy See, and discussed this in meetings with various civil and ecclesiastical lawyers. Surprisingly, their response was negative.[15]

The *privilegium Angliae* became a recurring theme from 1530 onwards, each time national autonomy was demanded. During these years another treatise appeared, written by representatives of the English Church, which sought to inform English subjects of the problems around the divorce and the attitude that the king had adopted to deal with them. *Articles Devisid*[16] (1533), which sets out to identify the people with their king, insists mainly on the pope's abuse of power, and justifies accordingly the refusal to submit to his commands. Like *A Glasse of the Truthe*, it anticipates one of the questions that would take on greatest importance from 1534, following the royal Act of Supremacy: the imperial doctrine justifying the divine right of kings, against the pretensions of the papacy to usurp their powers. This doctrine goes back to the medieval disputes over the powers of popes and emperors, and had taken on special relevance in the previous century. The French monarchs had defended their autonomy by claiming sovereign authority for themselves under the motto "*rex in regno suo est imperator*", and Henry VIII himself had adopted a similar attitude after he had taken Tournai in France in 1515, forcing its inhabitants to take an oath whereby they were subject to his authority alone. His criticisms of the then pope's attempts to intervene in the ecclesiastical administration of the territory had been emphatic, and in some ways foreshadowed what was to come.[17] Similarly, it was not without irony that many of the arguments that the Tudor king used in his defence had already been brought together in *The Sack of Rome: Dialogue of Lactancio and an Archdeacon* (1527), the work of the secretary to Charles V himself, Alfonso de Valdés. In this "dialogue", the emperor is pardoned for any and all responsibility in the sacking suffered by the papal city at the hands of his troops, while the pontiff is blamed directly for it:

> [Lactancio] told this to us, that since the Emperor, by defending his subjects, as is his obligation, the pope took up arms against him, doing that which he should not do, and unmade the peace and waged new war in Christendom. [N]or does the Emperor claim responsibility for the evil occurrences, since he did that to which he was obliged in defending his subjects; nor may the pope be without such responsibility, since he did that which he should not do in breaking the peace and waging war in Christendom.[18] (Translation by BD)

This idea was one of the pillars upon which Henry VIII (and his successors) based their attack on papal power.

In addition, *A Glasse of the Truthe* and *Articles Devisid* both emphasize the supremacy of the councils of the church over the Bishop of Rome, whose authority should be subordinate to the decisions made in them, so that any opposition by the popes to their resolutions constituted a clear act of heresy. England thus identified itself with the true Church of God in the face of the corruption of Rome:

> For howe may the byshoppe of Rome or any other primate be so bolde as to breake the canons the which every one of them voweth to kepe? And solemnly professed the same? . . . Who coulde thinke that one Byshoppe myghte destrue the actes of so many hooly fathers . . . Who coulde thynke that the churche of Rome, whiche in dede is but a doughtere of the churche universalle, myght destroye the lawe of her mother? . . . Therfore the pope of Rome oughte to rule the churche of Rome by the universall counsels and the lawe of gode: and no wyse the contrarye. (*A Glasse of the Truthe*, sigs D3v-D4r)

Hence, the papacy is blamed for the division of the Church,[19] and obeying the decrees of the general church councils in the interests of unity and carrying out internal reforms in the ecclesiastical structure are equally presented as urgent necessities. Both Henry VIII's rejection of papal authority and the taking of steps towards a renewal of the Church of England were thus justified (sigs D5v, D6r).[20]

The first of these steps had to be the dissolution of the illicit marriage, in order to free the people from the sin in which their king had been living for nearly twenty years. This was – or at least so it was presented – a question of conscience, in which Henry, unlike the pope, was merely following God's word and the opinions of the most learned persons of Christendom: "our prince wyl not . . . lyve an incestuous lyfe and abhomynable. These thynges be so contrarious to equitie, reason and iustice, that by his doinges it maye appere, what a maner a man he is, accordynge to a texte of scripture, whiche saith: *Ex operibus eorum cognoscetis eos*" (*Articles Devisid*, p. 8). The English people were called upon, therefore, to obey their king and offer aid to no other power in his kingdom (pp. 6–7).

The argument was taken even further, with a justification of disobedience towards any of one's superiors whose orders contradicted divine law. Although in this case the reference to the pontiff is obvious, this dangerous recommendation could have been extended to any sovereign who failed to fulfil his obligations to the people. Though here regicide or civil disobedience is not mentioned directly, this would also be the argument that when used by the Jesuits during the reigns of Elizabeth I and James I provoked such disquiet among Protestant ranks. The doctrine of which the Society of Jesus would later be accused was thus already expounded in the reformist polemics of the first years of the conflict, though here with the opposite intention to attack the pope:

> If he that is in power above the, as to whome thou owest thyn obedience, comaunde the to do any thynge that thou oughtest nat to do: there contemne and refuse his power. If he byd the do one thynge, and god an other: obeye god contempnynge hym. If that man byddeth, god forbydde: Shall I (sayeth saynt Bernarde) here man, and nat here and obey god? Therfore (as sayeth holy Basile) if we be bydde of any man to do that is contrarye to the commaundementes of Christe: there is hye tyme for us to saye, we be bounde more to obeye god thanne men. (*A Glasse of the Truthe*, sig. D8v)

This argument served to explain to the citizens their king's reasons for continuing conflict with Rome, despite the threat of excommunication.

Ann Boleyn's pregnancy precipitated the separation from Rome in January 1533, bringing with it the urgent need to legitimize the future heir. The king remarried on the 25th of that month, and immediately declared the Statute in Restraint of Appeals, which confirmed England's jurisdictional autonomy and established that all lawsuits and legal disputes – including that over the king's marriage – had to be heard and debated within the sovereign English state, without appeal to any other earthly authority.[21] On 23 May 1533, Archbishop Cranmer declared the marriage to the Spanish queen to be annulled, and on the 31st of that month the king's new wife was crowned. Condemnation from Rome was not long in coming, and gave the king a few months – until September – to reflect, and to accept Catherine again or risk excommunication.[22]

The Royal Council responded to this threat by rejecting the authority of the pontiff, who, they said, had insulted the English people because they "have [first] made holsome lawes, for the commoditie and welthe of our prince and realme, secondly, bycause they do preiudicate his worldly appetites and profyte" (*Articles Devisid*, p. 8).[23]

As could have been foreseen, the king continued with his plans, and made himself head of the Church of England in 1534 by proclaiming the Act of Supremacy. The office of supreme pontiff was relegated to the status of a mere bishop, and his authority was subordinated to that of the king. An appeal was made to imperial doctrine to legitimate the national ecclesiastical council, through which the separation of the Church of England from Rome had been carried out.

The internal reform of which so much had been said became a simple transfer of power, which greatly distressed both those who wished to maintain their affiliation to Rome and did not understand the reasons for the change, and those who, influenced by Protestant currents of thought arriving from Europe, held out hopes for more profound changes. Although anticlerical sentiment was deeply rooted and far-reaching, there were probably only a few who supported the royal decisions with enthusiasm, particularly the expropriation of monastic lands and the new fiscal policies.[24] These attitudes on the part of his contemporaries contrast with the idealized portrait of the English monarch that Richard Grafton paints in his *Abridgement of the Chronicles of Englande* in 1572:

> This Prince of personage was talle and mighty, in witte and memory excellent. Of such maiestie, tempered with humanitie and gentleness, as was comely to so noble a Prince. In knowledge of good letters, he farre exceded al kings of Englande before his tyme. For his magnificence and liberalitie, he was renowned throughout all the world, and in hys tyme was great alteration of things . . . whatsoever great things hee tooke in hande, the same he honourably atchyved and finished, to hys great fame, honor and praise.[25]

It is not surprising to find this type of comments in a work that summarizes the history of the nation and exalts the good deeds of its leaders, but one must also consider that Grafton was writing in the middle of the Elizabethan era, when Elizabeth's powerful propaganda machine reinvented the figure of Henry VIII as the origin and father of the Church of England. This idealized portrayal of his character thus legitimized his successors and the national and ecclesiastical project that they undertook.

Even so, the idea of creating a new church did not seem to have been part of the king's original plans; at no time had he rejected the unity of the Christian world. In fact – and despite the fact that the religious agenda that was set in motion just after the split was clearly influenced by Erasmus – it was not long before the king manifested a marked conservatism, which frustrated proponents of reform.

Anti-Catholic Discourse

However, this religious policy changed after 1538 due to the influence of the king's new secretary, Thomas Cromwell. The first acts concerning the sale of church lands, announced in 1536, were joined by a variety of laws that suppressed the worship of parochial and monastic images.[26] In 1538 the crown permitted the first public burnings of sacred objects, seen as acts that confirmed the new changes in doctrine and sought to create an identification between the people and the religious politics of their monarch. The English populace, nonetheless, was unprepared for such demonstrations of royal iconoclasm, and in 1538, when the second Act of Dissolution of the monastic orders was announced, the nation remained watchful in the face of the new laws against the idolatrous practices of Catholicism.[27]

The ambiguity of official policy provoked a rapid succession of events that were dangerous to the stability of the monarchy and the government. Hence in 1540 the king, conscious of the conflicts being generated by Cromwell's politics, decided to distance himself from the iconoclasm of the previous years.[28] The execution of the royal minister on 28 July of that year put an end to England's process of doctrinal evolution, and ushered in a period of religious conservatism that would last until the death of Henry VIII in 1547.

The accession of Edward VI to the Throne raised expectations among English Protestants, but the new king's coronation on 20 February 1547 already showed evidence of the difficulties of reconciling the figure of a monarch sanctioned by tradition with the demands of radical Protestantism

Aware of the contradiction between the iconoclastic denunciations of the influential reformist sector and an event characterized by medieval ritual and tradition, the Royal Council decided to cut short the coronation ceremony, "for the tedious length of the same which shuld weary and be hurtsome peradventure to the Kinges Majeste being yet of tendre age fully to endure and bide owte; *and also for that many poinctes of the same were suche as by the lawes of the realme att this present were natt allowable*" (my emphasis).[29] Nevertheless, the act of anointment was carried out without comment by the Royal Council; only Archbishop Cranmer saw it necessary to explain why ceremonial custom was followed in this particular case. In his opinion, they represented admonishments that were made to the king to fulfil his obligation as a monarch chosen by God, "not in respect of the oil which the bishop useth . . . The oil, if added, is but a ceremony: if it be wanting, that King is yet a perfect monarch notwithstanding, and God's anointed, as well as if he was inoiled."[30] This commentary reveals the impossibility of presenting the image of the monarch without alluding to what was, in the judgment of Protestant leaders, Catholic tradition. Hence, in spite of the attempts to strip the coronation of its ritualism, its resulting hybrid nature still caused problems.

The Reigns of Henry VIII (1509–47) and Edward VI (1547–53)

Moreover, the residual conservatism of the government remained in effect, as was demonstrated in the first *Book of Common Prayer*, produced by Thomas Cranmer and approved by parliament in January of 1549. Cranmer presented a simple English translation of the Latin liturgy, although he replaced the idea of the Mass with that of thanksgiving, and the doctrine of transubstantiation with that of communion as a memorial to the death of Christ. Its only novelty was its use of the vernacular, since the most orthodox clergy could still interpret the book within a Catholic sensibility.[31] In spite of the efforts of the Lord Protector Somerset to introduce many of the changes sought by reformers during the reign of Henry VIII, the parochial clergy's conservatism continued to be the primary obstacle to the eradication of the worship and traditions of the Church of Rome.

The discontent of a broad sector of the English people was reflected in the revolts that took place in 1548 and 1549. Though they arose for economic reasons, these uprisings also called for a return to the religious system of the reign of Henry VIII. Nevertheless, the fall of the regent Somerset and the rise of the Duke of Northumberland changed the political and religious panorama, since Northumberland's very position within the government depended upon the disappearance of the conservative elements that had characterized the previous era. The Catholic Bishops Gardiner and Bonner were deposed, and several measures were introduced to do away with the rest of Catholic worship. In 1550, Cranmer revised his *Book of Common Prayer*, by then influenced by Martin Bucer, one of the most powerful advocates of European Calvinism. The resulting edition was a midpoint between the earlier text and the most radical reforming currents, and envisaged a clean break with the nation's Catholic past. Although it was approved in April of 1552, the book's use was not permitted by the crown until November of that year, by which time it was too late.

Edward VI died in July 1553. During the six years of his reign, Parliament had imposed Protestant doctrine and liturgy on the nation, but had been unable to "naturalize" the principles of the reformed church among the population.[32] Even so, during the Elizabethan period, the image of the young monarch would be that of a zealous defender of the Reformation. A prime example of this is the anonymous portrait *Edward VI and the Pope* from 1570 (Figure 1), in which Edward appears as the inheritor of his father's project of reform (Henry is shown on his death bed, gesturing toward his son for the viewer's benefit). Edward's identification with the Bible (open next to him) is immediately made clear. Though he did not exercise royal authority throughout the whole of his reign, the portrait legitimizes his image as that of a sovereign who governs with the counsel of Somerset (positioned at his side) and the members of his Council, and with the official approval of his father. In the background is an iconoclastic vignette representing the destruction of idolatry during his reign. The reality was different in the final years: Northumberland's corruption and extreme ambition indirectly allowed a ray of hope for Mary Tudor, who, after the Duke's failed attempt to keep her from power, acceded to the throne as the first woman to wear the crown of England. Nineteen years later, Albion was once again Catholic.

From Anticlericalism to Anti-Catholicism: Origins of the Catholic Stereotype

Anticlerical sentiment had been deeply rooted among a broad sector of the English people since the fourteenth century, when the first voices of protest at the wealth and power of the ecclesiastical hierarchy had been raised.[33] For example, an explicit denunciation of the abuses committed by Catholic priests was made in the anonymous *The Lantern of Liʒt* (1410), particularly regarding the luxury and finery of their churches:

> Our material church that is ordained for parishioners, where they come together, shall be made with virtuous means and in honest measure. But in every respect it must be avoided that in this church any pride or luxury should show surpassingly, beyond the bounds of poverty, either in stone, timber or lead, either in glass, lime or plaster, either in bell, lamp or light, either in chalice, book or vestment, either in steeple, seats or painting, or other ornaments that belong to the church, and diligently this must be marked, that they bow to poverty, to eschew vain glory of this world, and glorify the cross of God.[34]

Such attacks were led by a substantial group within the laity, which demanded a more active role in the religious life of the country, and whose influence extended to every social level: the Lollards. Led by John Wyclif, they were characterized by their biblical fundamentalism and their critical attitude toward the traditional ideas of the Sacraments, the right of clergy to have worldly possessions, and ultimately the supremacy of the pope.[35] They insisted on the need to return to the simplicity of the Primitive Church and, most of all, to make the Scriptures accessible to laymen. Consequently the first translations of the Bible into English were made by Wyclif's followers, and carried out between 1382 and 1392.

The Lollard Bible establishes a clear connection between the worship of images and the clergy's supposed desire for riches by denouncing the profound economic differences between the ecclesiastical hierarchy and the laity, who were portrayed as victims of the priests' boundless ambition:

> Now men kneel, and pray, and offer fast to dead images that have neither hunger nor cold; and despise, beat, and slay Christian men, made to the

image and likeness of the Holy Trinity. What honour of God is this to kneel and offer to an image, made of sinful man's hands, and to despise and rob the image made of God's hands, that is, a Christian man, or a Christian woman? When men give not alms to poor needy men, but to dead images, or rich clerks, they rob poor men of their due portion, and needful sustenance assigned to them of God himself; and when such offerings to dead images rob poor men, they rob Jesus Christ.[36]

Convinced of the pernicious consequences of the seductive power of art in the church, and the temptations that this caused, they did not hesitate to encourage acts of iconoclasm and the expropriation of monastic lands, and so became dangerous elements for the ecclesiastical and political power structure. Lollardism retained its strength until well into the reign of Henry VIII, and continued to exist alongside Lutheranism when the latter appeared in the country in the decade prior to the Reformation. Once this had begun, the Lollards as a group began to lose the role of *provocateur* they had fulfilled for almost two centuries, since they became incorporated in the government's propaganda campaign. The fact that at the height of Cromwell's policies (1538–1539) many of the people were distrustful of the supposed Lollardist tendencies of their monarch is clear evidence of the assimilation of this group's ideals by the state.[37]

Anti-Catholic discourse, which ostensibly originated as a result of the schism, took advantage of the popularity of the anticlerical feeling that already existed within large segments of English society; Henry VIII did no more than exploit it. The anticlerical ideas that could be adapted best to monarchical interests were those regarding monastic property and the authority of the Holy See, points that the English sovereign sought to make use of in order to justify the Act of Supremacy and the expropriation of the monasteries. The state saw itself as the inheritor of the work of the first reformers, who until a short time earlier had been persecuted.

The texts analysed in this chapter are representative of the beginnings of English anti-Catholic discourse, and many of the principles that had defined Lollardist doctrine are echoed in them. Discussion of doctrinal aspects of the new faith forms the most significant element in most of them. Although the pamphleteers make use of many of these arguments in treatises that defend the position of the government, in other examples they draw away from this line of thought and are instead critical of various aspects of monarchical policy. As a result, one can see a definite distancing between the reformist pamphlets and the type of Protestantism that was championed by the nation's leaders. Anti-Catholic discourse, though it was employed by both tendencies, revealed that many gaps remained to be filled in this vision of an apocalyptic universe of opposing forces that English Protestantism attempted to create.

Following the separation from Rome, the need arose to justify the schism, and construct a Catholic "other" that would serve as an antagonistic counterpoint to the new Church of England. The evolution from anticlericalism to anti-Catholicism was a consequence of the new distribution of authority between the Church and the English state, together with the confrontational position with regard to the pope. The arguments remained similar; all that changed were the labels that identified the two sectors in binary opposition to one another. The opposing terms that had dominated the discourse of the first reformers – the collective of the laity against the ecclesiastical hierarchy – can be seen to be replaced by the Church of England and the Church of Rome. Hence, the description of the new enemy is articulated by means of one of the most traditional images in anticlerical discourse: the stereotype of a pliable clergy, characterized by its corruption, untruthfulness and hypocrisy, its love of wealth, and its clearly idolatrous tendencies.

The Church of Rome's unbridled ambition occupies a central position in the portrayal made of its representatives. In drama and in pamphlets, this extreme desire for wealth is attacked repeatedly – "When they smelled ryches and daylye coveted more and more, then was goddes worde laide aside. And afterwarde overcame they all things (as they do yet) with money . . . Lordes, dukes, emperours, Kinges, landes and people have made subiect to them"[38] – as is their tendency toward simony as a means of obtaining still greater financial rewards, as can be seen in the words of Avaritia in *The Three Laws*, by the playwright John Bale: "Father nor mother, Syster nor brother/ I spare not in my moode/ I feare neyther God, nor his ryghtfull rod/ In gatherynge of goode./ But howse and medowe, from the poore wydowe/ I spare not for to take/ Ryght heyres I rob, and as bare as Job/ The fatherles I make."[39]

Hence numerous parallels are also established between Rome and various biblical "others", whether peoples who were enemies of Israel, as in the case of the Babylonians (*The Beginning and Endyng*, sig. H3r), corrupt cities – Sodom (*The Beginning and Endyng*, sig. G3v; *The Three Laws*, sig. I4v),[40] Babylon (*The Three Laws,* sigs I2v, K2r-v, K3r; *King Johan*, I, 369), and Gomorrah (*The Three Laws*, sig. I4v; *The Beginning and Endyng*, sig. G3v) – or personages known for their impiety, such as Nebuchadnezzar and Simon Magus (*The Three Laws*, sig. F1v). Also, a particularly seductive and deceitful power is associated with the Roman church by likening it to female figures such as Jezebel and the Whore of the Apocalypse (Rev. 17), one of the motifs that was most widely used at the time to represent falseness and idolatry (*The Three Laws*, sig. F1r; *King Johan*, I, 369; II, 2414; *The Beginning and Endyng*, sig. H2r).

Criticism of Catholic superstition and idolatry in fact represents one of the principal links with Lollardism, and is a constant from the reign of Henry VIII onward. The sacraments and rituals of Rome were described as the fruits of its own creation, with no foundation in Scripture,[41] and a number of playwrights set out to parody Catholic ceremonies, as did John Bale, who included a song at the end of *King Johan*

The Reigns of Henry VIII (1509–47) and Edward VI (1547–53)

in which the attacks on papal corruption and idolatry were summarized in a burlesque tone.[42]

The denunciation of superstition and simony complement each other, and appear tightly linked together in the majority of the texts. Bale routinely includes them in long lists that would appear comical and ironic to the spectator:

> The dead sayntes shall shewe both visyons and myracles/ With images and rellyckes he shall wurke sterracles./ He wyll make mattens, houres, masse and evensonge/ To drowne the scriptures for doubt of heresye;/ He wyll sende pardons to save menny sowles amonge/ Latyne devocyons with the holy rosarye/ He wyll apoynt fastynges and plucke downe matrimonye;/ Holy water and breade shall dryve awaye the devyll;/ Blesynges with blacke bedes wyll helpe in every evyll. (*King Johan*, I, 996–1004)

In the Protestant view, these ceremonies constituted the principal form of manipulation that was used by the Catholic clergy to control their followers,[43] an ignorant mass, disposed to blind obedience.[44] The power and capacity for control that the Roman hierarchy possessed over its flock, the Protestant texts suggested, carried extremely dangerous implications, which led pamphleteers and dramatists to associate Catholic worship and tradition with illicit and treacherous activities such as magic and the theatre (*The Three Laws*, sig. C1v; *King Johan*, II, 2683; *The Beginning and Endyng*, sig. H2r).

In general, the authors are unanimous in characterizing the Mass as the principal event within which all these superstitious customs were put into practice. It is described as a show, a spectacle in which the original simplicity of the Word of God disappears to be replaced by idolatrous ceremonies in which entreaties are made to natural elements such as water and salt, and the cross and images of saints are worshipped (*The Hunting and Finding*, sigs A7r, B5r-v) The original meaning of the ceremony is adulterated and substituted by dramatization, which can only lead to wrong-headedness on the part of the believers. The metaphor of theatre, according to the Protestants, is made manifest in the strange vestments and dramatic gestures used during Mass,[45] which explains the concern of the Bishop of London during the reign of Edward VI, Nicholas Ridley, to do away with priestly robes for Protestant ministers. This polemic would be repeated at the beginning of the reign of Elizabeth I.

This controversy acquires a doubly ironic role in the case of plays. In the anonymous work *Albion Knight* (1537),[46] for example, the character Iniuri (Injury) appears on stage in overdressed finery. His ostentation characterizes the sense of sight as deceitful, and subject to being taken in by false appearances; against him are set the claims of auditory experience as the only means of knowing the divinity, as his opponent, Justice, declares at the beginning of the play:

21

O yet in apparell is great abusion/ If it be framed without dyscretion/ For in all apparell there may a great token bee/ Of fraylnes, of pryde, and instabylytie,/ If comen assyse therin use no measure/ For then is apparell a wanton foolysh pleasure/ And foly, best mede is of presumpcyon/ When nature or reason used resumpcyon.[47]

By relating the priests to dramatic acting, the authors attribute the same sinful character to them, discrediting them as deliverers of the Word of God or as intercessors on His behalf. This criticism took on a farcical nature when it was presented on stage and the forces of Catholicism were played by actors, who in some cases even used real priests' habits.

The frequent accusations levelled against theatre of immorality bind it closely together with witchcraft and the corrupt image presented of Rome. The association made between witchcraft and idolatry explains the constant criticism of transubstantiation, and the opposing insistence on the memorial and thanksgiving nature that the Communion ceremony possessed according to Protestants (*The Hunting and Finding*, sigs D6v, D7r). Thus, the battle against idolatry became a battle against the doctrine of transubstantiation, considered to be the worst perversion of the Christian faith.[48]

This type of denunciation was strengthened by comparing the pope and his Church with figures or groups from the Bible who were characterized by their idolatrous tendencies, such as the already-mentioned Nebuchadnezzar, and the Egyptians (*The Three Laws*, sigs F1r-v, I4v; *King Johan*, I, 1108–1110; *The Hunting and Finding*, sig. E3v). The latter were also associated with magic in geographical writings of the period.[49]

On some occasions the criticism extends beyond the Church of Rome, reaching the monarchy itself, mostly during the peak periods of religious conservatism. This is the case in *The Hunting and Finding out of the Romish Fox* (1543), which took the form of an extensive allegory through which to denounce the lack of thoroughgoing reforms within the Church of England. The author describes himself as a hunter in pursuit of a wild beast (sig. A2r). Such a monster – a "Romish fox" – represents Catholic holdouts that persisted in the kingdom, whose bishops – characterized as hunting dogs – had not taken part in the hunt but had instead hidden and fed their prey. The fox[50] remained obscured among the altars, covered by the rich garments of the Catholic priests, which thus impeded his discovery by the intellectuals from Cambridge and Oxford. The writer also gives the following enumeration of the Catholic traditions and beliefs that were still seen in the country:

> The Canon lawe is the lawe of the Popes chyrche, even at this houre, then yf the Canon lawe be the lawe of the chyrche of England, *the popes chyrche and the Englysh Chyrche are all one concernynge theyr ceremonyes and lawe, and then in what thynge do they differ?* . . . then muste the chyrche of

Englande also be a popyshe chyrche . . . But the pope is the heade of every popyshe chyrche, and by youre saynge the chyrche of Englande is a popyshe chyrche, *therfore the pope by yowre sayêg is the heade of the chyrch of England* . . . But in Christes and the Apostles tyme and in the tymes of the holy martyres was the moste perfect chyrch, therfore then was the perfytest lawe of the chyrch . . . But the canon lawe was not yet made in the Apostles tyme, therfore the canon lawe was not the lawe of Christes chyrche in the tyme of the *Apostles* . . . *Ye saye that the Canon lawe is the lawe of the chyrche of Englande, therfore ye saye that the chyrche of Englande is none of Christes chyrche.* (sigs B7r-v, B8r) (My emphasis)

In view of the gravity of these accusations, the pamphleteer avoids directly criticizing the monarch, but instead blames the bishops for having deceived the king in order to continue their practices; nonetheless, one can see an implicit denunciation of royal policy in these words, making the point that what had happened in England was merely a transfer of power:

ye [the bishops] fearynge that they shulde be dryven out of the realme with theyr father yf they were taken for the popes ordinances, by youre frendes ye procured and brought to passe, that the ceremonies whiche the pope made, *shulde no more be called the popes ceremonies, but the kynges ceremonies* . . . In doing of which thinge as myche as laye in yowe ye *made the kinge pope, for yf the popes actes and the kynges be all one, then is the kynge the pope or ellis partener wyth the pope.* (Sigs E1v, E2r) (My emphasis)

Carried along by intense anticlerical sentiment, the writer tries to soften his criticism of the monarchy by urging it to develop the reforming agenda further. To do so he insists on certain biblical parallels in which Henry VIII is described as the people's new liberator, chosen by God.[51] Allusions to the Old Testament were of great usefulness in anti-Catholic literature of the sixteenth and seventeenth centuries, at a time when the Book of Kings was employed to create a sense of continuity between the Tudor Dynasty and the first governors of Judah.[52]

In this way a process was begun of reworking the image of the monarch in order to justify his new role as head of the Church of England; this process, however, was fraught with contradictions, as it found itself intermixed with potential attacks on the sovereign's lack of responsibility in his commitment to the Reformation. The king was urged, therefore

to delyver hys subiectes from the bondage of the pope and . . . to dryve out of hys realme, abbotes, priores, nones, monkes and freeres whych occupied the most parte of hys realme and purposed to set ryght men in theyr places, as poor menes sonnes, to be afterwarde preachers of the worde of god . . . God dyd when he delyvered the chylderne of Israel from the bondage of Pharao, and drove out the Chanaanites of theyr lande that the true

Isarelytes myght have that land and succede them. (*The Hunting and Finding*, sig. E3v)

The monarch's Catholic tendencies are referred to again, in fact, at the end of *The Hunting and Finding*, when the author recognizes that he might be accused of treason because of what he has written. He then re-elaborates a new concept of treason associated with Catholicism that could be sustained, albeit peripherally, within the official anti-Catholic discourse of the state: "ye [the followers of Rome] be traytours and heretikes and unlearned asses, and haue no knowledge, but in the Canon lawe, and in olde gloses and fantasies of men" (Ibid.; sig. F7r). It is nonetheless significant that from the very beginnings of this process voices arise that seek to link the Catholic community with seditious activity. While this seems here to be a case of a defensive posture that reflects the pamphleteer's vulnerability to the power of the state, one can also see the need to project such fears and insecurities onto an adversary who – in a general sense, and given the short history of the reformist movement in England – could still not be considered a true "other".

Alongside the accusations of corruption, treachery and idolatry, Protestant authors also stressed other aspects associated with Lollardist discourse, which thus took on renewed meaning. Denunciations of the Bishop of Rome's abuse of power, cruelty and tyranny became more frequent, and demonstrate the progressive politicization of the Lollardist discourse, which, while it had indeed attacked papal supremacy, had always placed greater emphasis on the more doctrinal aspects of religious questions. The politicization of theological discussion would remain a feature of the era throughout the Tudor period, since the menace from the Holy See remained a constant, to a greater or lesser extent, up until the end of the reign of Elizabeth I. A new distribution of roles therefore developed within this discursive phenomenon, in which the pontiff acquired the persona of an antagonistic mirror to the sovereign of England. John Bale's works *King Johan* (1539) and *The Three Laws* (1547) echoed the tensions that the assimilation of this idea generated, and made use of anti-Catholic discourse to offer a critical view of the monarchy's policies towards the Holy See.

King Johan was written in 1539 and revised in the following decade during the period of the writer's first exile,[53] and he did not see his work published until 1558. The writing of *The Three Laws* took place in 1538, though it could not be published until 1547, thanks to the promising situation opened up for English Protestants by the arrival of Edward VI. However, despite the fact that they were only published several years later, these works were performed in the time of Henry VIII by a company of itinerant actors directed by the playwright himself, who enjoyed the patronage of the chief minister Thomas Cromwell and so collaborated with his propaganda campaign. Presumably these performances took

The Reigns of Henry VIII (1509–47) and Edward VI (1547–53)

place in town squares, inns or the homes of the nobility, the habitual venues for this type of professional companies;[54] documents exist, for example, that place the first performance of *King Johan* at the residence of the Archbishop of Canterbury, before an audience that included Cranmer himself, Cromwell, and the most distinguished figures in England's reformist circles.[55] There is no evidence that these plays reached the court, which could be an indication of disagreements between the monarch and his minister, who fell in disgrace soon afterwards.

Both these texts take the form of religious allegories, which allows their characters to be divided into two conflicting groups representing vice and virtue, which do battle for the soul or well-being of England and the survival of the Word of God in the kingdom. The association that is made between the vices and several historical figures (in the case of *King Johan*[56]) brings to the fore the same anticlerical and anti-papal tone that is predominant in the pamphlets, and with the same flat, undifferentiated depiction of the adversary.[57] The play equally underlines the connections of blood and friendship between the negative characters, who in turn are associated together by their use of certain objects and clothing, and also by their physical arrangement on the stage. Sedicyon, for example, is the cousin of Dissymulacyon, who, because of his dress and monastic trappings, is another manifestation of the clergy. This character brings Privat Welth onto the stage, who then introduces Usurpid Powre. The circle is closed when Sedicyon insists that Usurpid Powre carry him on his back. Thus their union acquires a clearly symbolic and parodic character when the latter three vices carry Sedicyon like a bishop to his throne (*King Johan*, I. 791–797).

The actors playing the vices also represent real persons, such as Archbishop Stephen Langton (in the case of Sedicyon) or the Pope himself (in the case of Usurpid Powre) (I. 834, 868). One such instance occurs when Dissymulacyon acts as a messenger for the English clergy, and goes to Rome looking for help. The Pope's response is to initiate the process of King Johan's excommunication, for which he leaves the scene and dresses in papal robes, while Privat Welth dresses as the Cardinal.[58] As Peter Happé has indicated, these masquerades operate not just as mere disguises, but also serve to establish an allegorical link that presents the Pope as the product of the union of Usurpid Powre and the Cardinal (later given the name Pandulphus), representing Privat Welth.[59]

In *The Three Laws*, in contrast, such associations are made thanks to the symmetrical structure of the work, which is divided into three distinct parts in which three pairs of vices are seen working to carry out their contract with Infidelitas to destroy the Law of God.[60] With this arrangement of actors and dramatic action, Bale extends his criticism to all sectors of society, from the nobility and the clergy – according to him, corrupt and idolatrous, and responsible to a great extent for the country's decadence – to the monarchs themselves – blinded by the desire for power and wealth – and, of course, the Church of Rome, which he considers to be the ultimate cause of the ruin of Christendom. The numerous parallels that are made in the play establish a strong link, especially, between all those who seek to destroy divine law, an idea that could be extended to a historical reality in which the Catholic faith was beginning to be associated with treason against king and country. The fact that the monarchs themselves are victims of supposed Catholic stratagems in the drama amounts to an indirect criticism of Henry VIII, who never openly declared himself a reformer. The connections drawn, by extension, between Henry and the Church of Rome remained a problem for the play. However, with the prospect of a new king with clearly Protestant leanings, such risks were reduced, and the text could even have had the opposite effect: that of strengthening the new king's image.

This kind of attack on different social groups also appears in *King Johan*, in which the playwright makes use of elements of historical drama to present more contemporary criticisms. The play's central figure is King John, John Lackland, who reigned between 1199 and 1216. He appears in the play as a historical parallel to Henry VIII, both of them distinguished by their opposition to the pope and their defence of monarchical supremacy in the face of excommunication. Although the real historical king remained a disputed figure,[61] the writer omits any incidents that might compromise his moral value. There is, therefore, a clear manipulation of the historical chronicles, in order to draw an idealized portrait of King Johan – and by association of the real-life king – who is described as a forthright man of deep religious convictions, and above all a victim of the ambition and corruption of the clergy and the country's nobility.

The identification of King Johan with Henry VIII is apparent at certain moments in the play, although an effort is always made to maintain a certain distance in order to avoid offending the English monarch or his successors. References to the King's Oath of Allegiance (I, 526; II, 2318), to his title as *Defensor Fidei* (II, 1521; II, 2427), to his excommunication (I, 118, 927–935, 1034–1051), to the Act of Supremacy (II, 4; II, 2431–2436), and to the danger of foreign invasion from France, Scotland, and Spain, are clear examples of the parallels established between the two figures. The character of Interpretour makes this association explicitly:

> Thys noble kynge Johan as a faythfull Moyses/ Withstode proude Pharao for hys poore Israel,/ Myndynge to brynge it out of the lande of darkenesse./ But the Egyptyanes ded agaynst hym so rebell/ That hys poore people ded styll in the desart dwell,/ Tyll that duke Josue whych was *our late kynge Henrye*/ Clerely brought us in to the lande of mylke and honye. (I, 1107–1113) (My emphasis)

As Peter Happé points out, Bale could not create a character named Henry VIII because the risk would have been too great, but these indirect references probably allowed him to exert a certain amount of pressure on the sovereign.[62] The fact that the work was published when Elizabeth came to the throne could be seen as one last attempt on the part of the dramatist to realize his reformist aims, since the lines of the play could be interpreted as a form of advice to the new queen so that she might not commit the mistakes of her predecessors.

Bale's use of allegorical and historical genres is complemented, also, by his deployment of many elements of the apocalyptic tradition. This takes on special meaning in *King Johan*, giving a forewarning from the very beginning of the play of the protagonist's suffering and death. The Book of Revelation had become a useful instrument to justify the schism from Rome. Protestant authors interpreted it as a historical text, as a prophecy in which God revealed his intentions. John Bale and his successors developed the doctrine of "The Two Churches" that had existed in parallel since the beginning of Christianity, one true and persecuted, the other false but powerful. This concept, derived from the two cities of St. Augustine, enjoyed great popularity among writers of the Tudor period.[63] Bale himself in fact wrote a long commentary on the Book of Revelation, entitled *The Image of Both Churches* (1541), in which he expounded this new theory. In both *King Johan* and *The Three Laws*, everything fits into this dual, apocalyptic vision of the Church and of a world in which the forces of good and evil are at war. This discourse of opposites very probably acquired considerable psychological force, and people learned to see their own history and identity in the light of this duality.

Bale was conscious of living in a historic moment, and so sought to establish boundaries: between an age of confusion and darkness that already belonged to the past, and another age enlightened by the Gospel that was opening up before him and his contemporaries. This description of his position is based, above all, on the allegorical structure of his works, in which the conflict between opposites always ends with the restoration of divine order. The Church of Rome is presented as a long and difficult interlude in the history of Christianity, as a dark age that has now closed so that God's original work might be resumed. The Church of England is entrusted with the task of perpetuating the principles of the first Christians, an idea that gains strength from the apocalyptic image of an old city that vanishes (Rome), opening the way for the new city, a new Jerusalem (England), free of Catholic influence (*The Three Laws*, sig. K2r). The playwright makes use of the power of Scripture and the theory of the invisibility of the True Church to legitimize the new Protestant faith and sidestep accusations of encouraging a schism. In so doing, he provides it with a history, a self-justifying tradition, as in the words of his character Evangelium:

> Theyr worshyppynges are, in outward ceremonyes/ That counterfet church standeth al by mens tradycions/ Without the Scriptures and without [?] hertes

affections/ My churche is secrete, and evermore wyll be/ Adorynge the father, in spyryte and in berytie/ By the worde of God, this churche is ruled onelye/ And doth not consyst, in outwarde ceremonye/ This congregacion is the true Churche mylytaunt/ Those counterfayte Desardes, are the berye Churche malygnaunt . . . / [it has existed] Sens the beginnynge, and now is in Christ returnd. (*The Three Laws*, sigs G3r-v)

The principal theme of *King Johan* and one of the central elements of the anti-Catholic critique in *The Three Laws* are constructed, therefore, on the basis of this binary arrangement of characters and dramatic action. The political threat that the papacy represented for Christian kingdoms, and the pernicious effects it could have on the stability of the state, become primary concerns in the drama.[64] Hence *King Johan* denounces the supposed machinations of the Bishop of Rome to gain power over sovereign monarchs:[65]

[SEDICYON] Tushe, the Pope ableth me to subdewe bothe kyng and keiser./ [KING JOHAN:] Off that thow and I wyll common more at leyser./ Trwly of the devyll they are that do onythyng/ To the subdewyng of ony christen kyng./ For be he good or bade he is of Godes apoyntyng. (I, 99–103)

According to Protestant authors, one of the political tools that the pope employed to know the minds and intentions of those in power was the sacrament of confession, which had already been denounced by the Lollards, who blamed it for engendering a heightened pride among priests and keeping the faithful locked in servitude.[66] This interpretation reappears in the dialogue between Sedicyon and King Johan:

[KING JOHAN:] Why, wyll ere confessyon soch a secret traytor be?/ [SEDICYON:] Whan all other fayle he is so swre as stele./ Offend Holy Churche and I warant ye shall yt fele;/ For by confessyon the Holy Father knoweth/ Throw owt all Christendom what to his holynes growyth. (I, 269–274)

The author writes sarcastically of the power that this sacrament accorded the Bishop of Rome, who was able to justify and forgive any act – including murder – committed in the service of his interests. When Sedicyon hears the confession of Nobility, he immediately absolves him of any sins he has committed in the name of the pope and encourages him to ignore the king's authority, which marks the beginning of the conflict that is dramatized in Act II (II, 1149–1189). The farce reaches its climax in the moment when Dissymulacyon is absolved of his sins just before taking the king's life (II, 2019–2049).

In the end, Johan succumbs to the pressures and tyrannical devices of the clergy and the Holy See. The foreign invasion that takes place in the second act (II, 1601–1638) represents an attack upon the subordination

The Reigns of Henry VIII (1509–47) and Edward VI (1547–53)

of monarchs to the pontiff, which had been a serious concern since 1538, when Emperor Charles V and King Francis I of France signed a ten-year truce under papal supervision. All three parties had ignored Henry VIII, who despite his best efforts found himself confronted by the threat of a General Council of the Church and an attack from Catholic Europe. At the beginning of 1539 the panic over the possibility of foreign invasion was in full flow – although, to England's good fortune, none of the enemy monarchs answered the Pope's call to arms.[67] Hence, Bale's work stresses the anxiety created by the threat of imminent war. Though the conflict that is presented in his plays is an internal one between the monarch and different social groups in England, in each case there is a search for an element outside the kingdom that can be held responsible for and accused of the divisions within the English nation, which will be overcome at the end when all groups in society swear obedience to the King. Nonetheless, we are left with a doubt as to whether the character Clergy keeps his word, and does not repeat his treasons of the past (I, 593–617). Bale maintains this irony into the very last scene, when suspicion is aroused even amid a supposed reconciliation.

Bale's two works exemplify the first steps in the elaboration of a Catholic stereotype, and the profound influence of Lollardism upon it. This discourse, however, was not limited to its own conceptual ends but also served as an instrument for more implicit denunciations of the monarchy's excessive tolerance of Catholicism. The fact that Imperyall Majestye restores order, together with Veritas, once again presents the concept of royal sovereignty as the only means by which to re-establish the true faith, and with it, the unity and stability of the country. Nevertheless, this could be interpreted as merely a fallacy if we look closely at the dialogue between these two virtues on the subject of the Catholic influence that still existed in the kingdom. The writer was probably aware, like Veritas, of the difficulty of establishing the new faith in a country whose spirit was still Catholic and whose monarch showed little coherence in matters concerning religion:

[IMPERYALL MAJESTYE:] I praye yow, take paynes to call our Commynalte/ To true obedyence as ye are Gods Veryte./ [VERITAS:]: I wyll do it, sir. *Yet shall I have muche a doo/ With your Popish prelates. They wyll hunte me to and fro.* (II. 2336–2340) (My emphasis)

Two other works, *Albion Knight* (ca. 1537–1538) and *Impacient Poverty* (1547), portray the Catholic revolts of 1537 and 1547 from different viewpoints, and leave behind doctrinal questions and, to some extent, the description of the Catholic stereotype that was so prominent in Bale's texts, in order to focus on political denunciation.

Albion Knight,[68] the work of an anonymous author, presents a conflict between Albion and Justice on the one hand, and Division and Iniuri

(Injury) on the other. The plot centres around the expulsion of the two vices from England, which they attempt to evade by creating a state of chaos within English society. The extensive use of symbols and iconology emphasizes the nature of the characters and the relationships that develop between them. Such is the case with the bloc formed by Justice, Peace, and Plenty, which evokes the iconology of Peace[69] and Alciatus' emblem CLXXVIII *Ex Pace Ubertas* – From peace, plenty – as an alternative to the instability which during those years made people fear for the prosperity of the country. The author appears to propose a relationship of harmony and concord between subjects and sovereign as the only means to put an end to the crisis that was enveloping England. The play could be seen, therefore, as an admonition to the monarch to change his economic policies and thereby calm the fears of the citizens:

> [INIURI:] This Iustice is a felow of a farr cast/ And dryveth such dryftes to rule all at the last/ And Peace is hys brother of one degree/ Which hath a fayre doughter that is called Plentie . . . / *And it is a comen saieng that Iustice Peace & hee [Albion]/ Will conclude a maryage with fayre dame Plentie/ And then wyll Albyon that olde soot/ With rest and peace so on her doot/ That than shee by her and her freindes/ Shall sayle in stormes at all wyndes.* (340–352)[70] (My emphasis)

The text criticizes the selfishness and irresponsibility of the king, the parliament and the clergy, who place their own economic interests before the people's well-being, as can be seen in the ironic words of Iustice to Albion when talking about the agreement with Iniuri at the beginning of the play:

> [IUSTICE:] Syr ye ought to be contented best of all/ Where iustice is treited with due equitie/ And where no favour nor mede shuld bee/ And when reason hath tried there every deale/ That such an acte were good for the comen weale/ *If therin anie losse may bee/ To the disadvauntage of Principaltie/ Such an acte leseth all hys sute/ With a lytle indoysing of reason astute/ And if it touche the Lordes spyrytuall/ Or be disavauntage to the Lordes temporall/ Fare well, go bett, this bill may sleepe.* (67–79) (My emphasis)

In effect, the English reformers had held out hopes that the lands and wealth confiscated from the Church of Rome would be used for good works, to construct colleges, set up foundations to aid the sick and the poor, and especially to improve the ecclesiastical infrastructure at the parochial level. These hopes were dashed with the advent of the act of 1536 which made the king and his successors the sole inheritors of these properties, which were thus due to bolster, not the interests of Protestantism, but the government's coffers.[71] The playwright shows the disillusion of the English people at the behaviour of their sovereign, and

The Reigns of Henry VIII (1509–47) and Edward VI (1547–53)

seems, to a certain extent, to justify the rebellions. Iniuri, in addition, makes a comparison between Albion and the proverbial goose[72] in order to highlight the king's ignorance and his loss of prestige in the eyes of other European nations:

> [INIURI:] Ye and what foloweth hereof maister Albion/ To your person universall derysion/ [ALBION:] Why to mee derision/ [INIURI]: *For all other straunge nacions/ They will raile on you with open proclamacions/ Saienge whosoever do as he dose/ Is halfe a man and halfe a wild goose/* [ALBION:] Why halfe a man and halfe a wyld goose./ [INIURI:] For with hie reason they saie ye can dispute/ And trie out perils with laborous sute/ And eke the treasure for the comen vaile/ As farr as wit or reason can assaile/ *But when all is done and your statute made/ Then foorth ye go in a wise trade/ To brynge it all to good conclusion/ And put it never in execucyon . . . / And for because ye study but for the begynnynge/ And never provide for a sure endyng/* Begynnyng lyke a man ye take great assay/ At last lyke a wyld goose even but to fly awaye. (88–103; 108–111) (My emphasis)

The course of action that is proposed from the stage is one of correcting such attitudes so that the country might prosper and gain in international standing. If the preferred choice of the main character Albion is England's national unity (118–119), his main enemy is surely Division, who personifies the internal divisions of the time, as revealed in the outline he gives of his plans to provoke social and political chaos. He will send two agents to carry out his schemes: the first, Double Device, will fuel the fire of animosity between the king and a public weary of paying taxes and getting nothing in return (269–274). This same spy will also attempt to corrupt the sovereign's relationship with parliament by creating mistrust between them. The attack made upon the abysmal administration of the monarchy, on the tensions within the House of Commons as a result of war policies, and on the generalized corruption within the country could not go unnoticed:

> Then the same spye shall use lyke doubleness/ And go to the comons and to them tell/ *That Principalytie with equitie doth rebell/ More to hys lucre in everie deale/ Applyeneng his affection then to the comen weale/* And how that he of *neglygence/* Doth not apply for theyr defence,/ Neither by Sea nor by londe/ Neither by hye wayes, neither by stronde/ But theves and raveners and murders eke/ Dayly true men they pursue and seke/ And that his lawes indifferently/ Be not used, but maintainenaunce and brybary/ Is suffred alone without reformacion/ *That the poore comons is in altercation/ Of this matter and wote not what to say/ Bringing them in opinion yt they ought not to pay/ To pryncypalytie theyr duety of very desarte/ Except lyke duetie be mynistred on hys parte.* (274–292) (My emphasis)

The second spy, Old Debate, personifies the age-old polemic over ecclesiastical authority, and revives arguments against the excessive powers of the Church in questions of affairs of state (297–313). Although the play was written ten years before the death of Henry VIII, there also seem to be references to Edward VI, as one can see in Division's speech in which he refers to the problem of clerical authority. This was probably an addition made after the play was first written, one intended to portray the disquiet that the accession to the throne of a child incapable of governing had provoked; in addition, a clear connection is established between the two reigns by the references to the problems that stemmed on the one hand from the power of the Church and, on the other, from the expropriation of monastic lands:

> That they [the clergy] ought by reason to rule thys land/ Because the powre of temporaltie/ Hath no knowledge in conning perdie/ *Neyther in youth will labour the passage/ Of paine for vertue to rule in age/* So that if they rulers wold bee/ They know not how, for in suffycientie/ Thus will I devide by thys proper trayne/ That peace amongst them shall not rayne. (314–322) (My emphasis)

The play shares, then, in a sense of social malaise that reached into the most disparate sectors of society, both Catholic and Protestant. The fact that the figures that provoke divisions within the country – Double Device and Old Debate – are related to the Catholic community does not mean that royal decisions escape direct and explicit attack. Since the text is unfinished, we cannot see exactly how these conflicts were developed in the course of the play, nor to what extent they were silenced in a final, conciliatory speech. But, be that as it may, their very presence in the play is in itself evidence of a provocative attitude on the part of the writer, as he gave voice to a country that was confused and disillusioned by the mistakes of the Reformation.

The also anonymous *Impacient Poverty*[73] proposes, in principle, a different solution to the conflicts generated by the revolts of 1547 (possibly the year the play was written), by making a direct appeal for order and obedience to the regime as the sole requirement for achieving peace in English society. This condition is presented in allegorical form in the play, and becomes the indispensable key through which the main character may attain salvation: "Exercyse youre selfe in vertue, from this tyme hence/ And unto peace evermore be obediente." (204–205).[74] In a corrupt world dominated by material values, Peace tries to save Impacient Poverty who, despite the temptations of Envye, Haboundance and Misrule, finally repents and decides to lead an honest life. A lasting peace is the only way for the country to leave behind its economic penury, as Peace declares at the outset of the play: "by peace they profyte in many a thynge/ Peace setteth amyte between kynge and kynge/ In time of peace merchauntes have theyr course/ To passe and repasse" (42–46).

Envye nevertheless questions these ideas, and demonstrates a certain mistrust of peace treaties, which in his opinion hide the true intentions of rulers, to continue to reap economic benefits without the need for confrontations. They are therefore deceitful stratagems, the main aim of which is not in any way to maintain peaceful coexistence between peoples: "Thou lyest knave by the masse/ For under colour of peace moch suttelte hath bene wrought/ And shyps are taken ye marchautes dere have boughte/ Was that for theyr promocyon/ Nay in tyme of war/ Such a knave durst not stere" (47–52).

The manipulation of the people by political leaders is denounced in the play, and Peace is ultimately discredited by Envye, who sets a trap for him in order to expose that he too can have revengeful feelings:

ENVYE:] Have ye any wyfe or no/ [PEACE:] Wherfore aske ye so/[ENVYE:] Bycause ye saye peace is moste expedyent/ If your wife made you cuckold you beyng present/ What would ye do/ [PEACE:] Geve her soche punishment as longeth thereto/ [ENVYE:] A false flatterynge horson loo/ Now thou sayest agaynst thyne owne declaracyon/ Yf thou fyght where is then peace become./ [PEACE:] I breake not peace with doynge due correctyon/ For correctyon shuld be done charitably/ *Irascemini et nolite peccare*/ [ENVYE:] I shall mete that at omnium quare/ Peace shuld forgeve, and not be revenged/ Hens horson by our lady of wolpit/ I shall rappe the of the pate/ PEACE: Go hence wretche, thou make bate/ It were almes to set the in newgate/ Howe mayster constable come nere/ Here is a wretche wythout reason/ Take and put hym in pryson/ With as many yrons as he may beare. (66–87)

Peace offers no convincing rebuttal to Envye's words, and only manages to quieten him by means of threats. As a consequence, Peace's true intentions are cast into doubt, and the spectator can easily feel a degree of incredulity at his subsequent actions. The need for forgiveness, one of the basic conditions for ending the country's internal divisions, is rejected by the virtue that here represents English reformers as a body. This play can be perceived, therefore, as a criticism of the intolerant attitude of the English crown, which did not seem to be prepared to consider the reasons of those who had rebelled against it.

The reference to "Thys noble audyence" in the epilogue (1064) may also support the hypothesis that the play was acted in the home of a nobleman by a company of professional actors. The scene featuring Misrule seems to be a typical example of the spectacles that were commonly staged as part of celebrations of the nobility, where guests ate, sang, and danced, as Misrule indicates as he tries to corrupt Impacient Poverty (by this point called Prosperyte): "[MISRULE:] Syr my name is myrth/ Beloved wyth lordes & ladyes of byrthe . . . / Syr ye must synge and daunce & make good chere/ I wolde ye had some propre wenche/ That were yonge and lustye at apynche" (644–645; 655–657).

Prosperyte's allusions to Calvinist doctrine stand in opposition to Misrule's urgings, suggesting that there may have been problems with the reception of the play by a part of its audiences: "Sith I to him dyd assent/ Had I never merye daye/ But lived in feare and drede alwaie" (671–673). The playwright thus emphasizes the cynicism and frivolousness of the audience, who would have been likely to share the point of view of the two vices: Misrule – who includes them in his celebration – and later, Haboundance – who perhaps personifies members of the court and noblemen made wealthy as a result of the expropriation of the monasteries.[75] The author is aware of the satirical and provocative character of the play, for which he seeks forgiveness at the end: "It is but a myrrour vice to exclude/ The maker hereof his entent was good/ No man to dysplease olde nor yonge/ Yet any faute be therin we desyre you of pardon" (1067–1070).

The fact that the audience could identify with one of the vices, representing the Catholic sector of society[76], betrays a less optimistic vision of the Reformation than those of other texts.[77] Beyond merely espousing a conservatism that proposes the obedience of the monarch's subjects as the only way out of political conflict, the play amounts to another wake-up call for the Protestant ruling classes who, carried along by the desire for wealth, were distorting and straying from the path of the Reformation. The ambiguous presentation of Peace and the values that he represents in the play further demonstrates such errors and the need for a change of direction in Protestantism in England. The arrival in power of Northumberland after quelling the revolts of 1547–9 did not resolve the conflicts that were threatening the English people, witnesses to new doctrinal changes that did not provide a solution to the corruption of those who introduced them.

The final text to be analysed here is more removed from political critique and is, instead, a clear example of theatre in the service of Calvinist doctrine. The play is *Iacob and Esau* by Nicholas Udall (1505–1556),[78] an advocate of the ideas of the Erasmian circle during the last years of the reign of Henry VIII. Although the date of its composition is uncertain – sometime between 1550 and 1557 – it is very likely that the play was first performed during the reign of Edward VI; however, it was first published in October of 1557, with a second edition in 1568. The reference that the playwright makes in the epilogue to the Queen (V, x, 121–126) and the clergy – "Now unto God let us pray for all the whole clergy,/ To geve them grace to avaunce gods honor and glory" (V, x, 119–120) – is probably to Elizabeth I and representatives of the Church of England,[79] given that the play's Calvinist tone would have prevented its being addressed to Mary I and the Catholic leadership. Although there is no actual evidence that it was performed at court, this would have been

The Reigns of Henry VIII (1509–47) and Edward VI (1547–53)

a feasible possibility, since Udall took part in the preparation of many such courtly performances. The suggestion that the play was performed in the home of a nobleman or in some public venues as part of a propaganda campaign by the Lord Protector (regent) Somerset is also credible. However, the most convincing theory is that the work was performed in a university or college, as an example of an adaptation from classical Latin comedy.

The play, structured in the form of several acts and scenes, deals with one of the most common themes of the Roman stage: the education of children. Udall's text examines this problem within England's new reforming context by contrasting it with the Calvinist doctrine of reprobation. The conflict that arises from the interaction of the two ideas is revealed in the words of Hanan, one of Isaac's neighbours:

> Alack good man, *what should he do more than he hath don?/ I dare say no father hath better taught his sonne/ Nor no two have given better example of life/ Unto their children, than bothe he and his wife:/* As by their yonger sonne Iacob it doth appeare/ He lyveth no looce life, he doth God love and feare./ He keepeth here in the Tentes lyke a quiete man:/ He geveth not hymselfe to wildnesse any whan./ *But Esau evermore from his yong childehoode/ Had ben lyke to prove yll, and never to be goo . . . / And wherof commeth this, of Education?/ Nay it is of his owne yll inclination.* (I, ii, 27–36; 39–40) (My emphasis)

The focus on education is subsequently displaced, then, by an almost exclusive analysis of the principle of reprobation, which is why the story of Jacob and Esau (Gen. 24, 25, 27) had been chosen for the play. Udall's work makes use of the biblical genre, which, handed down from the Middle Ages, remained common until the end of the reign of Elizabeth I. The influence on reformist allegories of this type of play, still familiar to the public, was obvious, and made it possible to comment on contemporary issues in the form of extrapolations from the Old and New Testaments.[80] Thus, the play's starting-point is the deep divide between the reformist group of the elect, represented by Iacob, and the group of reprobate Catholics, personified by Esau. Rebecca's description of her two sons fits within this same dual rhetoric:

> I remember when I had you both conceived,/ A voyce thus saying fron the Lorde I received:/ Rebecca, in thy wombe are now two nations,/ Of unlike natures and contrary fashions./ The one shal be a mightier people elect:/ And the elder to the yonger shall be subject. (I, iii, 35–40)

Although the association made between them and the Catholic and Protestant communities is not direct, Iacob's words about the pride of his brother, who refuses to accept his advice on the grounds of his greater age and authority, echoes the Catholic position and its emphasis on tradition as the source of power, against the young and inexperienced character of the Reformation: "But when doe him any thing of his fault tell,/ He calleth me foolishe proude boy with him to mell./ He will sometime demaunde by what authoritee,/ I presume to teache them which mine elders bee?" (I, iii, 9–12). The fact that Esau is the character condemned by God from the play's outset legitimizes the Protestant position, that authority is not bestowed by age but by the Word of God, to which Iacob makes constant reference in justifying his actions as responses to divine commands. However, this raises several problems, since the methods he uses to obtain his birthright do not meet the level of honesty expected of one of the elect. This is revealed in his doubtful and reluctant response to the advice of Rebecca[81]:

> Mother Rebecca, if withouten fraude I might,/ I would your advise put in vse wyth all my hart,/ But I may not attempt any such guilefull part:/ To buie my brothers eldership and hys birthright,/ I feare woulde be a great offence in Gods sight. (I, iii, 52–56)

Iacob takes advantage of his brother's being lost in the forest and weakened as an opportunity to buy his birthright from him in exchange for a plate of food (II, ii). His attitude is in contradiction to the merciful idea of feeding the hungry, a moral message that is again brought into question when Iacob, guided by his mother, deceives the blind man, Isaac, who mistakes him for Esau and gives him his blessing as firstborn. The fact that Iacob disguises his identity with a goatskin in order to imitate his brother's hairiness undermines the virtue of his actions, since this gesture could be seen as theatre, with its connotations of falsity. In addition, it also makes reference to the iconological emblem of Hypocrisy, which showed a woman dressed in a sheepskin, beneath which a wolf's feet could be seen.[82] The link established between the play's protagonist and this type of symbolic figure is direct, and underlines the immoral nature of his behaviour.[83] In spite of all this, his actions are ultimately justified because they are commands from God, and for this reason they are accepted by those who have been the targets of his deception (V, iv, 12; V, x, 63–68).

The end of the play is seen as a triumph for the doctrine of reprobation, though this is nevertheless unable to conceal all the resulting contradictions. Given that the audiences that would have attended its performances would have been predominantly Protestant, such paradoxes should not be seen as criticisms of these doctrinal points.[84] Rather, they reveal the difficulties that Protestants as a body encountered in occupying a central position in European Christianity, in marked contrast with the Church of Rome, which, after centuries in power, encountered no such obstacles. The appeal to the concept of the Two Churches and the supremacy of the Word and the Divine Plan in opposition to Catholic traditions were the only instruments by which the authority that was so desired could be accredited.

The analysis of these dramatic texts and pamphlets bears witness to the fact that England was a fragmented country that had not clearly decided upon the schism, and yet found itself irreversibly drawn into it. Henry VIII's attempts to placate the two main sectors into which the country's political and religious life had been divided were fruitless. Not only did he fail to garner support in either group, his own ambiguity and inconsistency – which arose among other causes as the result of his subordinating his decisions in religious matters to foreign policy and economic needs – discouraged those who did, in fact, have a definite programme for the country.

The first examples of anti-Catholic discourse appeared in writings on the subject of the king's divorce. A few years later it expanded nationwide, thanks to the propaganda campaign organized by Cromwell, who discovered theatre and the printing press to be two powerful political weapons. The task was to re-educate the public from the top down and this was what official propagandists set out to do, although the project could not develop effectively due to the previously-mentioned internal divisions and the attitude of a king who simultaneously defended the schism and his desire for a universal and united church. That part of the social scale that supposedly had to take on the role of educator appeared to be falling apart, as was demonstrated by the many accusations of treason (most of them false), conspiracies and executions that were seen in the last ten years of the king's life. It was necessary to normalize the separation from Rome, erase the memory of the people, and begin to write upon it again as if it were a *tabula rasa*, a process that would be extremely complicated for a nation exhausted by wars, taxes, and social revolts.

The hopes that the Protestant sector of society had placed in the heir to the throne were soon dashed, as the errors of the previous reign were repeated. Although some documents exist that refer to the performance of anti-Catholic plays at Edward's court during the early part of his reign,[85] courtly entertainments soon abandoned their commitment to the Reformation and opted instead for a return to the customary themes of the early years of Henry VIII, when theatre, at least in a court setting, had not carried any political implications. The playwrights and pamphleteers of the period not only expressed reformist ideals but also made use of the official discourse itself to expose its own inconsistencies and gaps and thus offer different responses to the conflicts of the age. Heirs to the Lollard tradition of the Middle Ages, these writers claimed for themselves an active part in the new era of political and religious transition that was opening up before them.

CHAPTER TWO

Mary I (1553–1558) and the Discourse of Victimhood

THE RETURN TO CATHOLICISM AND THE SPANISH THREAT

In 1552, Edward VI had become terminally ill, and rumour quickly spread that the regent Northumberland intended to alter the dynastic order of succession. To that end, he married his son Lord Guildford Dudley to Lady Jane Grey, the oldest daughter of the Duke of Suffolk and grand-niece to Henry VIII. Meanwhile, Edward, facing imminent death, was persuaded to name Lady Jane as his successor to the Crown and thus assure a Protestant succession to the throne. On 10 July 1553, less than a month after the death of the young king and with the approval of the Royal Council, which had been coerced and threatened by Northumberland, Lady Jane was proclaimed Queen of England.

Shortly after the proclamation, Northumberland had to leave London to deal with the threat still posed by Mary Tudor who, alarmed by recent events, had fled to Suffolk and from there demanded that the Council recognize her right to the Crown. The Council took advantage of the Regent's absence to take up arms against him. The Duke was not long in surrendering both himself and, in so doing, his plans for the future. Mary Tudor became Queen of England on 19 July 1553. Her predecessor had ruled a mere ten days.[1]

Changes were immediate. Northumberland's followers – Suffolk and Northampton – were excluded from the new Royal Council, as were those who had become unwitting accomplices of the Duke's regime, such as Cranmer and Cecil. In their place, Mary appointed Catholic figures who had faithfully supported her cause – Norfolk, Gardiner, Tunstall – as well as others who, without themselves having great religious convictions in her favour, or even in some cases showing Protestant tendencies, were disposed to accept royal authority. Gardiner was again ensconced as Bishop of Winchester and named as Lord Chancellor. Nicholas Ridley, the great defender of the Reformation during the reigns of Henry VIII and Edward VI, was deposed as Bishop of London, a post that was now conferred upon Edmund Bonner. In addition, Catholic Mass and Catholic ritual were imposed again, Protestant ministers were prohibited from preaching,[2] and an intensive programme was begun to encourage Protestants who rejected conversion to the Catholic faith to emigrate. This gave rise to the formation of a pro-reform movement that continued its attack on Mary's regime from exile.[3]

The first serious conflict the new queen faced arose as a result of her desire to marry and so provide an heir that would assure the continuation of the Tudor dynasty and the Catholic regime. In the first five months of the reign, conversations were held with the ambassadors of both France and Spain, in the face of the suspicion of the Commons.[4] But, Mary had already made her choice, selecting Prince Philip, the son of Emperor Charles V and future King of Spain, as the best candidate to bolster the Catholic faith in England.

Reaction against the engagement came quickly. The Royal Council opposed the marriage on the basis of the threat it posed of England's being governed by a foreign monarch, and attempted to persuade the queen of the need to marry an English nobleman. Nevertheless, Mary held fast in her decision and signed the marriage treaty in January of 1554, although it included a series of clauses whereby the Council sought to preserve the queen's autonomy and her authority over her husband. Even so, Philip was considered the real power in the government, despite the fact that neither parliament nor his marriage had given him any formal authority. This is confirmed by a letter sent by the ambassador of Savoy in September of that year, in which he wrote, "The King hears and dispatches state affairs, as it befits his dignity and authority that he should do so. He already has the same authority as his predecessors on the Throne of England".[5] Mary's union with Philip opened a breach between the queen and her subjects, who never forgave her for having handed the nation over to the interests of a foreign power.[6]

Nor did the English fail to notice Spain's association with Rome; they saw how, little by little and in spite of past conflicts with the Holy See, England could be returned to the Catholic fold. Confrontations had already arisen during the process of negotiating the royal engagement, and the Council had arrested several rebels accused of creating disturbances.[7] The most serious crisis, though, occurred on the night before the agreement was signed, with the revolt of Sir Thomas Wyatt and Lady Jane Grey's father the Duke of Suffolk, who attempted to block the engagement and so protect the interests of Protestantism. However, the queen's call to her subjects to show their loyalty to the monarchy resulted in Wyatt's surrender, which took place on London Bridge itself. As in the case of Northumberland, Mary Tudor took advantage of a moment of crisis to rouse and confirm the support of her people. A short time later, Wyatt, Suffolk, Lady Jane and her husband Guildford – both of whom had been locked in the Tower of London since Mary's accession to the Throne – were executed, together with others who had taken part in the revolt.[8]

Princess Elizabeth found herself drawn into the conflict, apparently unwittingly. Her detractors, in spite of having no clear proof, had her taken to the Tower of London, where she remained for two months before being taken to Woodstock and later Hatfield, where she lived, effectively under guard, until her sister's death.[9] Though the loyalty of the English people to Mary had been demonstrated, Protestant history subsequently consecrated Sir Thomas Wyatt as a great defender of English liberties and the Protestant cause, an image that was scarcely tainted by his disobedience to the Crown. As an example, almost twenty years later, the historical chronicler Grafton eulogized Wyatt and used him in evidence to reaffirm Elizabeth's innocence in the conflict, while also making clear his own position on the matter of treason against the queen:

> Before hys death hee (Wyatt) earnestly protested that the Lord Courtney and the Ladie Elizabeth the Queenes sister, were nothing gylty of hys doyngs, but utterly innocent therein. Thys Syr Thomas Wyat was a stout Gentleman, politique in warre, and of such excellence qualities, that he might greatly have profited hys Countrey, yf he had lyved as an obedyent subiect. (*Abridgement of the Chronicles of Englande*, p. 183)

Despite the people's show of support for her, their opposition to her marriage went unheeded by the queen, who continued making preparations. The wedding took place in Winchester in July 1554. The entry of the royal couple into London was a display of wealth and majesty intended to project the image of a powerful and mighty monarchy, capable of extricating the country from the state of corruption in which it found itself.[10] The description given by John Elder,[11] a Catholic sympathizer, of the different ornamental displays and stages set up by the London guilds reveals the manner in which the iconography of the two monarchs was constructed, particularly that of Philip, who was the subject of practically all the images represented in the *tableaux*. One of the main reasons why the City of London strove for such pomp was the need to make a good impression in the wake of the negative incidents that had occurred involving the Spanish retinue. The feelings of aggression and suspicion that Spain aroused guaranteed a harsh reception for Philip in the hearts of many Londoners. Despite the attempts to legitimize and justify his image, paradoxes and ambiguities were inevitable, whether intentional or not. Elder himself was unable to ignore a number of incongruous elements that complicated the acceptance of the image of Philip even among English Catholics.[12]

The first evidence of this was the appearance in the first part of the pageant of the characters *Corineus Britannus* and *Gogmagog Albionus*[13], displaying a placard to the king and queen summarizing the content of the first scene. It is highly significant that the chorus or narrator of the pageant adopted the third person when expressing the affection of the people of London, creating a rhetorical distance that contrasts with the use of the first person and the direct style of the pageants that would be created during Elizabeth's ceremonial entry into London at the time of her coronation in 1559:[14]

> O noble prince, sole hope of *Caesar's* side,/ *By God apointed all the world to gyde,*/ Right hartely welcome art thou to our land,/ The archer Britayne yeldeth the hir land,/ And noble England openeth her bosome/ Of *hartie affection* for to bid the welcome . . . / She [London] seith her citizens love thee on eche side,/ And trustes they shal be happy of such a gide:/ And all do thinke thou art sent to their citie/ *By th' only meane of God's paternall pitie.* (pp. 5–6) (My emphasis)

The new reign of Mary is compared in this address to the foundation of England – New Troy – which is characterized as an empire. Nevertheless, the text underscores England's reliance on the only figure that, the speech suggests, could guarantee such status to the country: Philip, heir to the Spanish empire. His presentation as a messiah sent by God to shepherd the English people no doubt caused adverse reactions among those subjects fearful of Spain's power. The paternalistic tone emanating from the stage contrasted, therefore, with the spectators' own patriotic feelings. Nor could the close association in their collective memory of Henry VIII (who had been affirming the imperial character of the English monarchy since 1534) with the new sovereign have been pleasing to many of the Londoners who watched the royal pageant.[15] The chronicler, however, does not mention the response of the people, who were kept silent throughout the drama and only alluded to in a general way in the verses written on the placard seen at the beginning.

The subordination of the English to their new sovereign seems, in fact, to be the implicit message of the third scene, in which the figure of Orpheus is shown playing a harp, surrounded by beasts that dance to the strains of the music. The words that describe the tableau are unsettling:

> The prince that hath the gift of eloquence/ May bend his subjectes to his most behove,/ Which in old time was shewed by covert sence/ In Orpheus whose song did wilde beastes move./ In like case now by the grace of speech so franke/ Doth comforte us, whose mindes afore were bleke,/ And therefore England geveth the harty thanke,/ Whose chiefest joye is to hear thee, Philip, speke. (p. 8)

References to the sovereign's eloquence mask a deep irony, in that they are potentially critical of a monarch hoping to curry favour among a people whose language he did not speak. The lines seem quite clearly to echo the view held by many of the English people that their country was being manipulated. The image of Orpheus controlling the wild beasts caused reactions such as that of John Foxe, who made use of this scene in his *Actes and Monuments* to emphasize the tyrannical intentions of the Spanish prince: "In an other Poetry King Philip was resembled by an Image representing Orpheus, and all English people resembled to brute and savage beasts, following after Orpheus's harpe and dancing after King Philips pipe".[16] Nevertheless, it should be kept in mind that the symbolic representations of the sovereign's eloquence in the form of Orpheus or Hercules were also a reference to the supremacy of the word over brute force, which further indicates their ambiguity and possible double meaning.[17]

Aware of the reservations of a broad section of the audience, the pageant's organizers also introduced another scene, in which they attempted to blur the prince's foreignness. They insisted on his dynastic link with the queen, and especially his English ancestry, which allowed him to share a common origin with his subjects and to some extend could neutralize the threat that he represented:

Englande, if thou delite in aunccient men/ Whose glorious actes thy fame abrod dyd blase,/ Both Mary and Philip their offspring ought thou then/ With al thy hert to love and to embrace,/ Which both descended of one aunccient lyne/ It hath pleased God by mariage to combyne. (p. 8)

The marriage thus justified, all that remained was to legitimize the restoration of Catholicism in England in the wake of twenty years of Protestant domination. For this purpose the final *tableau* employed one of the images with which the Reformation in England, and above all Henry VIII, its patron, had been most identified. The stage displayed a gathering of virtues – *Justicis*, *Equitas*, *Misericordia*, and *Sapientia* – each with its corresponding attributes, among which the character of *Veritas* stands out, holding in his hands a book upon which are written the words *Verbum Dei*. The scene unmistakably recalls the image that the King's Printer Richard Grafton had himself made of Henry VIII for the English Bible of 1539, in which the king appeared holding a book with these same words.

The Catholic queen thus appropriated a primary symbol of the Reformation; however, Elder barely mentions this detail, one that from a pro-Catholic position would be noted only reluctantly. The scene can hence be seen as a call to the queen to remain within the line of her predecessors, something that she had promised her people in a letter she had written during the days Lady Jane sat on the throne, when Mary's only hope lay in the support her subjects could lend her.[18] In this way, London's authorities took advantage of a public celebration to remind the queen of her most important commitment to the nation. Mary, however, ignored these demands and shortly afterwards convened her third parliament, with the goal of shaping a reconciliation between England and Rome.

The return to Catholicism would not be easy. Parliament acquiesced to the union with Rome, but in no way accepted that lands confiscated from the Church should be returned, even though the queen had an entirely free hand in matters of faith. On 18 December 1554, a law was announced that reinstated the fifteenth-century measures against heresy.[19] These allowed the bishops to bring charges against those they considered suspicious and to punish those whom the civil authorities found guilty with burning at the stake.[20] Each of the executions had to be authorized by the queen, who would have the benefit of any properties owned by the condemned.[21]

Pamphlets of the day reveal the unease that these decisions generated within the reformist community:

> In tymes past, it was the office of Nero and of other tyrantes to torment men to death for their faith: but now oure English bishops have taken upon them to put the tyrants out of that office. For they them selves condemne bothe lerned and unlerned for their faith and make you, right honorable lords [of the Royal Council], to execute the office.[22]

Old denounces the cruelty and tyranny of those applying such laws, and serves them notice of the wrath of God:

> And now, I trust your lordships do well understand and perceave, that this law by your consentes lately revised, made a law in force and strength, is contrary both to the doctrine and example of Christ and of his Apostles and Prophets. Wherfore it can not be but a wicked law. Woo therfore be unto you that make wicked lawes, sayeth God by his prophet Isaias.[23]

However, the effects of this persecution were not what the queen expected. She did not achieve the submission of the Protestant section of the population, but rather heightened its capacity for resistance and its defiance in the face of the regime. The deaths of Latimer, Ridley and Cranmer made them into icons of faith and bravery that inspired their followers to continue fighting for their beliefs: "The constant death of these preachers, amazed greatly many Englishmen and confirmed their mindes in that Doctrine which they had learned of them".[24] Years later, during the reign of Elizabeth I, the reformers adopted them as symbols of opposition to Catholicism; John Foxe's description of the tortures and executions they suffered in *Actes and Monuments* (1563) demonstrates clearly the influence that the discourse of Protestant victimhood under Mary would attain in the Elizabethan period. The author's emphasis on the men's humility and trust in divine Providence in the face of death – expressed in his account by means of a variety of dramatic gestures, such as a raising of the hands or glances skyward, in addition to continuous declarations of faith – places them in the tradition of Christian martyrs.

The pathetic details in the description of the deaths of the three churchmen, especially that of Ridley, who was burned at the stake only slowly, are chilling, and seek to transport the sympathetic reader to the place of execution:

> The fire burned first beneath . . . and that made him [Ridley] leap up and down under the fagots, and often desire them to let the fire come to him . . . For after his legges were consumed by reason of his strugglinge, with the payne . . . he shewed that side towards us cleane, shirte and all untouched with the flame. Yet in all this torment he forgot not to call unto God still, having in his mouth, Lord have mercy upon me . . . However it was surely it moved hundreds to tears, to behold the horrible syght. For I think there was none that had not clean exiled all humanity and mercy, whiche woulde not have lamented to behold the fury of the fire rage upon their bodyes. Signes there were of sorrow on every side. (fol. 1378)

This type of portrayal complicated perceptions of the individual involved, who were converted into idols whose clothing and possessions held an almost sacred character for their followers:

> Some other of his [Ridley's] apparel that was little worth he gave away . . . he gave away some other small things to gentlemen standing by, and divers of them pitifully wepinge . . . napkins, some nutmegs and ginger, his dial, and such other things as he had about him, to every one that stood next to him. *Some even plucked the points off his hose, and happy was he that could get any rag of him.* (fol. 1377) (My emphasis)

Lastly, the binary opposition between Cranmer/Ridley and the Catholic Bishop Edmund Bonner can be seen as a model of the contrast between religions, one common in anti-Catholic discourse, in which reformist faith is characterized as allied with the humbler social strata against Catholic abuses and cruelty. Ridley is quoted as saying:

> There is nothing in all the world that troubleth my conscience (I praise God), this only excepted. While I was in the see of London, some poor men took leases of me, and agreed with me for them. Now I hear that the bishop who new occupies the same place, will not allow my grants to them, [and] contrary to all law and conscience, has taken from them their livings, and will not suffer them to enjoy them. (fol. 1378)

Naturally, the martyr pleads for such individuals to be helped. To this is added the description of the fury, typical of the Catholic stereotype, that was shown by the followers of Rome when Cranmer reaffirmed his adherence to Protestantism:

As soon therefore, as the Popish party heard these things, they began to rage, fret, and fume; and so much the more because they could not revenge their grief; for they could now no longer threaten or hurt him . . . And then Cranmer, being pulled down from the stage, was led to the fire, accompanied with those friars, vexing, troubling, and threatening him most cruelly. (fol. 1501)

Religious persecution thus constituted the principal element that all the denunciations of Catholicism in Protestant texts of the later Tudor period took as their starting point. By the end of 1555, the total number of victims had risen to three hundred, and the pamphlets produced by exiled Protestants multiplied at an amazing pace, at the same time as rumours of possible plots against the queen, most of them originating in France.

Anti-Catholic Pamphlets: An Admonitory Discourse

The foreign threat revived English patriotism, which the Protestant pamphleteers tried to exploit to highlight the supposed connection between Rome and Spain. The three main themes that are seen repeatedly in anti-Catholic texts of this period are the discourse of victimhood or martyrdom, the need to practice one's faith openly ('outward non-conformity'), and the constant appeal to the England of Mary I to repent of its Catholic beliefs.

To articulate the role of victims convincingly, the authors of these pamphlets returned to the schema of binary opposites, but with one fundamental difference: while in the time of Henry VIII there was some confusion as to the identity of the opposing forces, due as much to the novelty of the schism as to Henry's doctrinal ambiguity, during Mary's reign the two sides were sharply distinguished from each other. The Protestant side was made up of exiles and martyrs for the reformist cause, chiefly Cranmer, Latimer, and Ridley,[25] and the Catholic faction by Queen Mary and her bishops, Gardiner and Bonner. Curiously, the Pope, for the first time, occupied a secondary position.

The anonymously authored pamphlet *An Apologie or Defence against the Calumnations of Certayne Men* (1555)[26] presents the perspective of an English subject exiled for religious reasons. The reason the author gives for writing the work is that of defending his decision to leave the country:

I wryte this because some men of that towne wyll reporte evyll of me and other men which be gone away, not for that they can laye anye wickednesse or ungodlye conversation to oure charge (God be glorified thereof) but only of an yll mynd, because we wyl not consente to theyr doynges, and ioyne with them in observing the order of this religion. (sig. B2r)

The pamphleteer describes the penury and rootlessness he must endure far from home and family, without work and with scarce means of survival. In spite of it all, he holds firm to his convictions, preferring to maintain a clear conscience with the help of Scripture (sigs A3r-A4r). As a result, he identifies himself with biblical characters who benefit from the constant support of Providence, such as the patriarch Jacob (sigs A7r-v) or Jesus Christ himself (sig. A4r), and he considers his exile to be a divine test of faith that will ensure his membership among the elect (sig. A4v).

Martyrdom also constituted an instrument for the propagation of Protestant doctrine. The various pamphleteers are aware of its effectiveness and the power of conviction given by self-sacrifice as a model of faith and conduct among the faithful. In the posthumous edition of the works of Nicholas Ridley, *Certein Godly, Learned and Comfortable Conferences* . . . ,[27] the author and Latimer are praised, because

> Theyre demed libertie of conscience with the bondage of the bodie and to save their lyves they wer content to lose theyr lyves. This was not the worke of the fleshe but the operation of goddess mightie spirite who hathe ever frome the Beginning not onlye builded but also enlarged his churche by the sufferance of his sainctes and sealed his doctrine with the bloude of his martyrs. (sig. A3r)

The fear of God is a dominant element in these writings, a vengeful God, one who condemns and punishes those who disobey Him. Thus the God of the Old Testament is invoked frequently in order to stress man's obligation to follow His will, and so avoid the possibility of reprisals: "Better is to suffer what crueltye they will putte unto us then to incurre goddess hyghe indignation" (sig. B5v). This idea is a direct link to the second basic theme of this type of text: the need to practice the Protestant faith in public. Throughout the religious persecution, the option was always available of outwardly converting to the state religion, but continuing to practice one's true faith clandestinely. However, such a simultaneous practice of two doctrines created a profound conflict for the country's religious authorities, who felt threatened by a potentially rebellious body among the apparently compliant laity as well as by the actual community of believers that openly defended their faith in spite of the punishment and persecution to which they were subjected. The latter group nevertheless rejected the adulteration or corruption that their religious beliefs would suffer if they were seen to be mixed with opposing rites and beliefs.[28] Criticism of outward conformity occurs, in fact, in all the writings:[29]

> Christianitie and true religion cannot be in him that is afraide to confesse Christe and hys gospel in the time of persecution . . . If in your heart you knowe but one God, whi with your external presence serve ye the thynge that

ye knowe is not god? If your faith see idolatri, whi doth your silence confes and profes the same? Two men in one, god loveth not. If the inward man know the truth. Whi doth the outward man confesse a falshod? ... The cause whi God was offended with this people [the English Catholics who converted to Protestantism during the reigns of Henry VIII's and Edward VI], was that outwardly thei confessed him, but their heartes were farre from him inwardly. (Hooper, *Whether Christian Faith*, pp. 3–4)

If the public demonstration of faith affirms the doctrine of those persecuted for their beliefs, outward conformity has the opposite effect:

By their such dissimulation, the very idolaters themselves have a confirmation and defence of their abhomination ... For this is true, that in all rites, sacraments and honoringes, whether they be of God or the Devil, there is a profession of the communion: so that anye man protested to be of the same religion that the rest bee of that be partakers with him. (Ibid.; sigs A5v-A9r)

In spite of the strength of the Protestant movement in exile, and even within England, where economic crisis and religious persecution had engendered deep social discontent, a large part of the English population continued to obey Catholic doctrine and follow its rituals. To combat this tendency, pamphleteers took advantage of the crisis that swept the country in 1557 and 1558 to revive their attacks on Mary's regime: "Dimnes and darkness, desperation and anguish, al horrible miseries and calamities, death and destruction draw fast on, which al thou maiest yet avoide if thou wilt turne at the loving calling of thy most merciful lord".[30] The call to repent before the wrath of God is, then, another constant within the anti-Catholic discourse of the period:[31]

Thou than o England, if thou have anie pitie on thy selfe, on thy grave headded fathers, on thy grave matrones, on thy swete children, on thy semelie maidens, and towardlie youth, shake of al sluggishness, sete no vaine shiftes, flatter not thy selfe in thy wickednes, heare not the blasphemous blustering of those helhoundes, that impute the losse of Calece [Calais] to the neglecting of poperi, as the heathen in S. Augustines times affirmed that the forsaking and despicyng of theyr goddess and goddesses, was the cause of the decaie, and ruine of the empire. Which theyr shameless and abominable affirmation, God incontinently revenged, with the overthrow, and burning of Rome the imperial citie. (Traheron, *A Warning to England*, sig. B4r)

A fourth theme, perhaps not seen as frequently as the previous three, is the repeated denunciation of the attitude of the English nobility who, according to the Protestant community, were supporting Mary's regime to protect their own property and privileges. References made in the chronicles of Grafton and Stow to the aristocracy's enthusiastic reception

Mary I (1553–1558)

of Prince Philip upon his arrival in London in 1554[32] seem to justify the pamphleteers' resentment toward them: "I pray God that ye may secke to set forth the glorie of God and not to destroye his worde which many noble men of late with many great learned men have taken great payne to promote and set forwarde" (Traheron, *A Warning to England*, sig. B1). Philip Melancthon went so far as to hold them responsible for the reintroduction of Catholicism into England, and John Old laid the blame on the laziness and lack of awareness of the Royal Council, allowing itself to be influenced by doctrines contradicting the Word of God and exposing the people to His punishment (*A Faithful Admonition*, sig. A4v; *A Short Description of Antichrist*, sigs A3r, D7v.).

In general, these writings express the state of uncertainty in which, yet again, the nation had begun to live. They point out internal divisions within the Catholic bloc in an attempt to discredit the validity of its actions and decisions which, from the Protestant perspective, were confusing to the people, who no longer knew what to believe.[33] The chronicles also echo the many revolts and conspiracies in which the Crown found itself entangled.[34] Particularly harmful was the accusation that the Queen had feigned a pregnancy in order to create a false climate of stability. The discovery of the truth, that she was not pregnant, came as something of a relief to those among the Protestant ranks, and at the same time produced a feeling of mistrust and scepticism that very likely affected all her subjects, even those of the Catholic faith. Grafton described the reaction of the English people as follows:

> At this time many talked diversly, some said the rumour of the Queenes conception was spred for a pollicy, some other affirmed she was deviced by a Timpanye, or other lyke disease, by reason whereof she thought herself with childe and was not. Some other thought that she was with chylde and that it dyd by some mischaunce miscarye, or else that shee was bewytched. But what was the trueth, I am not able to affirme. (*An Abridgement of the Chronicles of England*, p. 186)

For the most part the pamphleteers did not explicitly attack the Queen, although there were exceptions, especially among the writings from late in her reign. Some, for example, stress her supposedly tyrannical and cruel personality, accusing her of blasphemy and of having put many innocents to death, among them her cousin Lady Jane and her husband Lord Guildford, who had become standard bearers for the cause of English Protestantism (Traheron, *A Warning to England*, sigs A2v-A3v).[35] The pamphlets also denounce the deviant nature of her insistence on placing her own ambition and interests (her marriage to Philip) before those of her subjects:

> Thy ruler is disdainful and so proud that to be wife of an emperors sonne

and for hope that she shal once be called my ladie emperesse she is contente not only to make the as bare as a birdes taile, but also unnaturally to betraie the hir native countree and make the subjecte to a popish proude, unmerciful and ungodly nation. She is despiteful, cruel, bloodie, wilful, furious, guileful . . . with simulation and dissimulation, void of honestie, void of upright dealinge, voide of al semelie vertues. (Traheron, *A Warning to England*, sig. A5r)

Even so, despite all this, the bishops of London and Winchester were the primary targets of the pamphleteers. Both of them were blamed for the religious persecution and executions of the years since 1553, which had earned them the hatred of the English people: "The wolfe Winchester and blody butcher Boner fought once against many godly men . . . and they had all the power of the Realme serving their lustes" (Turner, *The Hunting of the Fox*, sig. A4r).[36] The pamphleteer B. Traheron painted Bonner as a corrupt and diabolical character, by means of an enumeration of adjectives and similes that liken him to mythological monsters known for their extreme cruelty:

Who can thinke on that bloodie beast Bonner, but a most grislie, ugle and horrible monstre shall be presented before his eyes, such a one as no Polyphemus in boisteousnes, no furies of hel with their snarie heares in al pointes of mischiefe, no Cerberus[37] in blasphemous roaring, no find in raging, in tearing, and in deuouring innocentes, can ouermatche. (*A Warning to England*, sig. A8r)[38]

Bonner's purported wickedness forms the central element in the anonymously written pamphlet *A Commission Sent to the Bloudy Butcher Bishop of London*, in which a series of delegates from hell visit the bishop to advise him of the plan that Satan has for him and through which he intends to carry out the destruction of the English realm. As part of this plan, he will have to corrupt its rulers (sig. B1r) and, above all, eliminate those who preach the true Word of God: "But besure that ye cease not til those gospell bablers be brought to the fier whiche they so longe looked and laboured for, and when they be burnt, then send to one of your proctours (the youngest were most metest) to garnishe invent and furnishe out some lyes of them in wrytinge, yea al cleane contrarye to that they sayde when they were aliue" (sig. B3v).

However, executions could only be authorized by the Queen, who was, contrary to the impression given by the pamphlets, the person ultimately responsible for such measures. Besides, Bonner had no influence at court and in fact was arrested by the Queen herself, who criticized his tardiness in carrying out the punishment of heretics.[39]

Like Bonner, Stephen Gardiner had been imprisoned during the reign of Edward VI. Mary rewarded his loyalty to the Catholic faith with a seat on the Royal Council, restoration to his former position as Bishop of Winchester and his appointment as Lord Chancellor. The fact that a member of the clergy was Lord Chancellor and as such responsible for worldly matters was unacceptable to some, as is seen in *A Short Description of Antichrist*:

> This miserable mischiefe ensueth and cometh of this misorder that the gouernaunce of this realme, by your lordships consentes, hath be committed and done away agaynst God, in makinge a bishop (that by Gods worde and appointemente was assigned to feed the flocke committed to his spirituall charge) to leaue his office, committed to hym by God to be executed and done, to be a chauncelour wher by he was occupied and busied in the hearing of the matters and affairs of this realme that he could no attende his flocke to feade them accordinge to Christes commaundemente. (sigs E1v, E2r)

The author concludes that it is impossible for someone who has rejected the role assigned to him by God to do anything positive for the country (sig. E2r). Other pamphleteers also accused Gardiner of having reintroduced Catholic customs and rituals into England (Turner, *The Hunting of the Fox*, sig. D1v) along with a great number of Catholic priests whose objective was to deceive the nation:

> But the Pope and his Sonne Stephen Gardiner with al the order of priests above named are false prophets wherfore they are all wolves . . . he is the principall wolfe and for a great parte the hole cause of the great and exceding number of wolves that we now have for al the while that he was hid in his denne the great number of wolves that go abroad nowe openly and worrye and kill euery where played the foxes in their holes. (sigs B5v, B6r)

Gardiner, however, had advised the queen to be cautious in matters of religious persecution. The bishop charged no one in his own diocese with heresy, and grew alarmed at the growing numbers of those killed elsewhere. In addition, he attempted to persuade the queen to adopt some other form of punishment, but was soon accused by other royal advisors of coddling the Protestants.[40] In effect, Gardiner and Bonner were used as scapegoats by the pamphleteers for the errors of the queen. The constant attacks and condemnations that these men were subjected to in reformist literature concealed more hazardous attacks for which the authors could have been accused of treason against the Crown.

The pamphlets resort to stereotypes to criticize the Catholic clergy and its followers, but the pope, except in Rudolph Gwalther's work *Antichrist* (1556),[41] remains relegated to a secondary role. For the first time, writers began to identify internal problems as the source of the conflict, problems seemingly created by England's own rulers. The Holy See, despite being an almost omnipotent presence throughout Mary's reign, was thus not portrayed as the coercive element of earlier periods. In this case the endorsement of the Tudor monarchy itself was so evident that the role of papal intervention, at least in the degree to which it was portrayed in pamphlet literature, was considerably reduced.

On the other hand, numerous criticisms were made in the pamphlets of Catholic doctrine, although they were less prominent by comparison with the testimony of religious persecution. Subjects such as transubstantiation, the Mass, and the value of the Scriptures above Catholic traditions continue to be discussed. The concept of the Two Churches is stressed, as is the importance of internal revelation above that of external ceremony. In addition, the pamphleteers exalted the figures of the apostles, the evangelists, and the Protestant theologians and pastors sent by God to light the way for reformists, while attacking the validity of the councils of the Catholic Church, since the latter were nourished by human, rather than divine, authority. The theological polemic was carried forward employing familiar arguments, which seems to indicate that the English Reformation had set doctrinal matters aside in order to focus its attention on the political aspects of the conflict at this time.

The emergence of the Spanish stereotype, absent in the previous era, began to take shape as a result of the marriage of the Queen and Prince Philip. Rivalries between the English and Spanish courtiers and others in the service of the future king were not long in coming. The Spaniards were often the object of intrigues and insults, as well as all kinds of loutish behaviour from the citizens of London, who complained that they were being made to feel like foreigners in their own land.

The pamphlet texts encourage just such xenophobic attitudes toward this new group, which England scarcely knew anything about, except for its trading monopoly in America and the terrible accounts of the Inquisition arriving from the continent. The Spanish menace, however, was already an established fact: "Take hede and beware in time of these godles alienes and Brutish Spaniards, which minde to conquer your nacion and to subvert the whole state thereof" (Melanchthon, *A Faithful Admonition*, sig. A1r). Melanchthon begins here by displacing his adversary from a central position in the conflict by assigning him the labels of foreigner and heretic; the threat lies in the words "brutish" and "conquer", through which the Spanish seem to be associated with the barbarity of the conquest of the Americas or with the conflict in the Low Countries, which could now spread, or at least so it was widely believed, to English soil.

The link that Protestantism establishes between Spain and the papacy already appears in one such pamphlet of this time, as a foretaste of what would become a constant fear of Spanish invasion, especially from the 1580s: "The Spanyardes com upon you, your cause and the cause of your wyves and your children is in hande" (Gwalther, *Antichrist*, p. 163). This pamphlet presents the first outlines of what would later become the Spanish stereotype: wickedness, cruelty, and tyranny.[42] The relation of the Spaniards with the Italians is significant, as an active connection between the Spanish Prince and Machiavellian government:

> For shall we thinke any man to be so folishe and ignoraunt, that he can not perceave, what malicious heartes the Italianes and Spanyardes beare to all Germanie? Is ther any man so deafe and doltishe, that he never hearde, how they raile against us? . . . Their manner is to burthen us also, with the horrible crime of heresye, yea they thinke it lawful for them to exercise all kynde of wickednesse, tyrannie, and merciles crueltie upon the Germaynes. (Gwalther, *Antichrist*, p. 167)

Philip's situation with regard to England had been problematic since the very beginning of negotiations for the marriage. However, he had no intention whatsoever of being implicated in religious matters, and even disapproved of the persecutions.[43] In fact, as soon as these began, he ordered his confessor, Alfonso de Castro, to write a sermon indicating Philip's rejection of such measures, in an attempt to improve his already damaged image.[44] However, the prince's opinions on religious matters failed to become known among public opinion, which only saw his influence behind the deaths of Protestants. Nor was his relationship with the Holy See as close as was alleged. It had actually been dealt a severe blow, with the ascent of Paul IV to the papal throne in spring 1555, since the new pope's hatred for the Hapsburgs and Spaniards were all too well known. The progressive worsening of the relationship between the pontiff and Philip erupted into open conflict after the latter became King of Spain as Philip II on the abdication of his father Charles V at the end of 1555, and in 1557 Philip was excommunicated, while Cardinal Pole, Mary's Archbishop of Canterbury, was accused of heresy by a tribunal of the Inquisition.[45]

The English were perhaps mistaken in considering the Spanish sovereign an ally of the pontiff, but they were not when Queen Mary broke part of her marriage treaty by throwing the entire weight of England's military resources into supporting her husband in the war against the papacy and France (1557–1558). The effects were disastrous. An acute economic crisis finally cast a nation that had lost faith in its rulers into despair.

In this state of socio-economic depression, extremist tendencies were exacerbated, and sought for those to blame for the terrible situation into which the country had fallen. Protestant pamphlets developed various strategies with which to elaborate an image of this group as the "other". The Catholic stereotype was thus joined with the Spanish stereotype to encourage the association that had been growing between Protestantism and English nationalism since the beginning of Mary's reign. To this was added a new element that would complete this process of marginalization of Catholics from the national community, at least until Elizabeth's accession to the throne: traditional misogyny. The Queen of England, because of her deep Catholic convictions, her clear pro-Spanish tendencies, and her being female, embodied these three opposing mirrors, in the light of which England's most radical reformers examined and defined themselves. The most representative exponent of this triple process of the creation of alterity or "otherness" is the work by John Knox,[46] *The First Blast of the Trumpet against the Monstrous Regiment of Women* (1558),[47] in which the author assumes the role of divine prophet: "And further, it is our duty to open the truth revealed unto us, unto the ignorant and blind world" (p. 2).[48]

The work proceeds with a logical structure that attempts to prove the writer's central premise: "To promote a woman to bear rule, superiority, dominion or empire above any realm, nation or city, is repugnant to nature; contumely [an insult] to God, a thing most contrary to his revealed will and approved ordinance; and finally, it is the subversion of good order, of all equity and justice" (p. 4).[49] Accordingly, he cites misogynous statements and commentaries from diverse authorities, among them the Bible, Christian theologians, and classical authors. Knox's attack on the rule of Mary Stuart in Scotland, then, stems from a broader criticism of women, who are defined in contrast to the male intellect:

> I am assuredly persuaded . . . that albeit the outward form of men remained, yet should they judge their hearts were changed from the wisdom, understanding, and courage of men, to the foolish fondness and cowardice of women. Yea, they further should pronounce, that where women reign or be in authority, that there must needs vanity be preferred to virtue, ambition and pride to temperance and modesty; and finally, that avarice, the mother of all mischief, must needs devour equity and justice. (p. 5)

The listing of such supposed defects stresses women's incapacity to govern, a premise that the author supports by allusions to nature and history:

> Nature, I say, does paint them forth to be weak, frail, impatient, feeble and foolish; and experience has declared them to be inconstant, variable, cruel, lacking the spirit of counsel and regiment. And these notable faults have men in all ages espied in that kind, for the which not only they have removed women from rule and authority, but also some have thought that men subject to the counsel or empire of their wives were unworthy of public offices. (p. 5)

This reference to a female stereotype associated with ideas of weakness and uncontrolled appetites is also connected in the text with the corrupt image of the clergy, and makes manifest the danger rule by women supposes: "wheresoever women bear dominion, there the people must needs be disordered, living and abounding in all intemperance, given to pride, excess, and vanity; and finally, in the end, they must needs come to confusion and ruin" (p. 6).

Once the chief elements of the stereotype have been enumerated, Knox proceeds to develop the various points that made up his initial premise, among them God's rejection of any government led by women, "first by the order of his creation, and after by the curse and malediction pronounced against the woman (by reason of her rebellion)" (p. 6). Man's authority is stressed, together with the point that any government opposed to the order established in Genesis must by nature be a usurper: "for he [God] has expressly forbidden them to usurp any kind of authority above man" (p. 8). Allusion to the ideas of rebellion and the usurpation of power connects the image of the woman ruler with the concept of foreign menace and, later in the text, with the threat of Spain (in the case of England) and France (in the case of Scotland). Knox also returns to the metaphor of the body as a mirror of the state, to refer to the chaos that could result, in his view, from women in authority:

> And no less monstrous is the body of that commonwealth where a woman bears empire; for either it does lack a lawful head (as in very deed it does), or else there is an idol exalted in the place of the true head. I call that an idol which has the form and appearance, but lacks the virtue and strength which the name and proportion do resemble and promise. As images have face, nose, eyes, mouth, hands, and feet painted, but the use of the same cannot the craft and art of man give them, as the Holy Ghost by the mouth of David teaches us, saying, "They have eyes, but they see not, mouth, but they speak not; nose, but they smell not; hands and feet, but they neither touch nor have power to go" (Ps. 115: 5–7). (pp. 12–13)

The denigrating likening of a woman to an idol associates her with the images that had been the target of attacks by Protestant iconoclasts. Knox thus connects the figure of the female ruler with Catholic idolatry, binding together both "others". This association allows the author to leave behind his general argument and focus his attack on the governments of Mary Tudor and Mary Stuart, each an example of Catholic women rulers who, according to reformist literature, had abandoned their people to enemy hands: "You shall be reputed a traitor if Englishmen hear you . . . and Scotland has drunken also the enchantment and venom of Circe – let it be so to their own shame and confusion" (p. 13). Their link to witchcraft through the mythological figure of Circe endows them with connotations of falseness and lust[50], and supports the presentation of both of them as belonging more to the rule of Satan than to that of God (p. 13). The author's description of the spectacle leading up to the coronation of the

Queen of England refers, in fact, even if indirectly, to the image of the Whore of the Apocalypse:

> The insolent joy, the bonfires and banqueting, which were in London and elsewhere in England, when that cursed Jezebel was proclaimed queen, did witness to my heart that men were become more than enraged; for else how could they have so rejoiced at their own confusion and certain destruction? For what man was there of so base judgement (supposing that he had any light of God), who did not see the erecting of that monster to be the overthrow of true religion, and the assured destruction of England, and of the ancient liberties thereof? (p. 14)

The criticism extends to the people who have accepted such a ruler, especially the nobility: "[they] see their own destruction, and yet have no grace to avoid it. Yea, they are become so blind that, knowing the pit, they headlong cast themselves into the same, as the nobility of England do this day, fighting in the defence of their mortal enemy, the Spaniard" (p. 14). Knox's sequence of defamations thus connects the three figures – Rome, women, and Spain – which become intermingled and form one single "other": "Finally, they [the English people] are so destitute of understanding and judgement, that although they know that there is a liberty and freedom which their predecessors have enjoyed, yet are they compelled to bow their necks under the yoke of Satan, *and of his proud mistress, pestilent Papists and proud Spaniards*" (p. 14) (my emphasis).

Knox concludes with a harangue aimed at all social classes, urging them to break their vow of obedience to the queen and remove her from the throne; to this end, regicide is proposed as the only way out of the country's critical situation. Once again, reforming discourse puts forward the same provocative images that years later would be associated with Catholicism. The defence of sedition against the legal government goes against previously accepted notions of social order and usurpation. Equally, this brings into question the role of radical Protestantism in England which, since its beginnings in the time of Henry VIII, and as would be seen again in the Elizabethan era, had shown itself to be a factor disruptive to the *status quo*.

Dramatic Literature: The Dark Side of the Reformation

Dramatic literature produced during this period distanced itself from the themes employed by reformist pamphleteers, and instead adopted the ideological line of the Marian regime. After twenty years of Protestantism, it was not an easy task to re-establish Catholic doctrine and rid it of the marginalized image it had acquired in the previous reigns. The nation was not, nor would it ever be, the same, as can be seen in the works *Respublica* (1553) and the anonymous *Welth and Helth* (1553–1555).

The author of *Respublica*, probably written in 1553, is unknown, although the play is most consistently attributed to Nicholas Udall, who, in spite of his connections with Protestantism, continued to play an important part in dramatic productions for the royal court. The prologue reveals that the play was performed by a group of children at Christmas of 1553. According to Peter Happé, it is quite possible that the manuscript was prepared as a record of this performance, and that it had not originally been destined for publication.[51]

The play depicts the state of desolation into which the female figure of Respublica had declined under the influence of the vices Insolence, Oppression, and Adulation, which, guided by Avarice, attempt to deprive the main character of the scarce property and wealth she still possesses. The virtues, Misericordia, Veritas, Iusticia and Pax,[52] attempt to halt their antagonists' schemes and save the nation from ruin. The principal themes that drive the dramatic action are, then, economic questions, similar to those already analysed in *Impacient Poverty* and *Albion Knight*. The financial motives concealed behind the actions of the vices[53] call to mind Northumberland's religious policy and the corruption that had emerged among Protestant ranks, as the character Avarice reveals: "Than Oppression here, to feather well his neaste,/ Cared not of theire livelood whom he dispossesste./ Bishops, deanes, provestes, yea poore folke from the spittle,/ Landes with churche and chapple, all was for him to little" (V, x, 33–36). One of this character's plans is to make his way into Respublica's court and there act as an agent to enable his companions to enter, one by one (II, ii, 50–69). The result of all this is a generalized state of corruption in which one can scarcely trust anyone, and a level of misery and crisis that extends to every sector of society:

> [AVARICE:] So, sir, nowe Respublica, the ladie of estate,/ Ye knowe nowe more latelye is left almoost desolate./ Hir welthe ys decayed, hir comforte cleane a goe,/ And she att hir wittes endes what for to saie or doe/ Fayne wolde she have succoure and easemente of hir griefe/ And highlye advaunce them that wolde promise reliefe./ Suche as wolde warraunte hir spirites to revive. (I, iii, 83–89)

The economic penury and state of desperation in which the protagonist finds herself make her easy prey for the vices. References to her blindness (II, ii, 13–23; V, ix, 95–100) are nonetheless significant, in that they recall an anti-Catholic discourse that criticized Catholics as blind and ignorant for allowing themselves to be led by the Roman hierarchy. In this case, Catholicism makes use of elements of the opposing discourse to justify its new, centralized position and silence the criticism that had poured out against it. At the beginning of the second act, Respublica's speech shows many characteristics that are in line with the discourse of the Reformation, such as nostalgia for the past – in the case of Protestantism, by evoking the early church, and here, in contrast, by alluding to the times before the schism (II, i, 3–4) – and particularly the need for good rulers capable of saving the people from ruin (II, i, 16–18).

The comparison of Protestant England with the wealth and splendour of Babylon (II, i, 11–12) takes on a profound irony, as it represents an obvious inversion of one of the well-established clichés of English Protestantism. Anti-Catholicism thus emerges as a discursive construct that based itself on the same broad repertoire that had been generated by the Catholic Church over centuries in order to present itself as the one and only true Church in the face of all dissenting voices. This discourse is maintained in a state of constant fluidity between the two opposing camps, which both use it in practically the same ways and for the same ends. All that changes is the point of view: in the case of *Respublica*, the Protestant community is marginalized so as to afford Mary I's Catholicism a central position. The need to legitimize a set of values and principles that up until a short time earlier had been vilified set in motion a method of self-affirmation that in the end was maintained by the same marginalizing process that had been used to delineate the Protestant Church during the reigns of Henry VIII and Edward VI.[54]

The presence of the virtues, led by Veritas, permits the salvation of Respublica, who quickly recognizes her mistake and the intrigues of which she had been the target (V, iii). Her character's association with Mary's reign – portrayed as *Veritas Filia Temporis* on the stages at her coronation[55] – is predictable, and anticipates the restoration of truth (i.e., Catholicism) in England by the Tudor queen. The symbolic union of the two characters underscores the providential nature of the return of Catholicism:

> [MISERICORDIA:] Iustice and Peace are appointed to descende,/ The one to kepe youe quiete, the other youe to defende./ As soone as wee fowre sisters togither shalbe mette,/ An ordre for your establishment shall bee sett/ By the eternall providence; yt is decreed soo. (V, iii, 47–51)

The direct result of the change is Respublica's transformation into Prosperity (V, iv, 32; V, vi, 16), which reproduces Alciatus' emblem CLXXVIII, *Ex Pace Ubertas* (From peace, plenty). Thus it seems that the author views the new period of transition with hope. The speech by the character People yet again denounces the oppressive nature of the fiscal policy of the former Protestant government and promotes the identification of the English people with the new Catholic regime. People, portrayed as a poor man of scarce economic means (V, vii, 16–18; 23–24), refers back to the circumstances surrounding the revolts of 1536–1538 and 1547 against the government's despotism, personified in turn here as the character Insolence, who treats People with contempt and is incapable of listening to his requests (V, viii, 6–15). English Catholicism thus proclaims its care of and support for the people, presented as wishing for political and religious transformation in the country. The restoration of Catholicism and the accession of Mary to the throne are described as the result of popular will: "[ADULATION] I will fall to speaking faire./ Butte of all this trouble we maie thanke People, this wretche" (V, viii, 41). The author thus puts forward a vision of a monarchy sustained on the basis of a contract between the queen and her subjects, with which suggestion the play ends.

The vices are finally unmasked by the virtues, and with the exception of Adulation – who is pardoned when he shows repentance – the three others receive various punishments in accordance with their actions.[56] Veritas compares the figure of Nemesis[57] (who appears in the final scene to mete out justice) to the English sovereign:

> Nowe ye see what thei are, the punishment of this/ Muste be reffered to the goddesse Nemesis./ She is the mooste highe goddesse of correction,/ Cleare of conscience and voide of affection./ She hath powre from above, and is newlie sent down/ To redresse all owtrages in citie and in towne/ She hath powre from Godde all practise to repeale/ Which might bring annoyaunce to Ladie Commonweale. (V, ix, 118–125)

The vengefulness of this character is problematic, since it seems to suggest the idea that Mary's government will be excessively strict, and incapable of pardoning its detractors. Though the period of religious prosecution was still some way in the future, one nevertheless could already get a sense from court circles that the return to Catholicism would be no simple matter.

The second work analysed follows a similar line to that of the previous text, although it focuses on one of the thornier questions of the first years of Mary's reign: the marriage of the Queen to the Spanish Prince. It was written sometime between 1553 and 1555, but the arguments that are expressed in the work seem to place it in the period prior to the signing of the marriage treaty in January of 1554. The text's publication in the middle of the Elizabethan regime (1565) suggests that it contained ambiguous elements that would have justified its revival. The most significant of these is the way its foreign characters are treated, which makes it possible to see a certain continuity in anti-Spanish and, by extension, anti-Catholic discourse.

In *Welth and Helth*, the role of the main protagonist is split between three characters, who function as a group throughout the play: Welth, Helth, and Liberty, who are committed by Good Remedy to remaining united in order to achieve prosperity for the country. The vices Ill Will, Shrewd Wit, and Hance[58] attempt to thwart their efforts. No reference is made to the salvation of the leading character's souls; instead, the motivating forces of the drama are very material, specifically, the stability and prosperity of the nation without the need for foreign support. This insistence could perhaps be an implied criticism of Protestantism, as had already been seen in Udall's work; even so, Good Remedy's description of the distribution of wealth betrays a certain degree of anticlericalism, with his allusions to the possessions that prelates of the church still enjoyed:

> The chiefe parte of all welth, lyeth in great estates/ Their substance and landes is right commendable/ Prelates of the churche is welthy of ryches/ Merchautes hath marchaudise & goods incomperable/ Men of law & franklins is welthy . . . / Thus welth of riches is devided diverse wayes/ And to these many charges, come now a dayes. (559–565) (My emphasis)

Thus it seems to uphold a view that is antagonistic towards those who controlled wealth, whether Catholic or not. In spite of this, the polemic is not pursued, since the text goes no further than mere allusions. The many patriotic references, on the other hand – "Consider Englyshmen, how valiant they be & ferce/ Of al nacions none such, when they have their helth/ No land can do us harme" (569–572) – reinforce the play's main premise, which could be summarized as an admonition to the queen to avoid marrying a foreign prince. To this end, stress is laid on the autonomy of England's:

> [GOOD REMEDY:] I pray thee go hence, for thou dost trouble me yll./ [HANCE:] Nen ic seker, ic wyl not gon, ic wold fain live hore stil./ [GOOD REMEDY:] *There is to many allaunts in this reale*, but now I/ Good remedy have so provided that English men shall/ Lyve the better dayly./ [HANCE:] . . . ic my selfe love descone Englishman./ [GOOD REMEDY:] Fie on ye flattering knave, *fie on you aliauts al I say/ Ye can wt craft & subtel tiget englishmes welth away*/ [HANCE:] O skon master, ic heb hore bin, this darten yeore . . . / [GOOD REMEDY:] *Must see so provide that welth from you have I shall*/ [HANCE:] Ic seg to you dat welth is lopen in an ander contry . . . / [GOOD REMEDY:] *ic understand the wel, yet thou liest lyke a knave/ Welth is here in England, & welth stil I trust we shal have.* (745–757) (My emphasis)

The fact that the character Hance is a Dutchman who insists on helping Good Remedy in dubious ways brings to the fore the conflictive relationship England had with the Low Countries, its chief rival in the international market. The reference to the many foreigners living in London in those years – in addition to those from the Netherlands, there were also many Germans and Italians – highlights the fears of many English citizens in the face of increasing commercial competition.

However, the most pointed attack is levelled against the Spanish, an ever more prominent group. The burlesque portrayal of Ill Will, who babbles nonsense in Castilian Spanish,[59] emphasizes the threatening image of Spain, which is thus seen to be associated with the heroes' antagonists:

> [ILL WYLL:] Qury cicis quest is un malt ombre/ Me is un spy&nardo compoco parlauere./ [HELTH:] Thou false chefe is thine English tonge gone/ As mischeuous is wil & shrewdwit, ye have destroyed mani on/ [SHREWD WYT:] Sir hurt not me, & wil tel you trouth anone/ This same is as false a knave as ever cam wtin saint Iohes/ [ILL WYLL:] Per amor de my as pi ca un poco/ Eo queris and ar your lagraunt creae so/ [GOOD REMEDY:] I can not tel what thou dost meae blabber/ But yu shalt speake English & confesse an other matter. (830–839)

The play depicts, therefore, the feeling of unease among a broad sector of the English people in the light of the perceived threat to their sovereignty posed by a foreign power. Religion occupies a secondary tier in preference to purely economic questions, although religious considerations cannot be concealed when they are linked – at least in the view of many in England – to the power of Philip II and of the pope. Hence we begin to see several characteristics that would come to form part of the Spanish stereotype during the Elizabethan period.

Although it is a matter of record that anti-Catholic and anti-Spanish plays were performed in the final years of Mary Tudor's reign, these performances were staged in the homes of noblemen and in locations far from the capital, and most likely never appeared in print.[60] Consequently, the majority of texts that have come down to the present day are plays that were intended to be performed at court and follow a more or less official line. The two examples we have analysed demonstrate, however, the desire on the part of playwrights to take part in the political decisions being made in that time of change, which explains the various demands that, implicitly or not, were regularly expressed in these theatrical productions. In addition, these plays attempted to legitimize the new Catholic government's position by making use of the same rhetorical weapons that had been seen in reformist plays. By criticizing the corruption of the Church of England, particularly regarding the improper use of expropriated monastic lands, they sought to appeal to certain sectors within the Protestant community who also rejected these practices. Nonetheless, English Protestantism in general felt more closely identified with radical reforming groups who, although they seemed indisposed to work toward social peace and stability, pursued similar doctrinal ends. Only after the clear establishment of the Church of England did such groups come to be viewed as subversive and problematic, and began to be marginalized in much the same way as the Catholics had been. This, however, did not occur until well into the Elizabethan period.

In 1558, the country was in an alarming condition. The queen saw how her subjects had forsaken her, and impatiently awaited her successor. Mary I died on November 17 of that year, and Catholicism would never again return to England. Later Protestant literature would take on the duty of keeping the memory of her victims alive, and references to the religious repression of this period would come to form a central part of anti-Catholic discourse from the reign of Elizabeth I onward.

CHAPTER THREE

Elizabeth I (1558–1579): A Failed Attempt at Reconciliation

The Iconographic Construction of Elizabeth I and its Anti-Catholic Implications

The construction of the public figure of Elizabeth I presented itself as a high priority in 1558. Not only was it necessary to justify the return to Protestantism, but also to defend a woman whose dynastic claim to the throne was unclear. Iconography would play a fundamental role in this process. We have selected here a text that describes Elizabeth's ceremonial entry into London as an example of the role of anti-Catholic discourse at the moment of defining the new religious order, as well as the image of the new ruler. *The Quenes Majesties Passage*,[1] was published nine days after the royal entry, and chronicled the several performances that were staged for the queen to celebrate her accession to the throne.[2]

Royal entries, like all forms of civic theatre, make it possible to observe the interaction of various levels of society, in this case at the moment when the monarch's public image is being created. These performances can, in principle, broach the people's demands, and may even dare suggest, by means of imagery and abstractions, the policy the authors wish their queen to adopt.[3] Elizabeth, who had witnessed her sister's failure, was determined not to commit the same mistakes.

In reality, the performances were part of an elaborate political propaganda campaign that was organized by city authorities under the queen's supervision.[4] She in fact provided part of her own wardrobe for use by some of the actors, and had given the end result her approval.[5] According to Helen Hackett, a celebratory tone for the event was enforced from the upper circles of power, so it is likely the displays of affection between the queen and her subjects were far less spontaneous than this chronicle suggests.[6]

The procession began at the Tower of London about two o'clock in the afternoon; from there, it headed toward Temple Bar, and finally to Westminster Abbey for the coronation. In the preparations for the ceremony, the concern to distinguish the incoming reign from the outgoing (and thereby demonstrate the superiority of the new Protestant regime by comparison with Mary Tudor's Catholicism) can already be seen, as one can gather from a document from the London City archives dated 7 December 1558:

> Item this day the Worshipful Commoners hereunder named were nominated, appointed, and charged by the whole court to take the charge, travail, and pains to cause at the City's costs and charges all the places hereafter mentioned to be very well and seemly trimmed and decked for the honour of the City against the coming of our Sovereign Lady the Queen's majesty that now is to her Coronation through the City with pageants, fine paintings, and rich cloths of arras, silver and gold in such and like manner and sort as they were trimmed against the coming of our late Sovereign lady Mary to her Coronation *and much better if it conveniently may be done.* (p. 19) (My emphasis)

Contradictions begin to multiply in the face of the need to resort to splendour and ceremony in order to convey an image of power to the citizenry,[7] since ritual bestowed an aura of spirituality on monarchs, one that sought to affirm their divine origin.[8] Elizabeth makes use of these devices to stress her image as an instrument of God, who will, in accordance with His judgment, install Protestantism in England. Though aware of the dangers of the use of imagery within the Protestant context, Elizabeth seemed not to have much choice. She presented herself to the multitude as a symbol overflowing with meanings, or as Il Schifanoya, the Venetian ambassador, put it: "dressed in a royal robe of very rich cloth of gold, with a double-raised stiff pile, and on her head over a coif of cloth of gold, beneath which was her hair, a plain gold crown without lace, as a princess, but covered with jewels, and nothing in her hands but gloves".[9]

The many connotations associated with this vision would have gone unnoticed by few in the audience, accustomed as they were to the language of allegory and symbols. On the one hand, they might recall the symbol of Magnanimity, who appears in Ripa as a "beautiful woman, with a clear, high forehead, a prominent nose, who dresses in gold, with the imperial crown upon her head". This quality is further described as the "ruler of even the vilest passions, who bestows generous favours for the benefit of others, with neither vanity nor the need for public applause".[10] These qualities would be directly associated with the queen, who would thus appear as generous, disposed to give her all for her people. On the other hand, the iconographical emblem of Virtue also dresses in gold,[11] and so this anticipates the message enacted on the second stage of the pageant, in which the queen was portrayed as an embodiment of the virtues necessary for good government. Nonetheless, the main image that this presentation of the queen would have called to the collective mind was that of the *Woman Clothed with the Sun*, from Revelation (Rev. 12), the antithesis of the Whore of Babylon and related by patristic texts to the Christian Church and, by extension, the Virgin Mary.[12]

The reforming discourse reinterpreted these images, making use of the opposition of these two apocalyptic figures to refer to the confrontation between the Catholic Church and Protestantism, an idea first propounded in John Bale's book *The Image of Both Churches* (1541), which describes the Whore of Babylon as the "proude paynted churche of the Pope" and the Woman Clothed with the Sun as "the poore persecuted churche of Christe, or immaculate spowse of the lambe".

However, the queen's own control of her public image was limited by the aspirations and desires of others who contributed to her royal iconography during her entry into London. Among them were Richard Grafton, the general coordinator of the pageant, and Richard Mulcaster, most probably the author of the lines the actors recited from the altars as well as of the previously-mentioned chronicle of the event. Both men were intellectual reformers and, as such, insisted on presenting the queen's commitment to Protestantism in a less moderated manner than she would probably have wanted.[13] The many anti-Catholic references clothe the interpretation of good government in religious code, which gives an indication of the distance between the interests of the representatives of the city[14] and the intentions of Elizabeth herself.[15]

The title of one piece was "The seate of worthie governance". In it there appeared a throne supported by four virtues: Pure Religion, Love of Subjects, Wisdom, and Justice; and at the feet of each of these were their respective opposing vices: Superstition and Ignorance, Rebellion and Insolency, Folly and Vainglory, and Adulation and Bribery (p. 25). Thus were summarized the principles upon which every Christian prince should base his government. These figures' symbolic meanings are obvious, as the author himself indicates in his chronicle: "every of them was aptly and properly appareled so that his apparel and name did agree to express the same person that in title he represented" (p. 25). Practically all the vices were represented in such a way that they would be associated with a stereotype of Catholicism. The most significant were those that appeared in opposition to Pure Religion: Superstition and Ignorance, traits that were identified with the Catholic masses that obeyed the doctrines of Rome.[16]

In spite of the relative religious conservatism that existed at many levels among the English people, Catholicism thus began to carry with it political values that supposedly ran counter to the well-being of the English nation – that is, to good government. The queen's moderate tendencies contrast with the lines that the actor directs toward her, warning her of the consequences of accepting Catholic principles: "she [the Queen's Majesty] should sit fast in the same so long as she embraced virtue and held vice under foot . . . if Her Grace did continue in her goodness as she had entered, she should hope for the fruit of these promises" (p. 26). The use in these lines of the conditional might be read as revealing the uncertainty of many English subjects regarding Elizabeth's future government.

A Failed Attempt at Reconciliation

In this admonition one senses the authority wielded by the city of London in determining the religious system of the country, as well as its style of government. The need to do away with Catholicism is proposed as an absolute condition for England's stability.[17]

The third part of the pageant was located in Soper Lane, where a stage with three arches was erected. Above the centre arch, set in the shape of a pyramid, were eight children, representing the Beatitudes. Their title, "The eight beatitudes expressed in the fifth chapter of the gospel of St. Matthew, applied to our sovereign lady Queen Elizabeth"[18] conveys a message to the queen, "which was the promises and blessings of Almighty God made to his people" (p. 26). The connection that is made between the queen and God's divine promise allows her to be characterized as his envoy. With this, the critics of female rule are silenced, since God is portrayed as ultimately responsible for Elizabeth's accession to the throne. The queen and her inner circle thus articulate a response to the polemic that had originated earlier in 1558 with the publication of John Knox's *The First Blast of the Trumpet against the Monstrous Regiment of Women*, analysed in the previous chapter. Faced with Elizabeth's accession to power, Knox attempted to reconcile his position with the new queen, although he maintained his same argument: "albeit that nature and Godes most perfect ordinaunce repugne to suche regiment . . . the extraordinary dispensation of Godes great mercy maketh that lawfull unto her, which both nature and Godes law denye".[19] In this sense, the *tableau* appears to follow the writer's advice, by stressing the role of divine will, which has resulted in Elizabeth's inheriting the Crown of England. The verses addressed to her from the stage explain the Beatitudes' significance, underscoring the queen's charitable and Christian image through the identification of civil power with the religion of the less fortunate.

The next stage portrays her as the representative and defender of the Protestant Church, the central pillar of her government, thus completing the two previous themes. The chronicler depicts the monarch's enthusiasm for and impatience to see the symbolic construction performed for her: "Soon after that Her Grace passed the Cross, she had espied the pageant erected at the Little Conduit in Cheap and incontinent required to know what it might signify. And it was told Her Grace that there was placed Time. 'Time?' saith she, 'And Time hath brought me hither'".[20] Elizabeth is identified with Truth, a figure who shortly afterwards appears on stage. Above this figure are raised two mountains, one on each side of the platform. One of them represents *Ruinosa Respublica*, a character who exemplifies ruin and desolation; on the other side is a mountain with the legend *Respublica bene instituta*, which "was made fair, fresh, green and beautiful, the ground thereof full of flowers and beauty" (p. 28). Between the two mountains appears the character Time, who

> appareled as an old man with a scythe in his hand having wings artificially

made, leading a personage of lesser stature than himself which was finely and well appareled, all clad in white silk, and directly over her head was set her name and title in Latin and English, *Temporis filia*, the daughter of Time . . . And on her breast was written her proper name, which was *Veritas*, Truth, who held a book in her hand upon the which was written, *Verbum Veritatis*, the word of Truth. (p. 28)

Time as the revealer of truth and justice was a common motif in humanist literature. Iconographic tradition had popularized a characterization of Time as a winged old man, according to the saying *Volat irreparabile tempus*.[21] Since the first years of the Reformation, Catholics as well as Protestants had adopted this *topos* in an attempt to reaffirm their respective positions and their defence of the true religion. Its use was especially common within reformist circles, who interpreted the figure of Truth in its religious sense and described Protestantism as the restorer of the Word and Law of God. The victim posture, which had so often characterized Protestant discourse, saw in the combination of these two figures an instrument capable of instilling confidence among English Protestants in the face of Catholic attacks.

The *tableau* attempts to convey, therefore, a certain optimism for the restoration of Protestantism following the Catholic interlude; and, once again, the need to do away with the vestiges of Catholicism is underscored as vital to the nation's prosperity. Although the author includes no commentary regarding the figure of *Ruinosa Respublica*,[22] the predominant language of the production is one of binary opposites, which permeate the entire celebration. Elizabeth could only be characterized in terms of the contrast she represented to her predecessor. In addition, the appropriation that is made of the motto *verbum veritatis* – used by Mary Tudor in her royal entrance in 1553 – constitutes, according to Helen Hackett, an act of aggression through which the foundations of the former regime were subverted: Elizabeth's identification with the truth implied that Mary Tudor's truth had been a fraud.[23]

This scene reaches its dramatic climax when the figure of Truth passes a Bible to a child actor who, in turn, surrenders it to Sir John Perrot.[24] As the last action of the *tableau*, he offered it to the queen, who, "as soon as she had received the book, kissed it, and with both her hands held up the same, and so laid it upon her brest, with great thanks to the city therefore" (p. 29). The political import of this theatrical gesture is obvious, and amounts to a declaration of iconoclasm on the part of the queen and the organizers of the royal entry with regard to the use of images that was a common feature of Catholicism. Special emphasis is placed upon the power of the Word as the sole conveyor of the truth, demonstrated graphically by the figure of Truth holding up the Bible. Nevertheless, the contradictions that this iconoclastic use of images throws up remain, despite the attempt to give them a moralizing purpose.

Almost at the end of the queen's progress, on Fleet Street, a square platform with four towers was erected. At its centre were three raised rows of seats, and above them, a throne. Seated on it was "a seemly and mete personage richly apparelled in parliament robes, with a scepter in her hand, as a queen, crowned with an open crown, whose name and title was in a table fixed over head in this sort *Deborah the judge and restorer of the House of Israel*. Jdic. 4." (p. 31). Six characters appeared beneath this figure: two representatives of the nobility, two from the clergy and two from parliament. The scene's title succinctly explains the symbolic reference: *Deborah with her estates, consulting for the good governement of Israel*. The images of castles and towers characterize London as heavenly Jerusalem (Heb. 12:22), and strengthen the link made between London (and by extension, England) and Israel, both of them God's chosen nations, which was a common theme in anti-Catholic literature but also an integral part of this type of ceremony which always drew a parallel between the royal sphere – the king and the city – and its symbolic correlate, the deified monarch of the New Jerusalem.

The symbolism of this tableau recreates a biblical scene: "And Deborah, a prophetess, the wife of Lapidoth, she judged Israel at that time. And she dwelt under the palm tree of Deborah between Ramah and Bethel in mount Ephrain: and the children of Israel came up to her for judgment" (Judg. 4:4–5). Professor Gómez Lara has analysed the allegorical interpretations associated with this figure on the basis of patristic commentary on the Book of Judges. In his view, the patristic texts depict this character as possessing masculine virtues, which would justify her role as protector against England's enemies:

> [The images employed to describe Deborah] could evoke the Virgin Mary, but only in the sense that Elizabeth could be interested in: as a prefiguration of the woman *viriliter*. The emphasis in the allegorical commentaries upon Deborah as a fighter against the Church's enemies and as the one who would bring about the triumph of the True Church over the Old Judaic Synagogue could easily be translated into those of the Catholic and the Reformed Churches.[25]

The need to refer to female historical figures who had governed successfully stresses again the uncertainty that a government led by a woman provoked among the English. The insistence that the queen governed with the backing of the nobility, the clergy and parliament further demonstrates this lack of confidence in Elizabeth's ability to rule.[26] The fact that the figure of Deborah is dressed in parliamentary robes – an attire in which Elizabeth was painted in several occasions – is significant, and leaves no doubt as to the rejection by London's representatives of the possibility of an absolute monarchy.[27]

On the way to Temple Bar, where the procession would come to an end, Elizabeth made one final stop, at the church of St. Dunstan, where the children of Christ's Hospital paid tribute to her. This hospital had been founded by Henry VIII after the expropriation of the Franciscan convent that had previously stood on the site, and since that time had been maintained with funds from the City of London. The policy of expropriating the lands of the Catholic Church, a central element in the reforms of Henry VIII, was thus seen to be linked with a promise of continuity into the reign of Elizabeth I, in a way that also emphasized both her social commitment to the people of England and her adherence to the tenets of Protestantism.[28] It is at this point in his chronicle that Mulcaster stresses the link between the Tudor Anglican monarchs, which is Elizabeth's source of legitimacy:

> This one spectacle yet rested and remained, which was the everlasting spectacle of mercy unto the poor members of Almighty God, furthered by that famous and most noble prince King Henry the VIII, Her Grace's father, erected by the city of London, and advanced by the most godly virtuous and gracious prince King Edward VI, Her Grace's dear and loving brother, doubting nothing of the mercy of the Queen's most gracious clemency by the which they may not only be relieved and helped, but also stayed and defended. (p. 32)

Knowing that the only thing that could perhaps keep England united was for the monarchy to have a conciliatory image, Elizabeth assimilated and deployed to the very end of the pageant the image of herself as mother-protector to her people. Catholicism became, therefore, a permanent reference point against which to define the image of the queen and her government. However, as we have seen, the impossibility of creating such an image without alluding, even if only indirectly, to Catholic tradition gave rise to numerous paradoxes. In addition, it provided a foretaste of the power struggles in which the religious and economic policies of Elizabeth's government would find themselves entangled.

The Quest for Internal Religious Conformity and the European Political Crisis

During her government's first decade (1558–1569), Elizabeth strove to achieve a degree of religious uniformity and to provide stability for the nation. Nevertheless, disputes soon arose between those inclined to accept the principles of the official church and those who sought either more profound changes or a return to Catholicism. The attitude of radical Protestant groups, those that came to be known as Puritans, was especially problematic. When the ecclesiastical authorities attempted to silence them, their response was to question the nature of the Church of England, which they considered to be corrupted by the presence of many Catholic traditions.[29] Some separatist groups were even more extreme, taking oaths of opposition to Protestant unity:

> I have now joined myself to the church of Christ wherein I have yielded myself subject to the discipline of God's word as I promised at my baptism . . . For in the church of the traditioners there is none other discipline, but that which hath been ordained by the antichristian popes of Rome, whereby the church of God hath always been afflicted, and is to this day, for which I refuse them.[30]

The association of the Church of England with Rome by means of apocalyptic discourse is clear: Anglicanism forms part of Babylon, and is one more of the heads of the Antichrist. The "other" is redefined according to the particular positions of each group. In this case, the English Church finds itself excluded from the elect when it affirms its continuity with Catholicism: "Antichrist, the Pope of Rome, this name is banished out of England, but his body, which be the bishops and other shavelings do not only remain, but also his tail, which be his filthy traditions, wicked laws, and beggarly ceremonies . . . yea, and the whole body of his pestiferous canon law".[31]

The situation of Catholics was generally very different, but it too was marked by internal dissension. The majority of English Catholics attended Protestant services in order to avoid paying the fine imposed upon those who did not. The problems of recusancy, direct challenges to authority by insisting on holding Catholic services, were almost always connected with, on the one hand, the surviving clergy from the reign of Mary, who refused to accept the basic principles of the new religious system, and on the other the Catholic nobility, who preferred to pay the fines and continue practicing their faith.[32] Not only that, they had a significant influence in local government, which created an important obstacle to the Anglican bishops' attempts at imposing religious uniformity.

Nevertheless, and despite the religious changes, English Catholics sought to remain at the periphery of political events during the first years of Elizabeth's reign. This attitude made for a relatively smooth coexistence between the Queen and her Catholic subjects, who could continue to practice their faith with scarcely any pressure from the state.[33] The first problems came from Rome. In 1562, the Council of Trent condemned the attendance of Catholics at Protestant services, although, curiously, this affirmation was not followed by any decree or law designed to enforce it, so that a large number of English Catholics ignored the warnings of the Holy See.[34] It would be as a result of tensions generated by events unfolding at the end of the 1560s that relations between the international Catholic community and England became icy.

If religious uniformity was problematic, there was another more practical and realistic means of achieving the desired stability: economic prosperity. The crown's investment in naval and military industries, alongside its promotion of trade and expeditions that were mounted by private interests, brought about significant economic development that did not take long to be manifested in other profitable activities. The sector that benefited most from this policy was foreign trade, to which Elizabeth's government was clearly committed.

The search for new trade routes had become one of the English government's priorities, one that it considered to be fundamental to its project of ensuring the nation's recovery, even though this might jeopardize England's moderating position in Europe. Elizabeth's supposedly peaceful intentions began to be subordinated to economic interests and religious commitments. The choice of Protestantism as England's official religion significantly influenced the queen's international policy. Her support for the three great nuclei of the Reformation in their conflicts with the two main Catholic powers meant that she was unambiguously situating herself among the Protestants. The most significant of these nuclei was perhaps the Calvinist movement in the Low Countries.

News of the massacres perpetrated by Philip II and the Duke of Alba in the Netherlands in the late 1560s reached England, heightening fears of a Spanish invasion. Anti-Spanish and anti-Catholic sentiment swirled together, and seemed to remind the English of the possibility that the persecutions of years past might be repeated. Elizabeth's intervention in support of the Dutch Protestants, despite the objections of conservative members of the nobility and of her own Royal Council, resulted in a serious antagonism with Spain that would, years later, unleash all-out war between the two countries.

Relations with France were probably even more problematic, since they had a bearing on the succession to the throne of England. With the death of her father-in-law King Henry II of France in 1559, Mary Stuart, Queen of Scots, had also become the queen-consort of the French nation, a position she would not hold for long, due to the sudden death of her husband King Francis II in December of 1560. During their brief reign Mary had been able to place her relatives, the Guises, in influential and advantageous positions around France, which allowed this Catholic family to intervene directly in affairs of state. Confrontations between the French crown and the growing Huguenot Protestant community began during these years, ushering in an era of religious wars that would last more than three decades.

The campaign against the Huguenots eventually reached Scotland, where Calvinism had begun to flourish. What began as a purely religious revolt eventually turned into a bitter struggle for political independence from France. In the summer of 1559, the Scottish nobility, led by the Calvinist John Knox, sought assistance from Elizabeth I in an attempt to thwart the French; and as she would do in the Low Countries, Elizabeth eventually chose to help the Protestant cause. It was the diplomacy of her chief minister William Cecil that, with the Treaty of Edinburgh, succeeded in removing French troops from Scotland, in exchange for the Calvinists agreeing to allow Mary Stuart to remain on the throne.[35] In 1561, Mary returned to Scotland with only limited powers, due to Protestant pressure. The first four years of her personal reign were relatively calm, but Mary refused to ratify the Treaty of Edinburgh, by which she would have been required to renounce her dynastic claim to the throne of England, and so Elizabeth continued to refuse to recognize her as her legitimate successor.[36]

The English Queen intuitively understood the effect of the succession crisis and of the conspiracies, most of them promoted by supporters of the Scottish Queen, that were being forged against her. Her fears were confirmed in 1565, when Mary Stuart married Lord Darnley, a part-English Catholic descended from the Tudor family, which consolidated Mary's claim to the Crown of England. The marriage proved disastrous, and ended with the mysterious death of the king consort in February 1567, when he was rumoured to have been murdered by Mary's alleged lover, the Earl of Bothwell. She was inevitably seen as involved. After long controversies, Mary found herself obliged to abdicate the crown to her one-year-old son, James VI, who was crowned that July, just before his mother was imprisoned. The Earl of Moray, leader of the Scottish Protestants, would govern as regent until the young king reached the age of majority. One year later, Mary managed to escape from prison and fled to England, where she sought asylum from Elizabeth I, who had no choice but to agree, in view of her cousin's royal blood.[37]

Elizabeth's excommunication by Pope Pius V in February 1570 also had a major effect on the English Queen's religious policy. Faced with the bull of excommunication, moderate stances no longer had much meaning, and though many Catholics converted to Protestantism, those who did not now became suspect of the charge of disloyalty to the crown. The damning words of the pontiff incited the Catholic faithful to rebel against her:

> But the number of the ungodly hath gotten such power that there is now no place in the whole world left which they have not essayed to corrupt with their most wicked doctrines; and amongst others, Elizabeth, *the pretended Queen of England*, the servant of wickedness, lendeth thereunto her helping hand, with whom, as in a sanctuary, the most pernicious persons have found a refuge. *This very woman, having seized on the kingdom and monstrously usurped the place of Supreme head of the Church of England* . . . hath again reduced the said kingdom into a miserable and ruinous condition, which was so lately reclaimed to the catholic faith and a thriving condition . . . [We] do out of the fullness of Our Apostolic power *declare the aforesaid Elizabeth as being an heretic and a favourer of heretics*, and her adherents in the matters

aforesaid, to have incurred the sentence of excommunication, and to be cut off from the unity of the Body of Christ. And moreover *We do declare her to be deprived of her pretended title to the kingdom aforesaid . . . and also the nobility, subjects and people of the said kingdom . . . to be for ever absolved from . . . all manner of duty of dominion, allegiance, and obedience.*[38] (My emphasis)

Rome's threats would not stop there. At the end of 1570, a new conspiracy against the Queen and her minister Cecil began to take shape, with the direct support of the Pope. Roberto Ridolfi, an Italian banker resident in London, was put in charge of organizing the enterprise, in which the Duke of Norfolk, Mary Queen of Scots and the Spanish ambassador in London Guerau de Spes were all implicated. Philip II and the Duke of Alba showed their lack of confidence in the plan from the beginning, but eventually promised their cooperation, though only after the uprising had begun. The plot proved a fiasco, due to the investigations of Cecil himself, who had suspected the conspirators and imprisoned Norfolk in time, forcing the rest to pull back. This new conspiracy strengthened the anti-Catholic sentiment of many English Protestants, as well as their antipathy toward the Queen of Scotland, the symbol of Catholicism in England, who was now accused of betrayal by part of the English people, who called for her head.[39]

All these factors increased tensions between England and the international Catholic community, and produced a radical change in perceptions of English Catholicism, and above all in the Queen's attitude toward its adherents.[40] One of the elements that helped fuel this situation was the initiatives that were being undertaken by English Catholics in exile. In the first years of Elizabeth's reign, the integrity of the Catholic faith in England was seen as threatened, on the one hand, by the physical and moral isolation of Catholics from the rest of Europe, and on the other by the campaign initiated by the crown to educate its subjects in the Protestant religion. The international Catholic community intervened, and a crusade against the so-called "church papists"[41] began in 1574, which took shape in the missionary campaigns led from the English College at Douai[42] in the Spanish Netherlands and later, after 1580, by the Jesuits. An intensive propaganda campaign was set in motion in an effort to strengthen the faith of English Catholics and avoid any contact between them and the Protestant religion.

In this first period of Elizabeth's reign we begin to glimpse the threat posed to the regime by both Catholics and radical Protestants. In effect, beginning in the 1580s, Elizabeth would be forced to confront both groups, who, though they espoused opposing positions and ideas, seemed to be evolving at the same pace, and occupied the same dangerous ground in relation to the state.

Responses to the *Status Quo*: Propaganda and Representation

The production of reformist literature increased considerably during these years, with the need to justify the restoration of Protestantism by a new government led by a woman. These texts heightened the feeling of unease that existed in England because of this political and religious transition. The pamphlets, which in general were critical of the established system and of many of the government's decisions, used anti-Catholic discourse to call for more dramatic reforms;[43] several playwrights also pursued this line, taking advantage of the denunciation of Catholicism to launch concealed attacks on royal authority.

Although interaction between the pamphlet and dramatic forms is a constant throughout this period – which accounts for the similar use that is made of stereotypes in both genres – it was the stage that most favoured the acting out of conflicts, particularly those that reflected the social and economic problems of the spectators. In other examples, it provided a space in which to debate certain Protestant principles, by setting them against other concepts or ideas which, though spoken by negative characters, could still attract the audience's sympathies. Theatrical works, then, were a means for the discussion not only of theological questions but also of the inclinations of disparate groups – moderate and radical Protestants as well as Catholics – within the nation's political and religious landscape.

The pope's renewed role as protagonist in pamphlet literature

The first key difference from the reign of Mary I is the resurgence of the pope as a central figure in anti-Catholic discourse. The same characteristics that had defined him during the reigns of Henry VIII and Edward VI[44] are evoked in order to underscore, on the one hand, the political threat that he represented for England and, on the other, the supposedly seditious nature of the Catholic community, denounced by radical Protestantism for their presumed collaboration in the pontiff's plans.[45] This indictment was based on the impossibility, according to the Puritans, of loyalty to two opposing powers,[46] an idea that suggests an inversion of the mechanism through which the dissident reformist minority of the era of Mary I had seen itself as God's chosen people and the victims of Catholic abuses. Now, the Catholic minority was presented as seditious, justifying the need for either their conversion or their exclusion in the interests of social well-being and political stability. The pamphleteer John Philips expressed this fear, and blamed Catholics directly for the state of unrest that existed in the country:

> Sundry causes have mooved me, though unworthy to take this labour in

hande: the one, the mutteringe of papistes, which mutter there and here, as opportunitie servith their turnes, strange lies, and news far distant from truth. Another cause is that the mindes of many men are disquieted and brought out of frame by the ungodly meanes of suche, as not only rebell against God and his worde, but also agaynst the estate of this Realme, our Queene and dignitie of the Crowne ... which not only purpose the ruine and spoyle of their naturall nourse and countrie but also as their uniust dealynges, their craftie attempts, and subtill pretences plainly showe and demonstrate the damage and decay of our moste gratious and excellent Princesse.[47]

Despite this, reactions to the Catholic threat were overall relatively mild. The author of *A Warning agaynst the Dangeorus Practices of Papistes* declares, for example, that his attack is only aimed at those Catholics who defended papal supremacy, and that he trusts that time will ultimately convert those subjects loyal to the crown who were still influenced by Catholic doctrine and ritual (sig. B4v).[48] One even senses a protective tone toward these Catholics loyal to the regime who, because of their religious preferences, could have been vulnerable to corruption by the defenders of the pope. Hence the author emphasizes the need to toughen penalties against the latter group, who could be impeding the conversion of many other undecided Catholics to the Protestant faith.

The queen's policy of tolerance seemed to help the supposed traitors by making them indistinguishable from the rest of her subjects. Because of this, a more rapid end to this lack of definition is demanded:

> Item that all advices to great personages, to persuade neutralitie or an enterteyning of contrary sides in religion with uncertaintie of countenace and favor is the way to supplant assured safetie, to make sure enimies and unsure frends, to lye open to parasites and traytors, to be unknownen to other, and to be unable to discerne what other be to them. (sig. B2r)

Not to do so would only enhance the traitors' ability to achieve their aims (sig. B2v). Thomas Norton adopts a defiant and admonitory position, reading Elizabeth's restraint as both irresponsibility and the direct cause of these rebellions (sigs B2v-B3v).[49]

Anti-Catholic discourse again serves to camouflage direct attacks on the crown. Catholics are blamed for the nation's internal divisions, and become scapegoats for the queen's alleged mistakes. Lack of unity among the English populace was, in the eyes of the pamphleteers, the main reason for the nation's precarious position in the face of the possibility of foreign attack. Criticism of Elizabeth's religious policy, therefore, hides a more generalized denunciation regarding the security of the entire country:

> As longe as ye be one in your selves of one hart there is none so strong nor so mightie that may avail by force to attempt your worthines. But as sone as

among your selves one is devided from an other, your enemies, though they be ful impotent of power they shal by processe of tyme plucke awaye the most fairest and the most thene fethers of your worthines.⁵⁰

Elizabeth's excommunication in 1570 lent substance to the identification of Catholicism as a political threat, barely hinted at in her reign's first decade. The pope resumed the central position in English anti-Catholic discourse that he had occupied earlier, and pamphleteers and playwrights focused on denouncing the supposed idolatry of the Catholic Church, its lust for wealth, and, above all, its abuse of political power.

Beyond their religious meaning, accusations of idolatry served as a point of identification for the Protestant faithful. Iconoclastic sentiment intensifies everywhere in the texts as a formula for identifying the Catholic "other", in spite of the fact that the Church of Rome had declared in the Council of Trent that all superstition should be avoided in the invocation of saints, the veneration of relics and the use of sacred images.⁵¹ These views were ignored by the reformist pamphlets, which were intent on erasing any doctrinal common ground between the two camps that might damage the binary rhetoric that sustained their arguments.

As a result of the excommunication, papal ambition and tyranny⁵² became the most frequent targets of anti-Catholic polemics, singled out as the cause of the internal strife that endangered peace among the country's people. Catholicism became synonymous with treason against the crown – "No marvell then if that he [the Pope] deale with mans decrees so ill,/ Discharging subiectes from their other"⁵³ – and the pope was redefined as the antagonistic mirror to the queen, in opposition to whom he stood as a rival for temporal and spiritual power. The playwright William Wager makes this opposition clear in *Enough is as Good as a Feast*, parodying the oath that the vices take to Covetous, who becomes their sole ruler and "spiritual guide":

[TEMERITY:] We take our leave of you, noble prince Covetise,/ The king, the emperor, yea, the god of all vice./ INCONSIDERATION:] O worthy visage, and body well compact,/ O goodly man in wit, work and fact,/ We simple creatures do show to you obedience,/ Being minded to depart under your patience. (589–594)

Philip Melancthon also writes about the tyrannical measures employed by the Holy See to humble those monarchs who might represent an obstacle to the achievement of its political objectives, with clear reference to the bull of Pius V:

The dragon comming forth of [arse?] of that popish asse, and casting out of his open mouth a great flame of fire, signified the horrible buls and the terrible lyghtnings of excommunication and the tempestious threatnings which the Popes and his adherents doe spewe out furiously upon all the worlde, when they doe see their ende night at hande, and that they must perish sodeinely.[54]

One can see here a resumption of the Protestant arguments of the 1530s, which insisted upon the necessity of depriving the pontiff of all earthly powers in order to prevent him exercising supremacy over the princes of Europe. As before, such authority was presented as an unnatural usurpation:

> The latter Bishops of Rome, being blinded with divelish desire of soveraintie, and swolne and puft up with such pride as the lyke was never heard of have not bene ashamed before God, nor before his aungels and the whole world, to advaunce themselves into that seate by simonie, *and to intangle themselves in secular kyngdome, and therwithall to withdraw themselves from the subiection of kynges and princes ordayned by God, to usurp other mens rightes, to beare both the persons of spiritualitie and temporaltie, and to chalenge to themselves the iurisdiction of both the swordes*, to suffer no man to be equall wyth them, and much lesse to be above them ... *to raigne over the Princes themselves, and to appoint them lawes, and finally to trample them under their feete, contrary to Gods* commaundement and the example of the Apostles.[55] (My emphasis)

The pamphleteers insist on the divine right of the English monarchy, and, indirectly, present Elizabeth's imperial status as head of state and the church as equivalent to that of the first Christian emperors. John Foxe, for example, compares her with Constantine in *Actes and Monuments* (1563): "yet wherein is your noble grace to him inferiour?" (fol. B2r). This idea is underscored by reference to the emperor's English origins – "Constantine the great and mightie Emperour, the sonne of Helene an Englyshe woman of this your realme and countrie (moste Christian and renowned Pryncesse Queene Elizabeth)" (fol. B1r) – and by portraying the queen as surrounded by the figure of a capital letter "C" – for Constantine – in the engraving "Elizabeth as a Second Constantine" (Figure 2). The engraving is from the first edition (1563) of *Actes and Monuments* by John Foxe. The author dedicated the book to Queen Elizabeth to celebrate the fact that, like Constantine, who had put an end to the persecutions suffered by the first Christians, the queen had ended the suffering endured by reformers under the regime of Mary I. Imperial power is accompanied by peace and harmony, represented by the fruits of the cornucopia. Elizabeth is seated on a throne; she wears the imperial crown (closed) and a sword, with her feet placed upon the tiara of the papacy. It is thought that the three persons at her side are John Day (printer of numerous reformist works), John Foxe and his agent at court and author of pamphlets, Thomas Norton. (For a more detailed analysis, see Hoak, *Tudor Political Culture*, p. 94; and Yates, *Astraea*; p. 43.) A royal order of 1571 required that all parish churches have a copy of Foxe's work available for their parishioners, and by that time it was already recognized as the official history of the Church of England.[56] And although history would have to await the second half of her reign to see the queen's imperial image fully developed, this was already familiar to her subjects, and benefited from the authority of one of the most emblematic texts of English Protestantism.[57]

Lastly, several pamphleteers explicitly associated Italy and Spain with the supposed tyranny of Rome. This was the case of William Fulke, who asked "and how is the Popish church able to gather general Councells at this daye? Who will come at her calling? Except a few Spaniardes, and a holy company of buckram bishops of Italie?" (p. 98). While this issue, as has been mentioned, was much more complex, and there is still no Spanish stereotype here nor any repetition of the criticisms launched against Spain in the reign of Mary, there is, in contrast, a series of indirect condemnations of the support that the Spanish monarch was giving to the papacy. The decade between 1570 and 1579 had begun with Ridolfi's conspiracy, and concluded with a failed military invasion of England by exiled English and Irish Catholics. Both episodes relied on the acquiescence of the Spanish monarchy. Spain's annexation of Portugal in 1580, bringing with it a complete commercial monopoly in America, highlighted the threat that Spain had doubtless represented for England throughout the previous era. While these pamphleteers had yet to produce the Spanish stereotype, their works already reflected a fear of this future enemy.

Anti-Catholic theatre and doctrinal problems

Like the pamphlet literature, dramatic works produced during these years played a vigorous part in the formation of the Elizabethan regime. Aware of the powerful influence of such works, Elizabeth stiffened her control over the theatre as soon as she ascended the throne. On 16 May 1559, a royal proclamation detailed the process by which theatrical works were authorized, and underlined the need for censorship of those that had anything at all to do with state politics or religion. However, this prohibition was not strictly applied, as is shown by a letter from the Spanish ambassador from 1562, in which he complains of the existence of many anti-Catholic books, farces and songs, in spite of the queen's promise to do away with them.[58] Hence one can see an ambivalent attitude on the part of the monarch with respect to the propagation of Protestant ideals in the country.

Elizabeth knew about the violence that reformist theatre had expressed during the reigns of Henry VIII and Edward VI, and was not inclined to tolerate such extremes. The fact that polemical drama was not prohibited at court supports this theory. Restricting it to the ideologically closed-off spaces of her inner circle seemed to be a way of controlling its capacity to cause conflict. This would also explain why plays performed outside this courtly circle, such as those analysed in this chapter, generally lack the anti-Catholic denunciations that years earlier had characterized the works of playwrights such as John Bale.

These dramatic pieces responded to the new guidelines by adapting their message to suit the different types of audience that attended the performances. Very often, plays were performed in public open spaces, which would to some extent explain the relative abandonment of doctrinal themes – prohibited by the government – and the greater emphasis on social and economic questions, which were probably closer to their audiences' lives. *The Life and Repentaunce of Marie Magdelene* (1558) by Lewis Wager, and *The Longer thou Livest the More Fool thou Art* (1559) and *Enough is as Good as a Feast* (1559–1570),[59] both by the playwright William Wager, formed part of the repertoire of travelling troupes of professional actors.[60] In the prologue to *The Life and Repentaunce of Mary Magdelene*, for example, the nomadic lives of these companies is mentioned,[61] and one gets a sense of a mostly rural audience, which is soon confirmed when the spectators are urged to pay for the performance.[62]

Only the first of these texts is of a religious nature, since, having been written in 1558, it was not affected by the decree of the following year. The other two, together with *All for Money* (1559–1570)[63] by Thomas Lupton, avoid direct conflict with Catholicism and focus on questions apparently far removed from religious polemics, such as the education of children and the value of money. Nonetheless, allusions are still made to the times of Mary Tudor and the Catholic menace, albeit more implicitly. In juxtaposition to these plays were works such as *New Custom* (1573)[64], which replaces political and social criticism with a theological discussion similar to that of pamphlet literature, and *The Glass of Government* (1575) by George Gascoigne, which combines the two aspects by elaborating Erasmian principles on education, though in a contradictory fashion.

Gascoigne's play does allow for reflection on various theological concepts, given the cultural baggage and social position of most of its the audience. The fact that the play is directed toward a younger audience highlights its didactic nature, as well as the way these themes are presented in the form of lessons from the teacher Gnomaticus. In one way or another, and even in the texts that avoid religious discussion, the overall perspective adopted is clearly Calvinist, and hence social criticism is inevitably passed through the filter of Protestantism. Consequently, anti-Catholic discourse, an indispensable tool of the Reformation, is insinuated in a more or less explicit manner through the themes presented in these dramatic productions, and at times comes to serve as a vehicle for more aggressive attacks.

The works considered here retain many of the features that characterized the anti-Catholic literature of earlier reigns, in particular their criticism of the social and economic problems within the English nation (*Enough is as Good* and *All for Money*), and the position of victimhood that had predominated in Protestant discourse during the Marian era (*Enough is as Good* and *The Longer Thou Livest*). In the works with the greatest doctrinal emphasis, a novel contrast with other periods appears: the apparent incompatibility of various Calvinist principles with the new governmental measures meant to educate the Catholic community in the Protestant faith. This question appears plainly in *The Longer Thou Livest, New Custom,* and *The Glass of Government,* and is glimpsed in *Enough is as Good* and *The Life and Repentaunce of Marie Magdelene.*

Enough is as Good as a Feast [65] and *All for Money*[66] are examples of the hybrid moral allegories that were characteristic of the decades between 1560 and 1580. *Enough is as Good* has been pointed to as a model of the so-called homiletic tragedies, didactic plays that portrayed the punishment of vices in accordance with orthodox views of the catechism and the homily. These works called for the punishment of the unrepentant individual, and usually ended in depictions of desperation or damnation in hell.[67] The primary difference between this and the traditional morality play is the absence of the repentance and renewal of the leading character, although this does not impede the final restoration of divine order.

By contrast, in *All for Money*, the common schema of three successive stages – the state of innocence, the state of corruption and, finally, the state of renewal or condemnation – is omitted. The figure of a main character is replaced by a portrayal of a world completely ruled by the vices, one in which corruption reaches into the farthest corners of every social stratum, as Damnation states near the end of the play: "For the most part of the earth do live so wickedly/ that they do thinke there is no hell to punishe sinne truely:/ In money they have great love, in pryde they do exceede,/ In gluttony and lecherie their lives they do still leade" (1414–1417).

The absence of a protagonist permits the double characterization of certain of the vices as both tempting and moralizing.[68] The character Sin, for example, not only attacks the virtues but is also critical of his son Damnation (291–300) and of Satan himself, with whom he does not wish to collaborate at a particular moment in the play (360–362). In a way, this is the only character that brings up the idea of conversion, an impossibility considering his depraved character (as a vice) and the connections he has established between the antagonistic figures by means of relationships of blood and friendship.[69] As a result, a type of unique universal character is produced, one that controls the action. These ties knit together a corrupt framework that includes every social class in the country, but especially the political and ecclesiastical authorities.

The words of Covetous in *Enough is as Good* also bring into question

Protestant policies which, in the eyes of the author, do not seem to be very distant from those of their Catholic predecessors: "For we have seen of late days this canker pestilent/ Corrupting our realme to our utter decay,/ *Ambition, I mean, which chiefly doth reign Amongst those who should have been example to other*" (240–243) (my emphasis). Neither does the reference made by Enough to the greedy attitude of some reformists go unnoticed:

> I know some in this realm which once were content/ With poorly enough which God to them had sent,/ Wishing of a good conscience, as they said verily,/ That God would once again restore the verity./ If it please thee, good Lord (said they) thy word to us again send/ And then truly our covetous lives we will amend./ But since it hath pleased God, them to wealth restore,/ They are ten times more covetous than they were before. (847–854)

The position of the playwright is not at all homogeneous, in keeping with the prevailing political climate of the day, and questions regarding the church are seen less and less from a doctrinal vantage point, as it appears more often as just another fixture in the social and economic fabric of the state. The most obvious example of this is the scene featuring Tenant, Servant and Hireling, in which the economic woes inherent to these three groups within the Elizabethan labouring classes are mentioned.[70] The first laments the uncontrollable rise in rents and the impossibility of renters' making their payments (970–982). In *All for Money*, the general rise in prices – the worst economic problem of all in the sixteenth century[71] – is criticized, and blamed on the lack of charity in English society. Once again, an appeal is made to religious and moral values in an effort to control, at least at the discursive level, the economic conflicts that affected the most humble sectors of the population:

> What husband man is he that abated the price of corne?/ Nay he rather buyes and keepes his own in store./ Many marchant man that is right simple borne/ With unsaciable gaines encreaseth more and more:/ He will not abate his price for helping of the poore./ Who will not prevent his neighbour with buying things over his head,/ All this is for money, so that love and charitie are dead. (66–72)

The references the character of Sin makes to the "new rich" that such a situation has engendered – "I am a wise yong man that feares to finde money./ In the covetous *churles* coffer I shall have him by and by,/ I am sure to find him at the *goldsmithes* stalls./ If there I misse him I shall never finde him at all" (503–507) (my emphasis) – points to a redistribution of wealth that was bringing into question the whole basis of the traditional social pyramid, which up to that time had been organized around land ownership. Both plays evoke, then, a world in which money begins to constitute the organizing principle around which the movement and disposition of social groups are structured.

The greater flexibility of the labour market and the relative religious stability during the first years of Elizabeth's reign led to an influx of foreign labour, which was soon portrayed as a clear threat to English workers, as is seen in the words of Tenant in *Enough is as Good*: "And specially strangers – yea a shameful zorte,/ Are placed now in England and that in every port –/ That we, our wives and children, no houses can get/ Wherein we may live, such prize on them is zet" (985–988).

The problem of xenophobia for strictly economic reasons was nothing new, but it intensified during the Reformation, as England became the country of refuge for the persecuted Protestant communities from France and the Low Countries. During the reign of Edward VI, more than five thousand people arrived in London,[72] a number that continued to grow due to Elizabeth's pro-immigration policies in the first decade of her government. Hence William Wager is referring to fears that were well known to the English, restless at the many changes that the development of trade and industry was causing within the country's socioeconomic structure. Such fears are embodied in the characters of Servant and Hireling, who protest against the difficulty and scarcity of their respective jobs (993–1002; 1011–1055). Their complaints to their landlords, represented by Covetous and Worldly Man, prove fruitless in light of these characters' greed (1109–1110; 1125–1130): "[COVETOUS:] So what care I, though to curse me the people do not cease,/ As long as by them my riches doth increase?" (1163–1164).

The criticism becomes more acute when allusions are made to the supposed legal backing that this kind of development received, promoted by the government as part of a strategy that generated capital and enriched state coffers, as Hireling declares: "You are happy sir; in your hands you have the laws" (1146). Thomas Lupton also includes an attack on judicial corruption in a final scene in which his character All for Money, dressed as a magistrate, sets about judging various of the accused (886–1314). The character's own financial interests predominate over all others when the time comes to pass sentence:

> I have had this day a trimme sorte of sweters:/ How many sent I away with money in their purses?/ My purse is nowe full even unto the brinke./ Nowe it is highe time for me to eate and drinke./ Have not I bene friendly to your grandfather Money?/ All such as he sent, they were dispatched quickly. (1305–1310)

Those individuals whom Money recommends are acquitted, regardless of the seriousness of the accusations against them, while those who show up without money are convicted, irrespective of the insignificance of the charges against them. Since he is a representative of the power of the crown, the magistrate's corruption extends to the monarchy itself, which is also implicated in the criticisms levelled against the ecclesiastical hierarchy that is under its protection, as the character Theology points out:

> So manie would not studie me but for money/ And thereby to live Lordly and in wealth:/ The Bishop, the priest, and the Doctor of divinitie/ Would give over their studie, not regarding their soules health,/ And use some other things, for as it appeareth,/ The artificer doeth leave his arte and occupying/ And becomes a minister for money and easie living. (15–21)

Representatives from every sector of society end up corrupted by money, which is venerated as an idol throughout the performance (125, 424).[73] In this way the image is given of a society with profound socioeconomic inequalities in which money plays an ever more important role. The playwrights' responses to this situation stress the need to content oneself with God's Providence (180–685; 702–703), and urge the spectators and society in general to view the new economic circumstances through the prism of Christianity: " . . . example may be/ To all men how their riches they shall use./ Make not that thy God which should be servant unto thee,/ For in so doing thou dost it greatly abuse" (1514–1517).[74]

The two main texts considered here nevertheless differ in the use they make of anti-Catholic discourse. While *Enough is as Good* follows more traditional lines, close to that of other works of the time such as *The Longer Thou Livest*, *All for Money* blazes a new trail. The introduction of the character Sir Laurence Livingless, the only example of a Catholic stereotype used in the play,[75] serves no purpose in the structure of the play nor in the arguments he puts forth. His presence is unnecessary for the development of the drama. The only function this character fulfils lies in his comicality. Hence, he seems to be part of a strategy to defuse the Catholic menace, by presenting it to the audience as the butt of jokes:

> [SINNE:] How manie Epistles did Paul write after he was converted?/ [SIR LAURENCE:] By the mass he writ to manie, I would they were all burned/ For had not they bene and the New Testament in English,/ I had not lacked living at this time I wisse:/ Before the people knewe so much of the Scripture/ Then they did obeye us and loved us out of measure:/ And nowe we can not go in the streetes without a mocke. (1186–1192)

Sir Laurence exemplifies the transition in the representation of vice to become the comic buffoon of classical comedy. The similarities he bears to classical character types so often ridiculed onstage, such as the slave trader (*lenos*) – for his greed, impiety, and stupidity – the parasite (*parasitus*) – for his love of food – or the aged Don Juan (*senex amator*) – for his lustfulness – serve to demonstrate the interaction between anti-Catholic discourse and the new changes in English dramatic forms.

Anti-Catholicism became yet another tool in the transition of the genre, by infusing the element of comedy into the lexicon of moralizing drama.

Enough is as Good and *The Longer Thou Livest*,[76] on the other hand, emphasize the idea of victimhood that had dominated Protestant literature during the time of Mary I. Their writers thus attempted to maintain this kind of characterization of Protestants into the Elizabethan period, when the centralism of the Church of England did not permit such a posture. Nevertheless, this language of victimhood continued to stress the Protestants' role as God's elect and so legitimize the reformist faith even after Mary's reign had come to an end. It established a clear opposition between a corrupt majority – "Which despise God and his counsel,/ As though there were no beatitude,/ No torments for sin with devils in hell" (*The Longest Thou Livest*, 1160–1172) – and a minority that forms part of the elect – "Yet God hath some good people, I dare say,/ Which pray devoutly, fast and abstain/ And call upon him night and day/ The wickedness of our times to restrain" (1193–1196) – and is silenced by the repressive apparatus of the Catholic government (1214–1220). The references that are made in the two plays to religious persecutions of the past stress the same idea, as we see in the words of Cruelty: "Again in providing your necessares,/ I will in such a sort canvas the law/ That such as be your adversaries/ Shall be brought to Coram and awe" (1465–1468).

Such allusions introduce a final reflection on the dangers of political tyrannies and their disastrous consequences for the people who endure them. The character Discipline[77] says:

When a fool is compassed with impiety,/ Which is the contempt of God and his ordinances,/ And such a fool erected to authority,/ The people must needs sustain many grievances,/ For there God cannot be duly honored . . . / Neither the public weal rightly governed,/ But all cometh to utter dissipation. (*The Longest Thou Livest* 1673–1677, 1679–1680)

Thus, the fear that Protestant England had experienced under the Catholic regime seems to continue even after the restoration of Protestantism:

[CONTENTATION:] It is often seen that such monstrous ambition/ As spareth not to spill the blood of the innocent,/ Will not greatly stick to fall to sedition,/ The determination of God thereby to revent;/ But God I trust shall disappoint their intent,/ And overthrow the power of fading treasure,/ And cause us all to wish for the heavenly pleasure. (*Enough is as Good*, 246–252)

These plays keep alive fears peculiar to a period of political and religious transition, at a time when things were no longer as they were, and the role of victim is preferred even when the circumstances had actually been reversed. Providence, in addition, is shown as guaranteeing punishment for all those who persecute the followers of the true faith, which allows for any methods of repression to be presented as divine justice rather than as the will of rulers: "If ever Covetous were in danger of punishment,/ He standeth now at the point of banishment . . . / I think the day of Judgement be now at hand" (381–382, 385–386).

The dualities of the apocalyptic viewpoint are expressed in reprobation, the most problematic of the Calvinist doctrines in these years. Though it had been represented in other dramatic works in earlier periods,[78] it assumed a new importance as it was placed in contraposition to the spirit and the instructions that the new Elizabethan government sought to uphold. The greatest paradox lay in the impossibility of combining two such opposing views as the doctrine of reprobation and the theories of Erasmus and his followers, which trusted in the human capacity to learn and improve one's nature. Calvinism espoused the vision of a world in which the damned could do nothing to achieve salvation. Whatever kind of teachings were applied to such persons they would only end in failure, since their spiritual blindness, stemming from their reprobate nature, prevented them from moving towards repentance and the forgiveness of God.

The Longer Thou Livest and *Enough is as Good as a Feast* initially offer the spectator a fantasy on the idea of free election. At the beginning of the former, the corruption of the main character Moros is shown as a result of the education he received from his parents (159–161); however, further on, Discipline recognizes Moros' incapacity to listen to the Word of God and, thus, to accept His Grace: "This folly is not his innocence . . . / But it is a malicious insolency/ Which proceedeth from a wicked heart" (254, 256–257).

The most conspicuous demonstration of the impossibility that the character could ever be rehabilitated is the failure of the plan for salvation that Discipline prepares for him, which presents a confrontation between Catholicism and Protestantism under the guidelines of anti-Catholic discourse:

> My counsel is that you fear God above all;/ Pray unto him to give you sapience;/ Cease not upon his holy name to call . . . / His ministers (priests and preachers/ Such as rule the holy church catholic)/ Obey, I mean such as be true teachers./ Company not with an heretic./ An heretic him holy doctors do call/ Which erreth in God's most sacred scripture,/ Which is blind and seeth not his own fall,/ But maliciously doth in error endure./ The greatest heresy that ever was/ Hath the Pope and his adherents published,/ Yea, the heresy of Arius it doth pass,/ For Christ and his benefits it hath extinguished./ Example by the wicked Mass satisfactory/ Which to Christ's death they make equivalent, . . . / Again, prayer to saints that be dead/ Which is a great point of infidelity,/ For they forsake Christ which is the head/ Who

taught to worship in spirite and verity. (283–285; 287–290, 292–300; 303–306)

The connection between the main character and the Church of Rome arises, then, from his Catholic background:

[DISCIPLINE:] But to you now, I pray you tell,/ Be these the best lessons of your parents?/ [MOROS:] No forsooth, I can ring the saunce bell/ And fetch fire when they go to matins.[79] / [DISCIPLINE:] Better it were to have no education/ Than to be instructed in any part of idolatry. (162–167)

This indoctrination seems to constitute the primary cause of the depravity of the character, who must move away from the doctrine of Rome if he is to be able to escape damnation.

In spite of the mutual exclusivity implied by this type of language, contradictions arise yet again. The reformists, for example, appropriated the authority and tradition of the term "Catholic" to justify the new Protestant faith, even though they felt a certain amount of uncertainty and disquiet at its use, which attests to the precarious state in which the Church of England found itself, still unable to break off its links with the Catholic Church: "His ministers (priests and preachers/ Such as rule the holy church catholic)/ Obey, I mean such as be true teachers" (287–289). Moros' irresponsibility and madness[80] is not a consequence of youth or inexperience but of his animadversion to the Reformation. His careless and disrespectful response to the words of Discipline make evident his rejection of God's commands, represented by the Bible that the virtues offer him. This scene embodies the reformist argument, since it is not long before Moros undermines the value of the message he receives by showing interest only in the book's illustrations: "God's santy, this is a goodly book indeed/ But there are any saints in it and pilcrows?" (469–470). This gesture seems a clear allusion to idolatry and confirms that he belongs to the Catholic community, which he therefore comes to symbolize.

From line 1201 of *The Longest thou Livest*, the appearance of the rest of the vices stresses this identification, especially that of Ignorance and Wrath, two of the fundamental traits of the Catholic stereotype. The fact that the first of these two assumes the name Antiquity and echoes the theory of the Two Churches makes it possible to introduce a devaluation of the Catholic argument of the supremacy of tradition over the Scriptures, a point that is made explicit when Antiquity is presented by Impiety: "This is another of your counsel,/ Whose name is called Antiquity./ His words are truer than the Gospel,/ A person full of truth and fidelity" (1309–1311). Catholicism's emphasis on tradition is thus proof of its ignorance and wickedness, since it denies the supremacy of the Word of God over the word of man (i.e., the councils):

[IGNORANCE:] The papists which the truth do know,/ Lord, how I have nuzzled them in my science;/ I have so taught them that howsoever the wind blow,/ They shall still incline to my sentence . . . / After every heresy and popery they are running,/ And delight daily to learn at new schools/ By ignorance they do themselves excuse,/ As though they know not that they did amiss/ When their conscience bear them record/ That their acts are wicked and evil. (1277–1280; 1283–1284; 1287–1290)

The corruption of Moros takes on more relevance as the play goes on, as his violence and aggression increase against those who oppose him, to the point that he physically threatens the virtues. The words of the character People at the end of the performance again bring forward the possibility of man's salvation after honest repentance, an idea that is rejected by Moros, who is incapable of responding to the last divine warning he receives by way of the character God's Judgement. His condemnation is, then, immediate and applies to his life on earth as well as his state after death (1847–1850). Since Moros represents the Catholic community, his earthly punishment can be read as a triumph of the Protestantism restored by Elizabeth I, whose regime is compared to the triumphal final stage of the homiletic tragedies, the restoration of divine order.

The mention of Catholic communities that were still unconverted in this new reformist age appears to prove the failure of the queen's religious policy, and the resulting need to apply stricter measures. Wager has little confidence in the possibilities of regenerating English Catholics in the light of their refusal to accept instruction in the Protestant faith, as God's Judgement points out at the end of the performance:

In our times we have known fools full of spite,/ And in this world have seen their reward;/ But contrary to nature and God's will/ They stop their eyes through wilful ignorance,/ They seek to slay, to prison, to poll, to pill/ Only for their own furtherance./ Of all fools indeed this is the worst kind,/ Whereof this time we have treated,/ Which to all mischief giveth his mind/ And refuseth to be instructed. (1869–1870; 1879–1887)[81]

Enough is as Good presents a similar structure, although the spiritual pilgrimage of the antihero is not portrayed through different stages of his life as in the previous text. The action is set in the present, lending more immediacy to the protagonist's seduction and the fragility of his moral state.

Once again, the virtues fail in their attempts to convert Worldly Man, who, having initially resolved to follow the advice of Contentation and Heavenly Man, soon shows himself to be incapable of heeding the Word of God, as is revealed by Temerity in referring to their plan for his conversion: "I warrant you the Worldly Man will soon be weary,/ For they will not suffer him once to be merry./ And verily he is inclined to nought;/ Therefore, think not that by them he will long be taught" (399–402). At times the spectator can nurture hopes for the protagonist's salvation: his constant references to the Bible (629–636; 658–659); his identification with Mary,[82] and his simplicity of dress characterize him as a symbol of innocence and purity, in stark contrast to Catholic artifice and ornamentation. The latter, in turn, is personified by Covetous, whose theatricality betrays his untruthfulness. The double entendres, the plays on words, as well as the reinterpretation of Scriptures and classical authors (781–798) confuse Worldly Man, who in the end proves incapable of differentiating between the Word of God and that of the vices: "Your words are even as true as the Gospel" (821). The Calvinist doctrine of reprobation is therefore reiterated, this time spoken by Enough: "The worldly man will needs be a worldly man still" (862–863). The absence of repentance, as a result of his reprobate nature, will lead him to eternal damnation (1325–1329; 1385–1392).

The Glass of Government (1575)[83] by George Gascoigne is probably the work that best represents the conflicts generated by Calvinist doctrine. In this play, two friends, each with two children, decide to employ a professor to instruct them in their duty to God, to family and to country. The children soon learn their tutor's lessons, but the older brothers begin to associate with a bad crowd and soon stray from the right path. To avoid disgrace, their respective fathers send them to the university of Douai with the idea that this will reform them, but only the younger children prosper. The first-born continue their wayward ways, and are finally punished for it, one with death and the other with exile.

Gascoigne's text is part of the tradition of prodigal plays, a genre fashioned on Erasmian lines in Holland in the first half of the sixteenth century. With clearly didactic intent, these works were performed in schools, and combined the format of the religious or moral allegory with particular elements from classical comedy.[84] *The Glass of Government* in fact begins with a defence of the role of education in producing virtuous citizens, a well-worn theme of the classical stage. Phylocalus, one of the two fathers, explains it thus:

> It hath pleased Almightie God to *bless us both with competent wealth, and though we have atteyned thereunto by continuall paynes and travayle, rising (as it were) from meane estate, unto dignity*,[85] yet doe I thinke that it were not amisse *to bring up our children with such education* as they may excell in knowledge of liberall sciences if we being unlearned, learned have by industrie heaped up sufficient store, not only to serve our owne use, but further to provide for our posterity, then *may they by learning aspire unto greater promotion, and builde greater matters uppon a better/ foundation* ... Al desire of promotion (by vertue) is godly and Lawful, whereas ambition is commonly nestled in the brestes of the envious. (I, i, 21–31, 33–34) (My emphasis)

The first step towards a reconciliation of the doctrine of reprobation with Erasmian ideas lies in a principle fundamental to all the teachings of the tutor in the play: love for and obedience to the Word of God. The first lesson is a clear affirmation of the Protestant faith, which, nonetheless, does not deny the utility of other types of writings:

> I would not have you thinke hereby, that I do holde in contempt the bookes which you haue redde heretofore, but wee will (by Gods grace) take in assistance such an so many of them as may seem consonant to the holy scriptures, and so joining the one with the other, we shalbe the better able to bring our worke unto perfection. (I, iv, 41–47)

Thus the aim of the lessons coincides with the principal propositions of Christian Humanism – "in theses foure chapters I trust (by Gods help) to enclude as much as shalbe necessary for the perfect government of a true Christian man" (I, iv, 96–98) – and resembles the ideas defended by Erasmus himself in his treatise the *Ciceroniamus*:

> As Christians, and for Christian listeners, would we express ourselves in the same way that the pagan Cicero spoke before pagans? Is it that all our behaviours should perhaps not conform to the standards that Christ indicated? ... [L]et us apply a truly Christian heart, and we will see how, with heavenly glory, the Name of Jesus sparkles in prayer and in the pages of the book.[86]

Cicero, a model of eloquence and rhetoric for the Dutch thinker, is also mentioned in Gascoigne's play (I, iv, 13–14, 23). The playwright presents, then, the humanist tradition as a possible answer to the need to integrate cultural and religious dimensions into the education of the young.

This process is complemented by the transmission of certain political and social values that ensure the stability of the state. The appeal to imperial theory and the required subordination of ecclesiastical power to that of the prince sent by God both connect the play with Elizabeth's excommunication, which had resulted in the Catholic community being branded as seditious. Such an assertion contributed to the heightening of anxieties felt by the faithful – Protestants – before a shadowy enemy:

> So that *he [the king] is to bee honored as the lieutenant of God here upon earth*, both because he hath power of commaundement, and chiefly because he representeth that heavenly King, who is king of kinges, and above all Kings to be honored. Even so *is hee also to bee obeyed in all seculer constitutions and pollitike provisions* ... Erasmus teacheth in his *Apothegmes*, that *obedience expelleth all sedition* & maynteyneth concorde the which may also appeare by *naturall reason* and common experience. (II, i, 28–33, 37–40)
> (My emphasis)

Nevertheless, the association of Protestantism with obedience to the queen was still not entirely clear, as the behaviour of certain reformist groups demonstrated. The problem of civil disobedience stemming from these groups and the ambiguous stance of the monarchy – which was supporting rebel Protestant groups in France and the Low Countries – may have presented obstacles to the assimilation of the playwright's message by a youthful and immature audience, who possibly remained unconvinced. The appeal to the audience's feelings of patriotism was one of the most commonly used tools for neutralizing such paradoxes. Religious and nationalistic obligations were mixed together, resulting in the only viable option, that of conservative Protestantism, which reflected the principles of the official religion and of the state. Consequently, both Catholics and radical reformists were left excluded from the group of the elect.

The emphasis on the obligation to obey the demands of one's homeland, even above those of one's own parents, further reveals a certain unease regarding the education that some young Englishmen were receiving. Until 1570 there was not, in fact, an aggressive policy against the educational programmes of the Catholic community, even though conflicts had already arisen at Oxford, where there was a large group of followers of the Roman church, and where an act had been announced in 1563 that required all tutors and professors to take a vow of allegiance to the regime. These measures were made tougher in 1571, with the establishment of obligatory conformity, followed by the closure of all Catholic schools in the country and the prohibition on Catholic youth attending the colleges founded by English exiles abroad.[87] The failure of such governmental dictates soon became evident. In the decades from 1570 to 1590, and even later, the presence of Catholics at Oxford and Cambridge, as well as the acceptance of students by schools on the continent, were a well-known fact, as was the existence of several clandestine printing presses and illegal schools. In addition, many of the nobility paid for the services of private tutors to ensure that their children were educated in the teachings of the Church of Rome.[88]

Gascoigne echoes the unease that the progress of Catholicism in education generated in Protestant circles and in the government itself. The playwright's insistence on the necessity of obedience to the nation above obedience to one's parents (II, i, 126–127) seems to anticipate some of the measures that would be taken after the arrival of the Jesuits in England, such as the removal of children from Catholic families and their re-education among Protestants. Gascoigne justifies this recommendation by declaring: "although thy Parents and proper family be overthrowne, yet (the common welth of thy countrey standing) thou mayst florishe and ryse againe: but the state of/ thy countrey being overthrowne, both thou and thy Parentes must likewise come to utter subvertion" (II, i, 129–133).

The second part of the play appears to contradict some of the ideas set out up to that point, by focusing on the exclusive nature of Calvinist doctrine on the question of salvation. The reprobate condition of the elder children is not so clear at first, as their tutor indicates on first meeting them: "Surely these young men give none euill hope of their towardness and declare by their seemly gesture and modest boldnesse to be both of good capacitie, and to have bene well enstructured hytherto in humanity" (I, iii, 42–45). Their sinful nature only materializes as a result of a process of temptation which is developed, as a moral allegory, by the characters of Lamia, Eccho, Pandarina and Dick Drumme,[89] who goad the young men to partake of earthly pleasures. Phylosarchus and Phylautus, the two elder sons, thus symbolize humankind's weakness before such worldly temptations, and are identified with the character of the prodigal son. The lack of any hope of salvation for both antiheroes brings into question the entire worth of the process of education that they received at the beginning of the play.

The contrast between the two pairs of brothers that appears at the end of the work is a cruel demonstration of the arbitrariness of Calvinist doctrine, and perhaps anticipated a difficult reception from a young audience still in the middle of their education. There appears to be no place for the Christian Humanism that had been advocated in the first part of the text within such a conception of the world. It gives, therefore, a bitter ending to the play, which only offers a distant hope of eternal salvation. Allusions to the problems caused by the education of youth, especially of those inclined toward Catholicism, represent a step further towards a vision of the Catholic as an enemy within – difficult to detect, and therefore doubly dangerous. The playwright points to this enemy as the same time as he warns of the uselessness of converting Catholics, since they are already condemned for being what they are.

In contrast to these works stressing the incompatibility of the doctrine of reprobation with the government's role as educator, *The Life and Repentaunce of Marie Magdelene* by Lewis Wager presents the spiritual evolution of its protagonist, Mary, a depraved soul who nevertheless still manages to renew herself and gain God's pardon. It offers, therefore, a more conciliatory view compared to those of other plays. The fact that this dramatic text also served as a vehicle for legitimizing a new woman-led government gave further impetus to this constructive and hopeful attitude.[90]

The Life and Repentaunce was written in 1558 and published in 1566 and 1567. The dates of its composition and publication coincide with different moments when the queen's capacity to govern was questioned by many in England; in 1558 due to the uncertainty brought by political change, and in 1566 because of foreign threats, embodied by Mary Queen of Scots. Hence it is significant that, alongside this play, several others appeared at the same time that also featured strong and constant female characters, who could evoke the image of the queen herself.[91] In these plays, the status as victim of the leading characters allows an obvious connection with Elizabeth I, the national symbol of resistance to Catholicism.

The Life and Repentaunce is an example of the adaptation of the medieval biblical genre for reformist purposes. The dramatist chooses the figure of Mary Magdalene, a model of loyalty to Jesus Christ in the Christian tradition, to demonstrate the Protestant concept of salvation, based on repentance and divine grace.[92] The idea of penitence determines the structure of the work and, as a consequence, Wager divides the play into two distinct parts: one which shows the moral degradation into which the character descends due to the pernicious influence of the vices, and a second one in which Mary, after meeting Christ, recognizes her sins and is converted. In addition, the playwright develops a secondary plot in this latter section in which Jesus, Simon the Pharisee and Malicious Judgement are the main characters, and which presents the conflict between the new, reformed faith and the Catholic Church. This second plot is intertwined with the first[93], and encourages Mary's repentance and so a happy ending for the play.

The play's allegorical structure also insinuates at a parallel with contemporary circumstances in England. The figure of Mary Magdalene would represent the English people, both in their corrupted state during the reign of Mary I and under Catholicism, and in their renewed state after the Protestant Reformation. Jewish law and its religious representatives can be identified with Mary's government, which had, in the eyes of reformist literature, brought about the moral downfall of her subjects. Lastly, the presence of Jesus Christ establishes the true faith – Protestantism – amid multiple Calvinist references.

The evolution of the character of Mary Magdalene forms the focus of the play. At the beginning, and in keeping with medieval hagiographic tradition, she appears as a capricious and arrogant, materialistic woman.[94] Her obsession with her physical appearance is extreme; she is proud and belittles those around her, as can be noted in the scene in which she curses her tailors for the awful work they have done on her dress:

> I beshrew his heart naughtye folishe knave,/ The most bungarliest tailers in this countrie,/ That be in the worlde I thinke, so God save me,/ Not a garment can they make for my degree./ Have you ever sene an overbody thus sytte?/ Nowe a mischief on his dronken knaves eare/ The knaves drynke till they have lost theyr wytte,/ And then they marre utterly a bodies geare./ I had liefer than xx shillings by this light/ That I had him here now in my fume and heate . . . / Nay but gis twentie shellings I dare holde,/ That there is not a gentlewoman in this land,/ More propre than I in the waste I dare be bolde. (57–65, 66–67)

These words characterize her as a variant of Mankind, since she represents human weakness, the inevitable point of departure for any morality play. Any state of innocence for the character is, therefore, nonexistent. The doctrine of reprobation makes appearances throughout the play, and explains the ease with which Mary submits to the temptations of Infidelity and his companions. In fact, the latter has only to mention the attachment Mary Magdalene feels to earthly things to initiate her progress towards corruption: "you [Mary] so tender & yong/ For marryng of your geare he is greatly to blame" (77–78). Infidelity's words emphasize Mary's inferior nature, both because of her sex ("tender") and her age ("yong"). These two elements constitute the main reasons why Infidelity initially has no trouble in deceiving the young woman and subjecting her to his will. This equally highlights her female condition – weak, changeable, and therefore easily manipulated:

> [MARY:] I can no lesse doe than love you with all my mynd,/ Redy to do you pleasure at your comandmentes./ [INFIDELITY:] *Verba puellarum foliis leviora caducis*,/ The promise of maidens, the Poet doth say, Be as stable as a weake leafe in the wynde/ Lyke as a small blast bloweth a feather away/ So a faire word truely chaungeth a maidens mynd. (119–125)

The play is rife with misogynistic dialogue, even in the scenes where Mary shows her loyalty to Christ, which is interpreted by Infidelity as further evidence of her instability (1203–1206; 1529–1532). These ideas formed part of the audience's interpretative register, and stressed the uncomfortable reality of being governed by a strong female personality who at times could be powerful within her humility.[95]

The other relevant trait of Mary Magdalene is her youth and irresponsibility, another common trope of the social literature of this period. Robert Potter has pointed out the growing tendency of moral allegories to interpret contemporary social reality through the prism of Humanism and Calvinism, and points to the "youth plays" written between 1520 and 1580 as prominent examples of this process of adaptation.[96] In these plays, the character of the young man (or woman) is presented not only as a metaphor for humankind's inevitable tendency toward sin, but also, especially after 1550, as a social problem.[97] He is, therefore, a conflictive character, one who must be strictly educated from an early age in order to avoid his being corrupted and becoming a blemish on society. *The Life and Repentaunce* echoes this unease, and blames Mary's loose morals on the education she received from her parents: "My parents brought me up in chyldhod/ In vertuous qualities, and godly literature,/ And also they bestowed upon me muche good . . . / But evermore they were unto me very tender,/ They would not suffer the wynde on me to blow,/ My requests they would always to me render" (162–164, 166–168).

These lines refer to an early period that could correspond to the character's state of innocence. Education in Protestant doctrine is seen as the only means by which youth may attain moral integrity and the possibility of salvation. The supposed carelessness of Mary Magdelene's parents explains her weak and sinful nature, and the ease with which she is corrupted by her wicked counsellors, as Infidelity says: "In faith I will tell you, you can not trust a wiser,/ You shall live pleasantly, even at your hearts lust,/ If you make me your counseller and deviser" (147–149). The instructions with which the four vices – Infidelity, Carnal Concupiscence, Pride and Cupidity – attempt to advise her (536–615) emphasize the need for artifice and ornament to highlight the beauty of Mary, who in this way is associated with the iconologies of Falsity of Love and Feigned Religion.[98] Although the cult of one's own image that is propounded by the vices suggests an obvious denunciation of Catholic ceremony and artifice, it also stresses the weakness of female nature. The work thus makes manifest some of the conflicts that the symbolic representation of Queen Elizabeth would create.

The first part of the play, which is entirely driven by the actions of the vices, allows for a greater dynamism and interaction with the audience, due to the theatricality of the characters, and could have prompted more or less conflictive readings of contemporary reality. One example of this is the discussion among the vices regarding marriage, one of the principal topics of debate during the first part of Elizabeth's reign:

[INFIDELITY:] . . . many incommodities truely be in mariage./ [CUPIDITY:] The bedde wherin lieth any maried wife,/ Is never without chidyng, braulyng, and strife,/ That woman shall never sleape in quiete,/ Which is maried contrary to hir diete./ [PRIDE:] Of all bondage truely this is the ground,/ A gentlewoman to one husband to be bound./ [CARNAL CONCUPIS-CENCE:] Trushe mistresse Mary, be ye not in subjection,/ Better it is to be at your owne election . . . [MARY:] . . . That will be a meane truly to lese my good name./ And so among the people I shal suffer blame. (652–660; 668–669)

References to this scene are not found in other texts on Mary Magdalene – not in the work of Digby, medieval dramatic texts, nor the gospel (official or apocryphal). It is, therefore, an original allusion, one that would be likely to grab an audience's attention. The question of marriage might refer to Elizabeth's need to resolve the problem of succession, but it might also call to mind the ill-fated marriage between Mary and Philip, interpreted from very early on, in the misogynistic pattern, as the result of the queen's female weaknesses. Although the play does not include specific references, this might easily have been the reading of a public receptive to such messages. The fact that Mary Magdalene argues in favour of marriage, even as a means of preserving honour, contrasts with the intentions of Elizabeth, who at 25 years of age was still unmarried and without an apparent desire to change her situation, even though she publicly acknowledged the need to provide the kingdom with an heir. The indirect connection drawn between the queen and the doctrine of the vices is controversial, and may, in fact, go beyond mere anti-Catholicism to a more pointed attack on royal policies.

Nonetheless, the author does not develop such a denunciation, and in an attempt to avoid problems with the censors soon introduces new characters that will make the doctrinal message stand out over and above the problematic issues of Elizabeth's government: the defence of the Protestant faith, as the only hope of salvation for the English people. The second half of the play consequently constitutes an exhortation in favour of Protestantism that practically nullifies any other social demand or denunciation. The stage is set for a clear confrontation between the virtues – Law, Knowledge of Sin, Faith and Repentaunce – who, led by Jesus Christ, will fight for Mary Magdalene's soul, and the vices, represented by Infidelity and Malicious Judgement, who will try to prevent her salvation.

The action of this second part of the play includes Mary's process of repentance after the intervention of Law, who, in keeping with the structure of moral allegories, reveals her sinful nature to her, along with her future damnation if she fails to remedy her position (1027–1062). She responds, sorrowfully accepting her depraved nature, and thus her inevitable condemnation, according to Calvinist doctrine:

> All men for synne by Gods sentence damned be . . . / It is beyond all mans possibilitie,/ To observe any commanundement in me required,/ Therby appeareth his weaknesse and fragilitie,/ Hapned through sinne, that against God he conspired. (1078, 1131–1134)

Acceptance of this doctrine must also have been difficult, as the words of Mary and Infidelity demonstrate. The humorous commentary by the vice would have aroused the sympathy of some spectators, who doubtless shared similar fears:

> [MARY:] If there be no more comfort in the lawe than this,/ I wishe that the lawe had never ben made:/ In God I see is small mercy and iustice,/ To entangle men, and snarle them in such a trade./ [INFIDELITY:] Feare not, their uniust God do you blaspheme:/ You see no remedy, but utter damnation./ Folowe my counsell, and put care away,/ Take here your pleasure and consolation,/ And make you mery in this worlde while you may./ Of one hell I would not have you twayne to make:/ Be sure of a heaven while you dwell here,/ Refresh yourself, and al pleasure doe you take. (1139–1142; 1146–1153)

After the many changes in religious policy, along with persecutions and economic disasters, the spectators in any town where the play was performed would probably have identified more with the words of Infidelity than with those of the virtues. The process of temptation did not end with the person of Mary Magdalene but was extended to the audience, who would have been reminded of their own failings.

Nor was the portrayal of Jesus Christ any simple matter. His opposition to the state religion turns him, on the one hand, into an object and victim of religious persecution, which allows a direct association to be made between his character and the Protestant community under Mary I. Allusions to his humble origins and his lack of formal education cause Malicious Judgement to doubt that he poses a real threat. Thus, the vice's words emphasize the position of authority based on historical tradition claimed by Catholicism, and link the character of Jesus with the Protestant tradition of victimhood:

> A beggerly wretch, that hath not of his owne,/ Once house or cabyn wherin he may rest his heade:/ His parents for poore laboring folks ar wel known . . . / And yet he taketh upon hym to teache men doctrine./ But within a while he will prove him selfe a foole,/ And come to utter destruction and ruine./ Is he able, thynke you, to withstande,/ So many bishops, priestes, and pharisies,/ Great learned men, and seniors of the lande/ With other people that be of their affinites? (911–922)

On the other hand, however, the rebellious and seditious position of Jesus with regard to the official religion is also underlined, which makes it possible to see a conflictive image of the character, since for its audiences the subversive elements would not be the reformists, but Catholics. References to the threat of foreign invasion strengthen this ambiguity: "All the multitude beginneth after him to ronne . . . / If you suffer hym till more people he hath wonne,/ Stranger shall come and take our dominion" (1938, 1940–1941).

Such contradictions are silenced with the arrival of Knowledge of Sin and Repentaunce, who assure salvation so long as there is sincere contrition. The emphasis placed on the Word of God (1405–1430) brings to the fore once again not only the principles of the Protestant faith that Mary should adopt in order to save her soul, but also the recognition of the role of human will in the process of salvation, which brings the argument closer to Protestant doctrinal themes. This contrasts with the theatricality and obsession with external appearances that Mary had shown at the beginning of the play. Her renunciation of the cult of her own image constitutes an act of iconoclasm that marks the climactic moment in the process of repentance. She strips her body of all artifice, and offers herself up in the service of Christ. What previously was the cause of her sinfulness and the source of others' temptation becomes an instrument of humility before God:

> But like as the parts of my body in tymes past,/ I have made servants to all kynd of iniquitie,/ The same iniquitie away for ever I do cast,/ And will make my body servant to the veritie./ This haire of my head which I have abused,/ I repute vile and unworthie to wipe my lordes fete . . . / These fleshly eies which with their wanton lookes,/ Many persons to synne and vice have procured./ They have bene the devils volumes and bookes,/ Which from the service of God have other allured./ Now you synfull eies shed out teraes and water,/ Wash the Lords fete with them whom you have offended . . . / Now would I gladly this oyntment bestowe,/ About the innocent feete of my saviour,/ That by these penitent fruictes my lord may know/ That I am right sory for my sinfull behavior. (1703–1708, 1711–1716; 1727–1730)

The characterization of Mary at the moment of her contrition – dressed in rags, kneeling and with her head bowed – connects her with the iconography of Penitence[99] and Humility,[100] which would have permitted instant recognition of the changes brought about in her character. Given that anti-Catholic discourse usually associated Catholics with the love of ceremony and ornament, Mary Magdalene's symbolic rejection of such vanities becomes, by extension, a general rejection of the doctrines of the Church of Rome. All vestiges of the previous regime, then, are eliminated, as Christ corroborates, since he contrasts Mary's humility and penitence with the arrogance of Simon the Pharisee (1751–1840).

Through his insistence on the observation by rote of external rules, Simon becomes a symbol of hypocrisy and falsity. His inability to understand the Word of God, together with his pride and tyranny, link him to the Catholic stereotype and place him in clear opposition to the central figure of Mary, as the character of Christ points out:

> I see who be hypocrites full of dissemblyng scorne,/ And who be persons of faith and simplicitie./ Where as you thinke you haue done me pleasure,/ In bidding me to eate and drinke with you here,/ Your intent was to shew your richesse and treasure. (1805–1809).

In contrast to other examples, the salvation of Mary is seen as the result of her repentance, providing a certain degree of optimism regarding the question of the conversion of English Catholics. The allegory thus constructed also suggests the same supplicatory attitude that was seen in the spectacle of the royal entry, revealing the worries and anxieties of the English people before the prospect of the new government. Equally, attempts are made within it to mitigate the unease caused by the presence of yet another woman on the throne of England, resorting to her similarities with female characters recognized for their strength and virtue.

The need to educate the public in reformist doctrine also appears in the final text to be analysed here, which is very similar in its approach to the most radical pamphlet literature of the period. The demands that the anonymous author makes on the government make it hard to imagine its having been performed in official or institutional circles. Its most novel aspect is that it visualizes the apparent distancing that seemed to have developed between the Church of England and the separatist and puritan sectors of Protestantism. If during the reigns of Henry and Edward the government had identified with many of the arguments of radical reformists – at least in theory – in the time of Elizabeth I the Church of England sought its own doctrinal space, from which it could present itself as the religious and political middle ground. And with that, a deep schism opened between the crown and these various communities, which were considered to be as dangerous as the Catholics.

New Custom (1573) recalls the situation of the less moderate English Protestants, and seeks to soften the queen's attitude toward them.[101] Initially, the play takes us back to the theological debates of Bale and the first reformers of the Tudor period, in what seems to be an attempt to demonstrate the link between contemporary radicals and their predecessors in the time of Henry VIII and his son, who, at least in the beginning, had supported the same ideas that the queen now condemned. References to the invisibility of the Church of England (Prologue 13–30; I, i, 92, 204–205, 225–230), the opposition of tradition and Scripture (I, i, 29–32, 153–160, 170–188), the emphasis on the Word over the image (I, i, 33; IV, i, 116–118), the defence of the use of the vernacular in religious services (I, i, 79–82), mention of the Calvinist doctrine of reprobation (II, i, 1–3; III, i, 63–68, 95–99) and the critical stance regarding the wearing of vestments by the clergy (II, ii, 37–46; II, i, 150–165) not only confirm the playwright's adherence to Protestant values, but also his condemnation of certain aspects of worship – clerical garments, the use of Latin, images – on which the queen herself remained ambiguous.

The play is structured around two clearly identifiable blocs. The confrontation this creates is the struggle between the vices (representing Catholics) and the virtues (personifying the reformers). The motor and final destination of the dramatic action is the downfall or consolidation of the Protestant faith in England. The portrayal of the two antagonistic characters, Perverse Doctrine and Ignorance, seen as "an old Popish priest" and "an older Popish priest," leaves no room for doubt, and the impression is confirmed with the appearance of Hypocrisy, Cruelty and Avarice, all characters associated with the Catholic stereotype. The fact that the character Ignorance is the oldest of the vices is not accidental either, and points to ignorance as being the primary cause of the propagation of Catholicism in the country. The origins of the Catholic faith can only lie in the lack of knowledge of its faithful who, blind and confused, follow whatever precept the Church of Rome tells them. The proposition is again put forward, albeit implicitly, that the indoctrination of Catholics in the new Protestant values should be carried out as the sole means of their achieving salvation.[102]

This is the viewpoint of New Custom, the principal character, who symbolizes the Reformation in its most extreme form. The association that Perverse Doctrine establishes between this character and the school of Geneva – "For since these Genevian doctours came so fast into this lande,/ Since that time it was never merie with Englande./ First came Newcustome, and hee gave the onsay,/ And sithens thinges have gone worse every day"(II, ii, 163–166) – and the portrayal that is made of New Custom do not fail, however, to present certain problems:[103]

> They rang to a Sermon, and wee chanced to be there./ Up start the preacher I thinke not past twenty yeeres olde./ With a sounding voyce, and audacitie bolde,/ And beganne to revile at the holie sacrament, and transubstanciation. (I, i, 20–23)

The conflict lies in the possible indirect association between this character and movements such as the Presbyterians, who were espousing the need for drastic reforms within the Church of England. The means the main character chooses to convey his ideas – "prophesyings", the type of sermon typical of Calvinist preachers – confirms this association, as does the didactic feel of the gatherings at which he speaks. These would therefore be controversial, since the play was framed in binary terms and could be felt to be an indirect attack on the monarchy that, as a persecutor of such a radical movement, would not be counted among the elect, but rather the opposite. The denunciation takes shape in the words of New Custom regarding the irresponsibility of corrupt monarchs towards their people:

> The doctours of the Churche, great faulte they dyd fynde,/ In that men lived not after their mynde./ First with the rulers as examples of sinne,/ Then with the people as continuing therin./ So that of them both this one thing they thought,/ That the people was not good, but the rulers were naught./ But in comparison of this time of miserie,/ In those daies men lyved in perfecte felicitie. (I, ii, 31–39)

References to contemporary politics ("this time of miserie") seem clear, since allusions to the government of Mary I are consistently placed in the past, as in the words of Avarice: "In Englande which my selfe plaied in the daies of queene Marie" (II, iii, 43). The author thus implies Elizabeth's irresponsibility, since she has not taken up the task of instruction, as is her duty, and instead blocks such efforts on the part of those groups who are committed to the propagation of reformist values. New Custom's words are an admonition to the queen to change her conduct with regard to these groups, who are presented – and this is another novelty in the light of the official, centralist discourse – as the sole guarantors of religious and political continuity for the Elizabethan regime: "But thankes be

Edward VI and the Pope, ca. 1570. Portrait number 4165, copyright © National Portrait Gallery, London.

George Gower, *The Armada Portrait*, 1588. Reproduced by kind permission of His Grace the Duke of Bedford and the Trustees of the Bedford Estates.

"Elizabeth as a Second Constantine." Engraving from the first edition (1563) of *Actes and Monuments* by John Foxe. Reproduced by permission of The Huntington Library, San Marino, California.

Crispin van de Pass, *The Jacket Portrait*, 1596. Reproduced by kind permission of the Parham Foundation, Parham House, West Sussex.

to God that such rulers doth sende,/ Whiche earnestly studie that fault to amende . . . / God direct their heartes they may alwaies continue/ Suche iust execution on sinne to ensue" (I, ii, 73–74, 77–78).

In contrast to the pamphlet literature of this time, traces of the Spanish stereotype have not been found within the theatrical works studied here, probably as a result of theatrical censorship. Despite their being subjected to stricter controls than in earlier periods, the texts considered demonstrate the variety of theme and genre that dramatic writing was beginning to acquire in those years. In broad terms, these plays are characterized by a return to elements of a prior time, such as the victimization of Protestants under Mary and the theological debates and attacks against the monarch during the reigns of Henry VIII and Edward VI. Also, in the light of a new and complex socioeconomic reality, an incompatibility is suggested between measures taken by the government and certain Calvinist doctrinal questions. Finally, the characteristics of the Catholic stereotype are developed and become more familiar to the English people. This explains its innovative use as a comic device, without it losing its value as an instrument of social and political condemnation.

The Church of England distanced itself more and more from the extremist tendencies of other Protestant groups at this time, which gave rise to a multiplicity of political and religious actors who employed anti-Catholic discourse to affirm or vindicate their central positions. The "others" were many and varied, which explains the variety and in some cases the ambiguity of literary responses to the reality of the times in England.

These ambiguities came to an end in 1580, with the beginning of a period marked by two clear characteristics: first, the continuous Catholic threat, and second, the rupture of the diplomatic stability that – with its ups and downs –Elizabeth had managed to preserve in her dealings with the two great Catholic powers in Europe. The tensions in the final years of the 1570s resulted in open war between Spain, which viewed the conflict as a crusade against Protestantism, and England, which emerged as a leading defender of the Reformation in Europe. In the second part of Elizabeth's reign, an appeal to nationalistic values and patriotic sentiment will, to some extent, put an end to the diversity of responses that had characterized the use of anti-Catholic discourse in the first half of the reign. The many and varied agents that had played a role in the construction of this discourse would become more homogeneous, forming two distinct tendencies that the Protestant literature of the period would attempt to project as messages for domestic consumption. In this way divisions within the nation would be avoided in order to fight a many-headed common enemy, which included Rome, the Society of Jesus, and Spain.

CHAPTER FOUR

Elizabeth I (1580–1603): Gloriana and the Victory of Protestantism

The Apogee of the Elizabethan *Status Quo*

The second phase of Elizabeth's rule was distinguished by the achievement of the desired centralization for the Protestant *status quo*, which meant the definitive marginalization of English Catholics and, in large part, the relegation of radical Puritan groups to a position of protest from the sidelines. The universe of opposites that dominated Protestant viewpoints, and their idea of victimhood, proved incapable of integrating the changing reality of those years and, especially, the effect upon the English imagination of an event as fateful as the triumph over the Spanish Armada in 1588.

Imperial theory, the concept of royal supremacy, which had been used by every reformist sector up to that point as part of the argument against the universal power of the papacy, became a fundamental instrument of the regime's propaganda machine in an effort to unite nationalist feelings with religious zeal. The political and symbolic consequences of Elizabeth's triumph were enormous, since, from a providentialist perspective, it was a *de facto* divine endorsement of the Queen's objectives (as well as those of her advisers), of achieving national unity and claiming England's rights to be a colonial power. The rhetorical key that allowed the construction of this imagery was the articulation of a three-headed foreign enemy that was now, supposedly, clearly identifiable: Spain, Rome, and the Jesuits. In order for this idea of England and all things English to take on the ring of truth, it was imperative that a seamless image of the Catholic "other" should take root in the popular imagination, an image recognizable both for its connections with the rival power, Spain, and for its seditious role in the service of the Pontiff. There is no doubt that this propaganda campaign was successful, since, despite serious economic problems and ongoing political crises, these years would be forever fixed in England's historical memory as the country's Golden Age.

Reformist and Catholic discourse in the face of accusations of disloyalty

In the spring of 1580 the first leaders arrived in England of a movement that would set in motion the Catholic apparatus that would be most active during the second stage of Elizabeth's rule. The priests Edmund Campion and Robert Persons and the layman Ralph Emerson began the second evangelizing campaign in Protestant England,[1] this time headed by one of the most committed and organized religious institutions of the age: the Society of Jesus.

In principle, the instructions that the missionaries brought from Rome forbade them from becoming involved in affairs of state, from participating in any type of political discussions by letter, or from criticizing the Queen.[2] As Persons himself indicated in his treatise *Confessio Fidei*:

> And that obedience which they [Christians] owe to their sovereign we inculcate not less but truly much more than does any of the Protestants. For we preach that princes should be obeyed not merely for fear of punishment or for the sake of avoiding scandal but for conscience's sake as well, and that he may be condemned who does not obey his prince even in the utmost secrecy of his closet [*in cubiculo suo secretissimo*] where no fear of punishment or scandal exists.[3]

William Allen suggests the same idea in his *Apology* (1581) and, after praising the rule of Elizabeth, defends the decision of many English Catholics to abandon the country for reasons of conscience. Allen argues that there is a clear contrast between the Catholic and Protestant communities (in his opinion, the only traitors to the crown): "Is our doctrine seditious? Be Catholics by nature or profession unquiet persons? Are they desirious of disorder, change and novelty, or weary of peace, order and antiquity? Are they libertines, despisers of authority, seekers of spoil, sack and garboil? Are they given to sacrilege, to irreligiosity, Epicurism, or atheism?[4] The first step on the path toward the missionary movement's self-legitimization in England was, therefore, to reiterate the Catholic community's loyalty to the Queen.[5]

Their main obstacle to credibility was the bull of excommunication against the Queen, which identified English Catholics as potential traitors to the crown. The Catholic community's reaction was to silence the effects of that document, either by avoiding mention of it or by denying its validity within England.[6] Numerous casuistic texts emerged with the aim of adapting Rome's norms to the circumstances in which the English Catholic community were living. Peter Holmes mentions two of the most representative documents written for this purpose, which were both linked to the leaders of English Catholicism of this period. In the first, from the early 1580s, stress is placed on the need for the followers of the

Church of Rome to obey royal dictates (p. 43);[7] the second, written between 1578 and 1579, reflects on the attitude that the individual Catholic should adopt when interrogated, and concludes by pointing out the duty of avoiding any compromising replies, especially concerning the temporal authority of the pope (p. 44).[8] Casuistic literature also attempted to defuse the mounting pressure applied by the government,[9] and appealed to the tolerance and understanding of the Catholic clergy itself, forced now to accept the occasional necessity of its faithful conforming to the state religion.

Such individual decisions were not at all uniform, but instead revealed deep divisions within the Catholic community. On the one hand, those who defended this outward conformity could justify Catholics' attendance at Protestant services, provided they did not repeat the liturgical responses that were called for in them, that they did not receive communion, and that they sat during the moments when the Protestants knelt. By these gestures they identified themselves as Catholics without disobeying the government's laws. On the other hand, a broad section of the clergy, headed by the Jesuits, argued for a clearer show of affirmation of Roman doctrine, whether through martyrdom or, as frequently occurred, by silence or evasive responses.

In spite of these divisions and the threats of the government, the Jesuit mission was able to integrate English Catholics into the international Catholic community and thus break their isolation of some twenty years. The spiritual support of the missionaries, aided by a magnificent cultural and theological education acquired in the seminaries of Douai and Rome, and a greater access to Catholic literature in England and on the continent, strengthened the principles and objectives of the community which, though it continued to maintain a passive posture towards the government, began to coalesce as a threat to the monarchy. Emergence from isolation also meant the consolidation of its connections with the papacy, which would soon extend further than Rome itself.

Nonetheless, beginning in 1584, calls for tolerance were abandoned, and the decision was made to pursue a more aggressive policy that sought the overthrow of Elizabeth, through the coordinated efforts of Rome, the Jesuits, and the European Catholic powers.[10] In the view of the Jesuits, military invasion was the only way to restore the Catholic faith in England, which explains the initiation of an intensive campaign aimed at inciting a popular rejection of the regime, leading to rebellion and civil disobedience. This idea of political resistance lasted until the mid-1590s, when the possibility of Spain conquering England faded away. English Catholics borrowed ideas that had been used in France by both the Huguenots and the Catholic League following the death of the Duke of Anjou, when they found themselves faced with the succession of a legitimate Protestant King, Henry of Navarre. For the first time during Elizabeth's reign, English Catholicism found a situation parallel to its own among the Catholic communities of the European continent.[11]

The main topics that are reiterated in all the Catholic texts of this period are the denunciation of religious persecution, the assault on Elizabeth's international policies for their anti-Catholic character, the defense of the papal cause in Europe's religious wars and, finally, the problem of succession to the Throne, which at first focused on Mary Queen of Scots. To all this must be added the vindication of papal supremacy:

> If princes have souls, they must needs be under the account and charge of prelates... The English statute making the monarch head of the church and a temporal common wealth: giving no less right to heathen princes to be governors of the church in causes spiritual, than to a Christian king: it maketh one part of the church in different territories to be independent and several from another. (Allen, *An Apology*, p. 195)

According to Allen, a monarch who set him or herself up as head of the church was a kind of national god, and therefore the veneration of Queen Elizabeth represented an act of idolatry that could only bring disaster upon the English nation (p. 198). The only means of avoiding such disgrace was to appeal to papal authority above that of princes. The Elizabethan government's tyrannical nature was a result of her heresy, and so she should be deposed before she brought condemnation down upon all her people; according to the author, the act of excommunication stripped the Throne of England of its legality.[12] The plan for resistance subsequently championed by the Society of Jesus was, therefore, a clear reversal of the ideas of loyalty that had been defended prior to 1584. Consequently, Catholicism would become the object of one of the most commonly recurring criticisms – that of rebellion and sedition – that had previously been aimed at Protestant groups, a reaction that led to no small amount of dissent among sectors of the Catholic community.

The death of William of Orange and Throckmorton's failed conspiracy on behalf of Mary Stuart in 1584 reinforced these notions, and also revived fears that Elizabeth might be murdered.[15] The feeling of paranoia towards Catholicism began to grow, and Protestant discourse, though aware of divisions among the Catholics, tended more and more toward broad generalizations. This led to a harshening of the punishments directed at English Catholics, who now became victims of the worst persecution of the previous twenty-five years. The machinery of government repression was not disposed to tolerate threats to the regime, and the various reformist sectors, though each possessing different agendas, agreed on the necessity of presenting a united front against Catholicism.[13] The conspiracies of Dr. Parry (1585)[14] and Babington (1586)[15] were of little help to a Catholic community which found itself in the monarchy's sights. Catholicism came to be defined as the primary evil afflicting the

English people, with the regime's stability and the Queen's very life depending upon its eradication. However, the words of the Jesuit Robert Southwell in his work *An Epistle of Comfort* (1587), echoing those of the martyrs during the reign of Mary I who were praised by John Foxe, warned that the task would not be an easy one: "Our prisons preache, our punishmentes converte, our deade quarters and bones confound youre heresye: You have laboured to suppresse us this 29 yeeres: and yet our ashes spring others and our dead bones, as Exechiell prophesied, are come to be *exercitus grandis* a huge army".[16]

The key figure in all these plots was Mary Queen of Scots, who could not escape the charges of treason levelled against her. As more details of the Scottish queen's plans came to light, the Royal Council decided to protect the right of James VI to the Throne of England in the face of the sentence of death given against his mother.[17]

On 1 February 1587, Elizabeth I signed the order to execute her cousin Mary. Her ministers Hatton and Burghley assembled the Council, which assumed responsibility for the death of the Scottish queen. Seven days later she was executed, away from the public eye, putting an end to the preeminent symbol of English Catholicism for the previous thirty years. The Queen of England's fury then fell upon her counsellors who, in her view, had brought about this chain of events. Once again, Elizabeth made use of her rhetorical powers to construct the image of a diligent queen, a martyr who sacrificed her principles for the well-being of her people.

The clearest example of this type of discursive construct was *The Copie of a Letter to the Earle of Leycester*, a clearly propagandistic pamphlet, written by Lord Burghley's son Robert Cecil[18] shortly after the death of Mary Stuart, in which the confrontations between the Queen, the Council, and Parliament are described in detail. Its most significant part reproduces the Queen's words justifying her actions and asserting her innocence in the matter. The Queen's declaration reiterates several points that already formed part of the iconographic construct she had cultivated since the beginning of her reign. As she had then, Elizabeth emphasized her position as a martyr, appealing to Protestantism's victimist tradition:

> And although there liveth not any, that may more justly acknowledge themselves infinitely bounde unto God then I, whose life he hath miraculously preserved at sundry times (beyond my merite) from a multitude of perils and dangers: yet is not that cause, for which I count myselfe the deeplyest bounde to give my humblest thankes. (p. 225)

The protection afforded her by Providence since the commencement of her reign identified her as an instrument of God, one sent to spread His message among her subjects and protect them from Catholic corruption and falsehoods. Her commitment to the Protestant faith, the only means of salvation for her people, explains her attitude toward Mary Queen of Scots. It refers, then, to the same mutuality of interests between the queen and her subjects as the procession through London in 1559, and explains the queen's position as the result of her commitment to the English people: "As I came to the Crowne with the willing hearts of my subjects, so doe I now after xxviii yeres Reigne, perceive in you [God] no diminution of good willes" (pp. 225–226). The fundamental difference is that in 1559 Elizabeth could only offer her good intentions, while now her very presence on the Throne, despite the Catholics' intrigues, was evidence of divine endorsement. However, this message, composed for domestic consumption, posed numerous problems in an international context.

The stress on her responsibility to her subjects makes way for an attempt to justify her lack of mercy for Mary: "Albeit I finde my life hath bene full dangerously sought and death contrived by such as no desert procured: yet am I therin so cleare from malice . . . as I protest it is and hath bene my grievous thought, that one, not different in sexe, of like Estate, and my nere kin, shoulde fall into so great a crime" (p. 226).

Elizabeth's identification with the former Queen of Scotland reveals, on the one hand, a clear awareness that after the death of Mary Stuart the international community could connect the Queen of England with acts of sedition against other monarchies. On the other, it seems to hint at the queen's fears of suffering a similar fate. A clear contrast is thus produced between the double personae, public and private, of a queen who had to sacrifice her personal interests for the sake of her duty to the Crown: "there were no more dependancie upon us, but mine owne life were onely in danger, and not the whole estate of your Religion and well doings, I protest . . . I would willingly pardon and remit this offence" (p. 226).

The anxiety that Mary's death provoked within the English government and monarchy shines through in two of the points stressed in this declaration: the transparency with which justice was carried out, and the participation of the best jurists in the process. The Queen of England, knowing her actions were being observed by the other monarchs of Europe, cloaks the act of regicide beneath the discourse of the duty imposed on a truly Christian prince.

References to her supposed feminine simplicity gain an ironic value, forming another reply to the attacks she expected to receive:

> These former remembrances, present feeling, and future expectation of evils, I say, have . . . taught me to beare with *a better minde these treasons, then is common to my sexe: yea, with a better heart perhaps, then is in some men*. Which *I hope you wil not meerly impute to my simplicitie or want of understanding*, but rather, that I thus conceived, that had their purposes taken effect, I should not have found the blow, before I had felt it: and though my perill should have bene great, my paine should have bene but smal and short: wherein as I would be loth to dye so bloody a death, so doubt I not, but God

would have given me grace to be prepared for such an event. (p. 227) (My emphasis)

The Queen's absence from Parliament places a question mark, to a point, over the moral validity of the execution of Mary Queen of Scots, since Elizabeth had refused to witness the declaration of the death sentence and, with it, the regicide: "Yet hat it not bene the doubt of any such daunger or occasion that kept me from thence [Parliament], but onely the great grief to heare this cause spoken of, especially, that such a one of State and kin, should neede so open a declaration, and that this nation should be so spotted with blots of disloialtie" (p. 228)

The Queen concludes with a discussion of the need to carry out decisions made in Parliament, "which shall serve to the establishment of his [God's] Church, preservation of your estates, and prosperitie of this commonwealth under my charge" (p. 229), goals that take priority over any moral or political question and which coincide with her duty to her subjects that she accepted at the beginning of her reign. Elizabeth once again demonstrates her rhetorical acumen by making use of many of the elements that formed her public image as protector of the English nation. Even so, the paradoxes and objections that continued to arise testify to the overall complexity of this process, as well as its inconclusiveness.

Elizabeth I as head of European Protestantism

The international situation had worsened in the previous years. In the Low Countries, the Duke of Parma, Philip II's governor in the region, continued to garner victories: the surrender of Flanders, a large portion of Brabant, Brussels and Antwerp – all between 1584 and 1585. Elizabeth had reason to feel threatened, aware that Philip II might ally himself with the Guises and use bases in Flanders to attack England. The murder of William of Orange in 1584 plunged Protestants into confusion, and made it difficult for the English sovereign to maintain her apparent neutrality.

In June 1585, the Queen received an embassy from the Dutch Provinces, offering her sovereignty over their territory in exchange for English involvement in the war against Spain. Although she declined the offer of sovereignty, Elizabeth promised military support, and sought to justify her decision in the pamphlet *A Declaration of the Causes to Give Aide in the Lowe Countries*[19], written by Cecil and Walshingham near the end of 1584, under the queen's supervision. It affirms the historical bonds between England and the Low Countries, as well as the kinship between the two nations,[20] which are due not only to religious reasons, but also, and above all, to their many shared economic interests, which form one of the fundamental motives for the English to lend their support.

References to Spanish tyranny are frequent in the text, which highlights the foreign nature of the Spanish officials, as compared to the bonds of

Gloriana and the Victory of Protestantism

brotherhood between the Dutch and England. The enemy is thus transferred to the periphery, to the status of alien, while the English government stresses its own median – and therefore justifiable – position in the conflict. The Spaniard incarnates the "other", the dangerous invader of anti-Catholic literature of the period:

> These Spaniardes being exalted to absolute goverment, by ambition, and for private lucre have violently broken the ancient lawes and liberties of all the countries, and in a tyrannous sort have banished, killed and destroyed without order of lawe within the space of a fewe monethes, many of the most ancient and principall persons of the naturall nobilitie that were most worthie of government ... And furthermore, to bring these whole countries in servitude to Spaine, these forreine governours have by long intestine warre ... made the greater part of the said countries ... in a manner desolate, and have also lamentably destroyed by sworde, famine, and other cruell maners of death, a great part of the naturall people, and nowe the rich townes and strong places being desolate of their naturall inhabitants, are held and kept chiefly with force by the Spanyardes. (p. 200)

Consistent with the queen's desire to avoid direct attacks upon other monarchs, the authors distance Philip II from the religious persecutions and attacks upon freedoms that were being carried out, blaming instead his officers in the Low Countries:

> But these Spaniardes, being mere strangers, having no naturall regarde in their goverment to the maintenance of those countries and people in their ancient and natural maner of peaceable living, *as the most noble and wise Emperor Charles, yea & as his sonne king Philip himself had, whilest he remained in those countries, and used the counsels of the States and natural of the countries, not violating the ancient liberties of the countries*: but contrarywise, these Spaniardes being exalted to absolute gouernement by ambition, and for priuate lucre haue uiolently broken the ancient lawes and liberties of all the countries, and in a tyrannous sort haue banished, killed and destroyed without order of lawe within the space of a fewe monethes many of the most ancient and principall persons of the naturall nobilitie that were most worthie of gouernement.[21] (pp. 199–200) (My emphasis)

Nevertheless, the justification that is given of the Dutch rebellion contradicts this statement, and reveal the difficulty of Elizabeth's position. In spite of all the praise for the King of Spain, military support for the Protestants in the Low Countries could only be seen as an attack on the Spanish monarchy. Also, the defense of a people's right to political resistance would be received with perplexity by English Catholics, who had been persecuted and punished for the same positions that are defended in the text:

As a good loving sister to him [Philip II], *and a natural good neighbour to his lowe countries and people, wee have often, and often againe most friendly warned him, that if hee did not otherwise by his wisdome and princely clemencie restraine the tyranny of his governours and crueltie of his men of warre, we feared that* the people of his countries shoulde bee forced for safetie of their lives, and for continuance of their native countrie in their former state of their liberties, to seeke the protection of some other forreyne Lord, *or rather to yeelde themselves wholy to the soveraigntie of some mightie Prince, as by the ancient lawes of their countries, and by speciall priviledges graunted by some of the Lords and Dukes of the countries to the people,* they doe pretend and affirme, that in such cases of general injustice, and upon such violent breaking of their privileges they are free from their former homages, and at libertie to make choice of any other prince to bee their prince and Head. (p. 201) (My emphasis)

In this manner intervention in Holland is disguised within the discourse of political victimhood and the right to self-defense that so often characterized anti-Catholic writings. On 20 August 1585, the Treaty of Nonsuch was signed, by which England committed itself to send an army of five thousand soldiers, commanded by the Earl of Leicester. Though still without a formal declaration, war with Spain had begun.

The actions of European Catholicism had grave consequences for the English Catholic community, which had fallen victim to a progressive hardening of the laws directed against it, as well as the growing suspicions of being a fifth column. The reality, though, was much more complex. English Catholics distrusted Madrid's supposed connections with the Holy See; they did not feel compelled to support Spain in its indulgence of the Pope – who only promised to pardon them in the event the queen was murdered – and they were also aware of the animosity between Philip II and Pope Sixtus V, and the hesitancy on the part of the latter to collaborate with the House of Austria.

Equally, though, Elizabeth's suspicions regarding the close relationship between the English Catholic community and Spain were not unfounded. The Spanish court had assumed the role of sponsor to many English Catholic families, and financed the schools and seminaries that undertook the training of new students and priests, many of whom had intentions of joining the Jesuit missions in England. It also promoted the publication and distribution in the Low Countries of apologetic works in English, and awarded generous grants to refugees who supplied information regarding the Queen of England. For Elizabeth's court there was, therefore, clear evidence of the ties between the Catholic community in her own country and the Spanish Crown. For his part, Philip II had little confidence in the usefulness of such people in his invasion plans, and remained suspicious of them.[22]

The Spanish threat took physical shape on 29 July 1588, when the

Spanish Armada arrived in the English Channel after a difficult journey that had begun in Lisbon on 18 May. A detailed description of the complex political circumstances that terminated in the sinking of the Spanish fleet off the coast of England[23] would be broad and long, so discussion here will be limited to what this event meant for the project of English nationalist identity, and the way it definitively tied that identity to the existence of a multiple "other", which was Catholic, Spanish, and defeated.

In the first place, pamphleteers used the threat of invasion as an instrument to forge strong ties of kinship among the English people, irrespective of religious convictions: "let us imbrace christian unity and concord, the which also will make us invincible against all our enemies that seek to invade us".[24] Several authors relegate questions of faith to a second tier of importance, pointing to practical reasons to justify the desire for unity: "The doubt to lose life, lands and goods, will cause us to agree".[25] The Spanish menace provides a unique opportunity for England to unite against a common enemy; as such, the image of the nation as a ship on the storm-tossed seas of discord is revealing:

> And seeing God hath placed us English men here in one common wealth, also in one Church, as in one Ship together: and no storme so daungerous to a Shippe on the Sea, as is discorde in a weale publique. Let us shunne it, as the skilfull Mariners doo the two daungerous Rockes, Scilla and Charibdis. Let us seeke peace and earnestly imbrace it. (Tymmes, *A Preparation*, sig. B7r).[26]

One gets an uneasy sense that certain sectors among the population would support the Spanish cause – "They [the Spanish] hope perhaps to have, some helpe within this Ile" (*An Exhortacion to all English Subiects*, p. 1) – but trust is placed in the nation's courage.[27]

This portrayal contradicts the image of inferiority that had often been seen: "Let us altogether Ioyne handes as bretheren against those abhominable Idolaters ... who trust in their multitude, and presume altogether upon their strength: whereas the race doth not always belong to the swift, nor the battaile to the strong" (Tymme, *A Preparation*, sig. B2r). England's weaknesses and internal divisions – which made possible the support for the invaders, and the idea of legitimizing Elizabeth's overthrow– serve, nonetheless, to reinforce the image of Providence as the country's protector:

> The furious Foe enthralld in thirst of Blood/ Whos Ravenous Rore, outreacheth Seas and Lands,/ Still Raging, seeks Subversion of the Good,/ By Mighty Meanes of stearnfull Armed Bands:/ *But God Regarding his true Peoples plight;/ Prevents their wrong & makes prevail their Right/* No Councels, or Complots of Men, may stand:/ Or stratagems, of strange invented Ill:/ Or Strength by Sea, or Puissant Powre by Land,/ To strive with

God, or straine beyond his will./ *God fights for us & shields our Lives from Thrall:/* What skils it than, who be our Foes at all?[28]

The war is described as a crusade, in which religious and nationalist motives are inevitably bound together, and victory is England's reward for its struggle for the Protestant faith:

> Let therefore the hartes of the Nobles and Captains of this noble lande bee strong, valiant, and of a good courage to fight the Lords battails, against the sworne enemies of his truth and Gospel. Let every true English man bee in a readines with bowes, billes, morispikes, and gunnes, to march on in a warlike araye, lyke true soldiers, *for the maintainance of y Gospel of Christ, for the preservation of our noble Queene Elizabeth, for the defence of our countrey, our landes, our children, our wives and our lyves: and to repress the pride of straungers, which seeke to invade us, and thereby to possesse our goods* to force chaste matrones, to deflower virgins, to kill our children, and to make us their drudges and bondmen for ever. The quarrell wee see is iust: *the cause is Gods.* (Tymme, *A Preparation*, sigs B1v-B2r) (My emphasis)[29]

The most obvious example of the interaction of these two interests is the portrayal of the queen as God's emissary[30] and guide for her people, two ideas conveyed by the use of allusions to light: "The glory of the Kingdome shall remaine as the sunne in the sight of the Lord: and as the Moone in the night season, so shall our Elizabeth give light unto her people" (Marten, *An Exhortation*, sig. F1v). The first simile no doubt refers to the apocalyptic figure of the Woman Clothed with the Sun – "Then came the Queene . . . atired like an Angell bright" (Deloney, *The Queenes Visiting of the Campe at Tilsbury*, p. 1) – the symbol of the reformed Church, with clear evangelical and anti-Catholic connotations, and integrated into the iconography of the monarch from early on. On the other hand, the meanings associated with the moon – virginity,[31] feminine power and immutability, among others – form an indispensable metaphor that underscored Elizabeth's authority and her longevity in the face of the many conspiracies against her.[32] Marten also reproduces Ripa's emblem *Eternity or Perpetuity*, in which there appears a woman with a sun and a moon in each hand,[33] which, in this context, again stresses the queen's strength and, by extension, that of her people.

This type of image used in reference to the queen would be a recurrent theme until the end of her reign, as is shown by one of her most popular portraits, the *Rainbow Portrait* of 1600, in which the queen represents the sun that brings forth the rainbow. Elizabeth is holding it as a promise of peace after the storm. The motto *Non sine Sole Iris* (without the sun, there is no rainbow) supports this reading.[34] In most of the texts analysed there are, in effect, references to the peaceful character of Elizabeth's government. Thomas Tymme, for instance, gives thanks to God for that long peace which by the gracious gouernment of our peaceable Salomæ, we have long enjoyed . . . This peace, hath brought forth plentie of riches in our land. The Lord hath opened to us his good treasure, euen the heauen to giue raine to our land in due reason, and hath blessed all the worke of our hands. (sigs A3r-v)

Kyffin presents the defeat of the Armada as divine recognition of Elizabeth's policies, which guaranteed not only the moral well-being of her subjects but also their prosperity (sigs D3v, D4r). England's naval power is revealed as a chief instrument of colonization and the production of wealth – "I may not heere omit in Silent Sorte,/ Her Royall Ships strong wrought for stearnfull war,/ (Whereof all worldly Realmes doe raise report)/ Through raging Seas discovering Regions farre" (sig. A4v) – supplanting the Spanish fleet and the empire of Philip II. Thus Elizabeth becomes "the Sole Empress of the World" (sig. D4v). Comparisons drawn between her and military figures, both female – Bellona (sigs D1v, E1v), Amazon (sigs D4r-v) – and male – Mars (sig. D1v) – emphasize her power and military prowess, and thus seek to eliminate doubts or scepticism about the competence of a female ruler in times of war. Identification is also sought between the queen and her subjects, united against a common adversary.

The most meaningful examples of these arguments and images are found in two pamphlets – *The Queenes Visiting of the Campe at Tilsburie*[35] and *Elizabetha Triumphans*, both from 1588, and by Thomas Deloney and James Aske respectively – which describe a visit by the queen to the encampment at Tilbury, shortly before the final battle of the campaign. Both combine in their portrayal the queen's majestic character – "Her royall grace with all her traine,/ was landed there with great renowne" (Deloney); "She thence some-way still marching Kinglike on,/ The Canons at the Blockhouse were discharg'd:/ The Drums do sound, the Phiphes do yeeld their notes,/ And Ensignes are displayd through-out the Campe" (Aske, sig. D2r) – and her humility and simplicity:

> Her faithfull souldiers great and small,/ As each one stood within his place:/ Upon their knees began to fall,/ Desiring God to save her Grace./ For ioy wherof her eyes was filled,/ that the water downe diffilled./ Lord blesse you all my friends, she said,/ But doe not kneele so much to me:/ Then sent the warning to the rest,/ They should not let such reverence be. (Deloney)

In this case, the image of her tears recognizes her as a woman without bringing with it pejorative connotations; instead, it shows the gratitude of the queen, who promises similar loyalty to her subjects in return: "For in the midst of all your troupe,/ we our selves will be in place:/ To be your ioy, your guide and comfort,/ even before our enemies

Elizabeth I (1580–1603)

face" (Deloney). As in the procession before her coronation, the relationship between queen and subjects is seen in terms of mutuality, as an exchange of favors: "Yet say to them that we in like regards, / And estimate of this their dearest zeale, / (If time of neede shall ever call them foorth / To dare in field their fearce and cruell foes) / Wilbe our selfe their noted Generall" (Aske, sig. E1v).

Elizabeth's "feruent loue" for her people is echoed in an almost melodramatic farewell, in which the sadness of the troops in the encampment at the queen's departure extends to the whole of Nature. Elizabeth adopts the role of sentimental heroine for her subjects, which softens her clearly masculine military attributes. Once again, the authors maintain a tense balance in describing the strength of the queen in wartime, without undermining her conciliatory feminine nature:

> Which sayd, she bow'd her princely bodie down,/ And passed thence unto the water-side . . . / And there euen the fore-white mant'led Ayre,/ From whence the Sunne shed foorth his brightest beames,/ Did cloathe it selfe with darke and duskie hue,/ And with thick Clowdes bar'd Phaebus gladsome streames/ From lightning then the Earth with glorious shew/ It powres foorth showers in great and often droppes/ Signes of the griefe for her departure thence. (sigs E1v-E2r)

As a result of the failure of the Armada Elizabeth became the focus of an idolatrous cult,[36] which in many ways shaped subsequent relations between the queen and her court. It should thus come as no surprise that this episode was, from that time on, an essential point of reference for English Protestantism, especially at decisive moments. The image of the queen would for centuries remain linked to the defeat of the Spaniards, which to this day retains its providential character.[37] The *Armada Portrait* of Elizabeth (Figure 3), in which the Spanish ships are seen to advance but are held back by the powerful monarch presents us with the queen as the religious, nationalist and imperial icon that she had become by the end of 1588.

In George Gower's *The Armada Portrait* (1588) Elizabeth is seen between two windows, through which are portrayed the arrival and the defeat of the Armada, respectively. The Queen is presented as the world's new empress, as demonstrated by the imperial crown at her side and her hand resting on the globe. (For more information, see Roy Strong, *The Cult of Elizabeth. Elizabethan Portraiture and Pageantry*, London, Thames and Hudson, 1977, p. 43.)

Elizabeth appears in the Armada dress in several portraits. One of the most significant is that known as *The Jacket Portrait* (1596) by Crispin van de Pass (Figure 4), in which she is portrayed as the inheritor of the imperial ideal of Charles V. The Pillars of Hercules (which refer to the opening of her empire to the New World) support this idea. The pelican (a symbol of Christ's sacrifice) indicates the queen's role as the mystical mother of both the nation and its Church; the phoenix, a reference to Christ's resurrection, depicts her as chaste and unique, the last of her dynasty. Behind her is seen a map of England, with forts defending the people from foreign invasions. The Queen is seen, in fact, wearing the Armada dress and with sword in hand, ready to fight for the Protestant faith – behind the sword is a book with the inscription *Posui Deum Adiutorem meum* (I have made God my helper) – and for her political and economic interests.[38]

This image was repeated yet again on the funerary sphinx made of the queen following her death; this was a representation of the monarchy's "political body", while the tomb upon which it rested contained the earthly remains of the deceased queen.[39] The image that was passed on to posterity was thus none other than that which was produced after the victory over the Armada.

The triumph of Gloriana

These military triumphs did not erase religious dissent, although there was a clear weakening of the Catholics as a body, divided over questions such as the possibility of deposing the queen, a Spanish invasion, and the dynastic succession.[40] Jealousies among the English Catholic clergy grew in the face of the progressive advance of the Society of Jesus, since, by around 1593, the Jesuits controlled all the English Catholic schools on the continent.[41]

The English Catholic laity felt themselves excluded from the evangelizing mission, and in many cases did not share the ideas of civil resistance propagated by the Jesuits during those years. Also problematic were the conflicts between the Jesuits and the *appellants*, a group of Catholic priests who had declared themselves loyal to the Crown and criticized what they regarded as the seditious attitude of the Society.[42] Disputes over the structure and distribution of roles within the missionary movement in England were another source of disagreement, such as the one that originated in Wisbech, where Catholic prisoners, divided by questions of power within the community, split into two camps, or the one in the seminary in Rome, where serious confrontations occurred between the students and the Jesuit administration.[43]

The Puritan movement, on the other hand, had since 1580 achieved a high degree of organization, and had succeeded in taking its demands to Parliament in spite of the queen's refusal to discuss matters related to her religious policies. They exerted a notable influence on public opinion, and were one of the principal sources of pressure on the ruling system.[44] With the naming of John Whitgift as Archbishop of Canterbury in 1583, however, the Presbyterian project saw its forces undermined. In October of that year, several new laws were announced that were aimed at both

Catholics and Puritans, which showed the determination of the monarchy to finish with those who did not accept religious uniformity.

As a result, the years 1584 and 1585 witnessed an extensive Presbyterian campaign, through pamphlets that attacked the foundations of the official Church. Their aggressive character unsettled the regime, which wasted no time in imposing severe censorship on all texts printed in the country. Even so, the Puritans continued their efforts clandestinely, and intensified the tone of their attacks not only against Catholics but also against the hierarchy of the Church of England.[45] The attacks levelled against Anglican bishops in the *Martin Marprelate Tracts* (1588–1589) caused serious consternation among the ecclesiastical leadership, who found themselves unable to control the threat posed by such writings. However, their radical tone failed to benefit Puritans as a whole, since they had lost credibility in the eyes of public opinion and begun to be associated with acts of sedition.[46]

In August 1589, a series of actions taken against hidden printing presses were successful, and were followed by a meticulous investigation of those implicated. As a consequence of this increase in governmental persecution, by the beginning of the 1590s the Puritan movement had lost both its level of organization and the efficacy of the previous decade. An effective pamphlet program in defense of the official religion seriously weakened the foundations of English Puritanism, whose representatives abandoned the active struggle in order to focus on more pastoral labours.[47]

The last decade of Elizabeth's reign was not an easy one for the people of England. The economic crisis brought about by expenditure on wars, inflation, the exploitation of commercial monopolies by the nobility, and the loss of successive harvests created a generalized state of unrest.[48] Concern over political change and the succession to the Throne added to the anxiety of the English, who were quick to show their dissatisfaction. The Catholic and Puritan communities hence awaited optimistically the arrival of a new sovereign who would listen to their demands. Desires for change – above all with regard to war policy – were mixed with apprehension at the end of an age.

On 24 March 1603, Elizabeth I died, and with her, England's Tudor Dynasty.

Pamphlet Literature in the Second Phase of Elizabeth's Reign: The Multiple "Other"

Anti-Catholic literature of the second half of the reign of Elizabeth I takes a somewhat different tack by comparison with the works of previous years. The most notable example of this is the abandonment of theological polemics.[49] Mention of the Word of God is only made when it is needed in order to justify the imperial theory of sovereignty, and with it the power of Elizabeth in relation to the Pope. Given the bellicose state of the international situation, it is not surprising that anti-Catholic authors replaced doctrinal elements with descriptions of Catholic aggression in order to encourage a collective act of rejection. There is no doubt they inflamed public opinion and increased hatred and fear of the followers of Rome, who were now more organized and more committed to their cause – especially the followers of the Society of Jesus.

The characteristics associated with the Catholic stereotype are the same as those in earlier reigns, although the repertoire has broadened, particularly with the appearance of a new "other," which practically acquired a monopoly as the target of these attacks: the Jesuit. In general he shares many attributes of the Catholic type, but takes on new elements that turn him into the powerful transgressor-figure that rivals the menace posed by the Pope himself. Finally, with the gathering war with Spain that would begin in 1585, the Spanish stereotype also assumes an even stronger form.

In response to both internal conflicts and the international threat, Elizabeth I would be presented as Astraea, the head of a strong and stable monarchy, the protector of her people in the face of the forces of the papacy. Reformed England was the image of a new Golden Age, whose benefits would be shared by all humanity. In this way, from within a discourse of defensive resistance, England's right to expansionism in the face of the Spanish *status quo* could also be made visible.

The Society of Jesus

The introduction of the figure of the Jesuit into the Catholic stereotype only increases its menace. The pamphlets of the time in general point out the role of the Society of Jesus in the nation's political and religious instability; this attitude, however, was not the exclusive domain of Protestant authors, but also appeared among other Catholic groups, both in England and abroad.[50] In spite of this, these opinions were irrelevant to reformist writers, who preferred instead to blur any points of distinction that might question the unified character of the enemy.

Within the portrayal of the Jesuits, political elements are preeminent over matters of religion or doctrine; from this emerges the role of spy, which is often conferred upon them within Protestant literature:

> The old saying was, let the shoemaker meddle with his slipper, the smith with his anuill, and the priests with their prayers; but the Jesuites . . . are in at all. *He is not worth a rush amongst them that is not able to manage a kingdome. Matters of state, titles of princes, genealogies of kinges, right of succession, disposing of scepters, and such affaires are their chiefe studies. Some feare they are more cunning in Aretine, Lucian and Machiavell* . . . assuredly *they*

doe not behave themselves, like any other religious men ... There are few kinges courts in Europe, where some of their maisterships doe not reside, of purpose to give *intelligence to their generall at Rome*, of all the occurrents in these parts of the world, which they dispatch to and from by secret cyphers, having either a Jesuite, or someone Jesuited, in the most of those kings counsels, *who ... must without scrupples deliver to them, the secret of their soveraignes* to their uttermost knowledge.[51] (My emphasis)

This association with Machiavelli emphasizes the Jesuit's hypocrisy and lack of scruples, questioning his loyalty to any established power: "The Jesuites will be Spaniards or Frenchmen, or whatsoever else, if opportunitie be offered thereunto ... the Iesuites change and rechange their rules and lawes, at their owne good will and pleasure ... [they are] fit for all times, all places, and all companies" (Bell, *The Anatomie*, p. 58).[52] Jesuit casuistry[53] also made it possible for the Society's members to use particular forms of self-protection that included falsehoods and disguise – "A little before the comming of the Spanish fleet, they sent their spialls, among them some that were priests, in disguised garments, with instructions".[54] This could also be accounted for by the Jesuit defense of methods such as simulation, which was enough for the Protestant ranks to insist on the Society's capacity for manipulation. The Spanish Jesuit Pedro de Ribadeneira explained the process in this way: "Simulation is really two arts. The first, of those who, without cause or advantage, lie, pretending that there is what there is not, or that there is not what there is; the other, of those who, without evil intent to deceive and without lying, prudently allow a thing to be understood as something else, as he sees the need or usefulness".[55]

Simulation, or equivocation, posed a serious threat to any political authority, since the Jesuits cloaked themselves in it in order to deceive or to hide the truth, justifying such actions by their freedom of conscience. Pamphleteers pointed this out to warn of the danger posed by this group within England:

No one thing breedeth greater danger and hatred to all catholikes in England, then the Iesuits abuse of Equivocating, making it indeed nothing else but an art of lying, cogging, foisting and forging, and that without al respect of matter, time, place, person ... And this doctrine of the iesuits, touching equivocation, hath already bewitched so many of the lay Catholiks, that impossible it is, for any (that is not a Iesuit) to know a Iesuits hart, & so no man is able to bind upon any words of theirs, they have so many shifts, and so little conscience in speaking truly, except it bee one of themselves to another.[56]

Nevertheless, the English Jesuit Robert Persons recommended that Catholics use this device only in cases of extreme necessity. According to

Persons, the Catholic community should demonstrate honesty and thus earn the trust of the rest of the English people: "In opinion likewise, and estimation of others, . . . the word of a Catholicke man ought to weigh more than the oath of an other, and the oath, or promise of a Catholicke, more then any band or obligation of an other, which for the most parte I doubt not, but is so already taken in England".[57] This was not entirely correct, since many Protestants continued to distrust many of the Society's methods.

Besides identifying them with spying and with Machiavellian politics, the pamphlets also contributed to the myth of the Jesuit as seducer, a common motif even before their arrival in England; English reformists merely added this new element to the collection of vices that already made up their stereotype. In Europe, many Jesuits were spiritual counsellors to ladies of the nobility, who in turn became their benefactors, a fact that aroused the envy of other orders – especially the Dominicans – and provoked all kinds of comments about them. However, despite attempts by some of these women to join the Society, the Jesuits always refused, considering them to be a potential temptation before which they might succumb, which contradicts the image of seducers that was so often used in propaganda against the Order.[58] According to such propaganda, the inherent weakness of women explained their attraction to the Society, whose interest lay in obtaining both sexual and economic favors: "So silly women more devout than discreet . . . poore soules do mightily dote and run riot after them . . . and the ignorant multitudes of the Iesuites do use most women gospellers, trumpetters of their praise, & with these women tatlers and women gospellers, the Secular Priests are much troubled" (*The Downefall of the Iesuits*, p. 41).

Women represented one of the principal connections between the Jesuits and the nobility, and so the pamphleteers also pour scorn on their love of wealth and power: "He [the Jesuit] is richly apparelled, and attended on with a great traine of servants, as if he were a baron, or an Earle" (Bell, *The Anatomie*, p. 34).[59] To this, Robert Southwell answered that the salvation of souls was much more important than his vestments,[60] and Persons and Campion, in fact, were instructed before beginning their mission to wear modest and sober clothing.[61] Nevertheless, leaving aside the greater or lesser comfort of their living conditions, the Jesuits did seek protection and a degree of economic security, so that the first guidelines they received stressed the need to convert the aristocracy. This was expressed by John Gerard, one of those in charge of the earliest activities of the Society in England: "The way, I think, to go about making converts is to bring the gentry over first and then their servants, for Catholic gentlefolk must have Catholic servants".[62] This idea, however, was not shared by other Jesuits, such as Robert Persons, who criticized the Society's concentration in the south and center of the country, where the Catholic aristocracy was most influential. Although, with the passage of time, efforts were made to broaden their area of influence, regions such as the west of England and Wales never felt the presence of the Society.[63] Protestant authors mentioned this tendency, and pointed out the Jesuits' lack of commitment to the humbler elements of the country.[64]

The Jesuit also constituted a threat to patriarchal authority, by challenging the power of the father,[65] of the husband,[66] or the lord in the houses of the nobility:

> The Jesuites so rule in all gentlemens houses where they reside, that no lease must be let, but by their advice; the tenants must either please them, or repent at leisure. Such fines must be taken, as they thinke convenient . . . in effect they doe so rule and . . . as scarcely can the master or the mistress of the house, give a piece of bread at their doors, but it must be done with their approbation. (Bell, *The Anatomie*, p. 31)

Given the recurring use of the parallel between familial and social order during the sixteenth and seventeenth centuries, the Jesuit was seen as a threat, one that shook the foundations of English society by questioning such traditional domestic power structures. The relationship of a noble lord to his servants could be extended to that between a monarch and his subjects. Hence, if the head of the domestic household could be threatened, in the broader social context, this threat could also lead to the theory of tyrannicide.

The Jesuit Juan de Mariana, one of the principal champions of this doctrine, explains in his work *De Rege et Regis Institutione* (1599) the risk that tyrannical monarchs run before a discontented people, fully capable of rebelling against and killing them. He consistently places the good of the people before that of the monarch, so it is not surprising that his words were unsettling to the princes of the era, including Elizabeth I:

> And must we allow the tyrant to vex and torment our country at his leisure, the country to which we owe more than to our own parents? Such evil and such villainy are far beneath us. It matters little that we must place in danger wealth, health and life. At all costs, we must save our country from danger; at all costs, we must save her from ruin.[67]

The Jesuits' association with this doctrine was a constant in Protestant writings of the period, which sought to expose the tyrannicidal tendencies of groups that resisted religious conformity. As one example, the French minister Antoine Arnauld accused them of the many rebellions in France, and of an attempt on the life of King Henry IV at the behest of the Pope:[68]

> Their [the jesuits'] purpose and burning zeale is to murder the living: was it not in the College of Jesuits at Lyon, and also in the College of Iesuites in

Paris, that the resolution was last taken to murder the king in August 1593. Are not the depositions of Barriere executed at Melun, notorious to all the world? And do not those depositions make all true French hearts tremble and quake, all them I say, that have not built their plottes and hopes upon the death of the King? Was it not Varade principall of the Iesuites, so chosen by them, as the honestest and best Iesuite, that exhorted and encouraged the murderer, assuring him that he could not doe a more meritorious worke in the world, then to murder the King though he were a Catholike, and that for this deed he should go straight to Paradise? (pp. 11–12)[69]

In the eyes of the pamphleteers, the French wars of religion and the assassination attempts against French sovereigns – Henry III and Henry IV – were a warning for Elizabeth to remain alert to the Society's activities and to toughen restrictions against it.[70]

The control of confession is another of the most repeated topics used to present the Jesuits as a dangerous influence: "it is these bold confessions, (where without witnesses they paint not the faces but the hearts of their scholars with the painting of rebellion against their Prince and Magistrates) that filled so many places, and so many dignities with Spanish hearts, enemies to the King and his state" (Arnauld, *The Arrainement*, p. 14). Their alleged capacity for manipulation reached the point of denying absolution "unlesse they would vowe and promise to bande themselves against their Soveraigne" (p. 9).

Although criticism of the papacy continued, a gradual shift in the focus of the attacks made by Protestant authors came about, as they became more and more focused on the Society of Jesus as the primary agent – sometimes more so than the pope himself – of the Catholic menace. The effectiveness and perfect organization of their each and every activity seemed to evoke not just fear among the Protestant rank and file, but also hidden admiration for their evangelizing and political capacity. Their confrontations with other sectors of the Catholic church, often mentioned in anti-Catholic literature, failed to weaken the powerful and unified image that many Protestant authors attributed to them from 1580 to the end of the seventeenth century. The mirror of comparisons once again indicated the weaknesses of English Protestantism, this time in relation to the polemical Jesuits.

The Spanish stereotype and the Black Legend

Beginning in 1580, an important movement also developed within pamphlet literature that laid emphasis on the equation of Catholicism with the interests of Spain, and interpreted religious non-conformity in terms of treason. The Spanish monarch is commonly described as an instrument in the hands of the papacy, in whose every action political and religious interests run together:[71]

> *Philip* therfore taking the Pope for Peters successor, *suffered himselfe to bee led and ruled by this man of sin* [the Pope], *holding his preceptes for oracles* . . . yet *Philip is so blinded*, as he hath not an insight into this their iugling, for that hee is taught by theyr doctrine that the Churche of Rome is the supreme Church . . . Soothing himselfe uppe in these heresies, *being so feared the frowne of the Pope and his Cardinals, doubting to bee excommunicated with some paltrye Bull, that what they demande bee graunteth, as well in matters of temporall estate*, as in Ecclesiasticall rightes and Ceremonies . . . perswaded by the Pope, and them of the Ecclesiasticall sorte: *he provided a great Armado*, his shippes huge and monstruous, his men the chosen Cavaliers of Spain, Portugal and Itale, and other Provinces.[72] (My emphasis)

The pamphlet literature once again takes up the Spanish stereotype that had taken shape during the reign of Mary I, in order to identify its every characteristic with the generic figure of the Catholic. This parallel particularly insists that all followers of Rome, even if they were born in England, were sympathetic to Spain. Many of the vices previously associated with Catholics were now attributed to the Spanish, who were accused of cruelty both in pamphlets and in plays, especially in their treatment of the indigenous peoples of the Americas,[73] the Low Countries (Orange, *The Apologie*, B2v, C1r-v, F1v, F4v, G2v-G3r, K1v-K2r) and foreign monarchies (*A True and Perfect Description*, pp. 23–24). Spain's alleged support for political tyranny[74] explains the hatred that was felt for it in Portugal,[75] France (Lewkenor, *The Estate of the English Fugitives*, pp. 120–124), Italy (p. 114) and England,[76] as well as among the other peoples who shared the Iberian Peninsula, the Catalans, Aragonese and Valencians, among others (*A Treatise Paraenetical*, p. 16 and *A Fig for the Spaniard*, sig. B4v).[77]

Faced with the aggressive attitude of imperial Spain, different authors seemed to take comfort in the promise of divine punishment – "But say that neither these plagues of swelling sedition, or pinching famine, happily sent by God himselfe to none other ende, but to relent his stonie heart, and set him at peace, with other princes that seek after, and delight in peace, can quallifie his hautie humour or quence his hot desire of revenge" (*A Fig for the Spaniard*, sig. C3v)[78] – in the progressive weakening and diminishing of Spain's human and material resources – "Who is ignorant of the great slaughters of Spaniards, that have beene committed within these foure yeares? Who is ignorant of the huge losse, both of men and ships he hath sustained in this last Indian voyage" (sig. C3v) – or in the formation of an international alliance against Spain (Chilmead, *Thomas Campanella*, p. 115).

As with the Catholic stereotype, unbridled ambition is portrayed as the principal cause of Spanish tyranny. References to the defeat of the Invincible Armada are abundant in pamphlets and later dramatic works as confirmation of both the suspicions of the English and the illegitimacy of Spanish aspirations. Hence the defeat of the Armada acquires a central role and value, since it is proclaimed from an English position supposedly sanctified by God – "Our foes like friends, will faine to come for our soules health,/ But God doth know their soule pretense: they shoot but at our wealth" (*An Exhortacion to all English Subiects*, p. 2). In keeping with its ambition, Spain is animalized through comparisons with the fox (*A Pageant*, sig. B1r),[79] the horse,[80] the tiger (Ashley, *A Comparison*, pp. 21, 23), the lion (Ibid., p. 23, *A Pageant*, sig. B1r) and the rooster (B1r),[81] each of them related symbolically to the image of cruelty and hunger for dominance.

Spain's presumed disingenuousness and hypocrisy (Orange, *The Apology*, sigs B2v, F4r y G3v) explain these authors' warnings against any sort of political alliance with such an adversary, whom they describe as cunning (Ashley, *A Comparison*, p. 21; *A Pageant*, sig. B2v; Chilmead, *Thomas Campanella*, pp. 122–123), traitorous (A *True and Perfect Description*, pp. 9–10) and disloyal (*A Fig for the Spaniard*, sig. B3v; *A Treatise Paraenetical*, p. 22; *A Pageant*, sigs B1r, B3r-v). Although an image of the enemy as powerful permeates the majority of the texts analysed – especially those produced immediately before or after the defeat of the Armada (Marten, *An Exhortation*, sig. B4r; Aske, *Elizabetha Triumphans*, sigs C4r, E3r) – this portrayal of superiority is sometimes questioned in order to bolster the confidence of the English people: "The fame of him [King Philip of Spain] is farre greater than his force, and there is not this daie anie prince in the whole world, whose estate standeth more tickle and readie to ruine than his, and there is no cause why we should feare him, but many why he should feare us" (Lewkenor, *The Estate of English Fugitives*, p. 87).[82] This explains why in some cases the Spaniard might see himself as inferior, and be jealous of his English adversary (Wilson, *The Three Lords*, p. 40). While the purpose of this type of commentary was to relieve the tension being felt in England, it was not too far removed from the truth. Mattingly has explained that the fleet of Philip II was not as excellent as the Spanish made it out to be, and many of the English maintained.[83] In fact, the author points out the lack of optimism on the part of the Spanish admiral, Medina Sidonia, and his chiefs with regard to the Armada's chances of success.[84]

The enemy's efforts to maintain an external appearance of strength and invincibility merely hides, therefore, an internal weakness: "[their] discourse is like the Cipres tree, which being great and high bringeth foorth no fruite" (Ashley, *A Comparison*, p. 25). External appearances here serve as a sign of arrogance and vanity:

> In a place of garrison, where nothing is to be done but bragging and domineering, there turn a loose, he will play his part, he esteems his skil, far to surpasse all others, but no sooner doth he heare the thundring rumor of *Los Enemigos*, or see them plant their Tents and standards with any advantage,

before his residence, he is in a moment wholly metamorphosed, his heart shrinkes like a peece of wet leather by the fire, all his Lyon like courage banished like smoake, for that from a Lyon he becomes a Hare, yet he will seem to cloake it. (*A Pageant*, sig. B1v)

Cowardice is another common failing of which the Spanish are accused, and one of the few that sets them apart from the stereotypical Catholic (Ashley, *A Comparison*, pp. 32; Wilson, *The Three Lords*, pp. 48–49). It stands in sharp contrast to the aforementioned arrogance and vanity, and thus magnifies the sarcastic impact of the portrayal. The metaphor of the peacock, the very symbol of arrogance and conceit in Renaissance emblem literature and iconology,[85] lends credence to these accusations: "Signior being in the streete, or any other publicke place his first gestures, are to bend the head, turne the eye, and Peacock-like to behold himselfe if nothing be amisse" (*A Pageant*, sig. A4v).[86] The wantonness and illicit sexual habits that were previously attributed to the Catholics are now extended to the Spanish as well (*A Perfect Description*, pp. 27–28, 33–34; *A Treatise Paraenetical*, p. 56; *A Pageant*, sig. B2v), characterized as irrational beasts governed by primal impulses (Ashley, *A Comparison*, p. 21, Orange, *The Apology*, sig. E2r). The frequent references to lust and gluttony[87] aid the portrayal of the Spanish as inconsiderate and disrespectful individuals, who treat those around them with contempt whatever social class they may be from (Wilson, *The Three Lords*, pp. 46, 48). Such impressions point to the corruption of the Spanish empire and, further, to the internal weakness that will ultimately destroy it.[88] References to the Spanish as moors, negroes, or mestizos (Ashley, *A Comparison*, pp. 19–20; *A True and Perfect Description*, p. 35; *A Treatise Paraenetical*, p. 24) confer upon them the same sense of alterity and inferiority that were attributed to these peoples in the geographical discourse of the day. Hence, the lack of purity of blood was emphasized, an idea intended to undeline their corruption and, thus, the perversion of everything they did.

The texts examined here are an example of the development of the Black Legend in England during the second part of the Elizabethan government. There was a significant interest in equating the figure of the Catholic with that of the Spaniard, and to unite them beneath the label of "other" as a strategy to calm English Protestants. This device was useful insofar as it allowed the definition – to a greater or lesser degree – of a concrete enemy against which the English needed to be united, in contrast to the invisibility of the Catholic adversary of earlier times. This stereotype was, therefore, a reliable rhetorical construct for the duration of the Anglo-Spanish conflict – a peace accord with Spain was signed in 1604 – and even beyond. It was only dramatic literature, which experienced a spectacular peak during this period, which would use this instrument for aims that transcended mere anti-Spanish or anti-Catholic criticism. The complexity of the political panorama allowed for many responses that escaped the iron grip of the censors and managed to adapt themselves to the political and religious needs of a restless society anticipating the conclusion of the Tudor era.

The imperial image of Elizabeth I

As has been mentioned, following the defeat of the Spanish Armada England witnessed a widespread development of the cult of Elizabeth I, in which anti-Catholic/anti-Spanish discourse fulfilled an important function. English Protestant propaganda justified the Queen's imperial authority as an intellectual heir to the legacy of Charles V of Spain, and called upon her to rise up against Rome and take the place of Philip II, who had betrayed his father's imperial policy by allying himself with the Pope. Criticism of Rome and of the Spanish, therefore, masked the English monarch's intention to take over Spain's position as Europe's great empire.

The struggle for European supremacy represents a central axis around which the majority of dramatic and pamphlet texts revolve. Hence they revisit the concept of the monarchy as it was represented in the Common Law, which defined the sovereign as *imperator in regno suo*, with the corresponding rights of self-government and of creating and interpreting the nation's laws.[89] The imperial nature of her rule legitimizes the English queen's power before Rome, as is shown by the implicit analogy drawn between her and Emperor Constantine:

> So after his [Christ's] triumphant resurrection, and glorious Ascension, the spitefull heathen Emperours of Rome, having the whole power and iurisdiction of all Asia, Africa, and Europe in their hands, intending utterly to abolish his name, and extinguishing his religion for ever, as before they had crucified the heade, fought still by all meanes possible with most grievous afflictions, painefull torments, and horrible kinds of death, to persecute his poore dispersed members, for the space of 300 yeares together: till the Lord of his fatherly affection, taking pitie of his poore dispersed flocke, raised up that godly and famous instrument, Constantine the great. After their long and lamentable troubles to snaffle Satan and set them in quiet rest and safetie.[90]

Since this doctrine associated the monarchs of England with the first Christian emperor, Wright's description of Constantine as a restorer of order within Christendom extends to Elizabeth herself,[91] stressing the queen's divine origins and the need for obedience on the part of her subjects (Wright, *The Hunting of Antichrist,* p. 23; Bunny, *A Comparison,* p. 58).

However, such absolutist ideas with regard to the state were not very popular in England and were only accepted in particular instances, such as in relation to the struggle with Rome.[92] This period in general can be seen as one such exception, but nevertheless some authors still appear to have been uncomfortable with this doctrine, insisting on the need for a mixed government in order to avoid such concentrations of power. William Chauncie, for example, speaks of the necessary collaboration between the Queen and Parliament, and devotes a chapter of his work to the different laws and statutes produced by various English sovereigns and their respective Parliaments in order to limit papal supremacy.[93]

The Protestant schism, when seen as the result of centuries of struggle between Rome and the English Crown, represents a clear link between the reforming Tudor dynasty and its predecessors. Elizabeth is extolled as the victorious heiress to her ancestors' imperial ambitions. Parliament's support legitimizes monarchical decisions, in contrast to the tyrannical attitude of the Holy See; but, at the same time, hidden within this praise is the implicit admonition to the queen that she not fall into the same errors as the pope. These associations are clear, and their validity is further reinforced in the light of the English people's supposedly unanimous and positive response to the Reformation. As for internal dissent, the pamphlet literature constructed a model of stability, with the hope of transferring this to the religious reality of the nation:

> The Noble Prince therfore, King Henry the eight, seeing and considering these detestable enormities, and wicked usurpation of the Pope of Rome, did utterly banish his counterfet authority out of this realme of England, with the appurtenances of it. Which having him selfe begun in part to doe, *he had it confirmed with the consent of the whole realme*, by statute and lawe made in the eight and twentie yeare of his reigne, *at a Parliament holden at Westminster, to the great comfort of all his faithfull subiectes, to the reviving of the dignitie of his imperiall crowne, and most of all to the true honour and glory of the Almightie*. After this noble King, there succeedde the godly worthie Prince his sonne, King Edward the Sixth ... And of late again (albeit) *some interruption grewe in the time of Queene Marie*, Our Most vertuous and gratious Sovereigne, Queene *Elizabeth, following the godly steps of her noble father and brother*, had it inacted in her first parleament, that the authoritie of the Bishoppe of Rome, and of all other foraine power, and potentates, spirituall and temporall, should utterly be driven away. (Chauncie, *The Rooting out of the Romishe Supremacie*, pp. 127–128) (My emphasis)

The criticism of papal power thus sustained an image of the strength of the monarchy that was indispensable in such a time of crisis. In the ten years after 1570, amid the uncertainty created by plots against the Queen and the bull of excommunication, there had already been several demonstrations of support for the monarch. Local celebrations of her accession to the Throne and her birthday began to take the place of the earlier Catholic festivals, and soon another date was added to the calendar of festivities: 19 November, the date of the Armada's defeat.[94] The spread of this type of celebration also coincided with a fundamental change in the meaning of other spectacles, both civic – the Lord Mayor's Show – and courtly – St. George's Day, feast of the patron saint of the country and the Order of the Garter – which began to form part of the cult of the Queen.[95] Elizabeth was converted into an object of adoration for pamphleteers and playwrights alike. Exhausted with the questions of succession, they, together with other participants in the process – among them, the queen herself – elaborated a complex and powerful iconography that sought to keep the country united.

Many elements of imperial theory coincided with the apocalyptic readings that were recurring themes in Protestant tradition, and which provided assurances that the Queen of England would be victorious over the dark forces of Rome. The clearest examples of this type of discourse appear in *The Estate of the English Fugitives* (1596). The imperial virtues of the queen – "She like a princely, zealous, and loving mother carefully tendereth, fostereth and preserveth her subiects by *wisedome and fortitude* from forreine violences, & by *clemencie, religion and iustice*, from inward mischiefes" (pp. 121–122) (my emphasis) – underline the importance of mercy as one of a monarch's principal political and moral virtues, as opposed to the cruelty and despotism of the pope or the Spaniards:

> This is in deede extreame tyrannie, and not that which her maiestie useth, who is alwaies readie to receive into grace and favour, those of whome she hath anie hope that they will become good subiectes, & had, as I have heard, offered (after that by lawe they were condemned) her princely mercie & favour to some of them, if they would have promised to become good subiects. (p. 73)

Elizabeth represents the new Astraea, who has brought a Golden Age to the English nation:

> Let us from this hell of miseries cast backe our eyes upon that heaven of blissefulness which wee doe enioy at home, under the fortunate and happy governement of our most excellent and incomparable soveraigne, there we shall finde an other estate of matters, all things flowing in plenty, peace, comfort, quietnesse, pleasure, and tranquilitie".[96] (p. 121)

Opposition to the pope and to Spain, therefore, is the product of an adaptation of the earlier imperial discourse to the current socioeconomic and religious necessities of the country.

Nonetheless, peace and plenty were scarce commodities in time of war, and Elizabeth was involved in several of them. Writers could only stress

England's defensive stance, and insist upon the necessity of these conflicts as a means of defending justice and the true faith: "Her warres are just, charitable, and defensive, for maintainance of which, besides the trust that she reposeth in God, she is allied in strait league, friendship & confederated with the most victorious and Christian King of France, with the Kings of Scotland and Denmarke . . . & with sundry princes and estates of the empire being her neighboures" (p. 121). Political and economic motives are concealed, and everything is reframed in religious terms in an effort to assert the righteousness of these conflicts. The emphasis placed on her subjects' love for the queen, and especially the naming in detail of the monarchs who supported her, nonetheless allows us to see a certain anxiety or fear regarding the possible outcome of such bellicose policies. One could only trust in the power of Providence, a consistent theme in Protestant literature.

The author of *An Answer to the Untruthes Published and Printed in Spain*[97] introduces a similar idea, although he includes a disturbing element within his discourse, that of feminine weakness: "They were invited, by the sight of a tender woman, being the first that put hirselfe to such a travell, for Christendome, the peace of hir Countrie, and for the quietnes of hir subjects" (p. 4). This pamphlet was published a year after the defeat of the Armada, with the country in full patriotic fervour; hence, it is likely that this reference does not conceal concerns over a female-led government as much as convey a certain ironic tone regarding those who doubted Elizabeth's abilities. Comparisons between her and a variety of heroes – Mars, Hercules and Hannibal (p. 4) – and emperors – Julius Caesar and Charlemagne (p. 4) – confer upon the Queen masculine and imperial virtues that she, as monarch, ought to possess. On the other hand, the parallels that are suggested between her and female biblical figures, characterized by their faithfulness to God and to their people – Deborah, Esther, Ruth and Judith (p. 4) – soften the sovereign's image as an exception and a transgressor. Lastly, such an enumeration of comparisons also emphasizes the diversity of her roles – military, imperial, vigilant and maternal – in a way that refers back to the symbolic needs that she must satisfy as queen and as a woman.

The process of construction of the royal image that had begun at the time of her accession to the throne was reoriented towards the evolution of the figure of Elizabeth as head of Protestant imperialism in Europe. The detailed description of her new enemies – Spain and the Jesuits – enriches this portrayal of the monarch, which reaches nearly mystical heights in the last years of her reign. This also produced an undesired effect, since the queen's age imbued this praise with an unavoidable feeling of twilight that could only presage the end of an era.

Anti-Catholic Discourse and the New Theatre

The opening of the first theatres in England in 1576 brought a radical change in the conditions in which performances were made and, above all, in the conception of dramatic action. The idea of commercial theatre emerged, and changed definitively not only the way works were produced and the role of the audience, but also, and especially, the theatre's function as a center of social interaction, where public opinion was created and modulated. The *Acte for the Punishment of Vagabondes* (1572), which severely punished all "players in interludes, and minstrels, not belonging to any Baron of this Realm, or towards any other honourable personage of greater degree",[98] was decisive, since the various acting troupes had to form around a nobleman, who could ensure them not only legal protection but also protection against censorship. Theatrical activity was also affected by a progressive distancing of the city from the court, which doubtless influenced the various genres, themes and messages that the dramatists depicted.

We have selected two works by John Lyly, one of the most significant court poets of the period, *Endymion, The Man in the Moon* (1591) and *Midas* (1592), which both make use of the classically-inspired allegorical play to reflect upon the theme of empire. The presence of the queen among the audience would have permitted a multiplication of the levels of dramatic interaction and would, in principle, confirm the defense of monarchical values that the two works supposedly present. With the exception of the allegorical play *The Three Lords and the Three Ladies of London* (1590), which was probably performed in an Inn of Court, the other four plays that will be analysed here were performed in public theatres, which allowed for a more obviously explicit use of anti-Catholic and anti-Spanish discourse. The variety of genres reveals the efforts made to adapt to the increasing demands of an enthusiastic and receptive audience: *The Spanish Tragedy* (1586–1587) is a revenge tragedy; *The Massacre at Paris* (1594?) and *A Larum for London* (1602) could be seen as examples of history plays (though they were based on quite recent events), and *The Life of Sir John Oldcastle* (1600) is an example of the tragedies dealing with reformist martyrs, plays that gained great popularity near the end of the reign of Elizabeth and at the beginning of that of James I. Anti-Catholic discourse found a home in each of these different genres, demonstrating not only its popularity but its value as a dramatic device.

Anti-Catholic discourse at court

Although anti-Catholic and anti-Spanish discourse is seen in the works by John Lyly (1554–1606) that we intend to examine, interest in the theme of empire at times relegates the criticism of Rome and Spain to a secondary level. The queen's attendance in the audience shifts the cult or worship of monarchical principles to the plane of immediate reality, and thus extends the space represented by the stage to the entire Elizabethan court. The result is that all relationships – including that between the playwright and his queen – are interpreted in theatrical terms. Hence, these works are not only an affirmation of the imperial nature of the English monarchy, they also touch upon the "dramatic" – and therefore artificial – links between the queen and her subjects.

The exact date of the composition of *Endymion* is not known.[99] Helen Hackett places it in 1585,[100] while Bevington points to the end of 1587 or beginning of 1588.[101] This last possibility certainly seems the most correct, since there are documents that attest that its première took place on 2 February 1588, during the celebration of Candlemas.[102] The fact that the play was performed on this day underscores two characteristics of the sovereign's public image that have already been mentioned: her virginity and her role as England's mother-protector. In effect, the play's leading character, Cynthia/Moon, is associated with Diana, Goddess of the Hunt and symbol of chastity, who, though in Ovid's legend she falls in love with a mortal and shows clear signs of weakness, in this work appears as a powerful woman, secure in her virginity, who at no time feels tempted to fall in love with any of her subjects.[103] The eulogy to the monarch, Cynthia and Elizabeth, nonetheless reveals a certain feeling of restlessness and frustration on the part of the character (and on that of the playwright) at her inaccessible and distant nature, which draws into question the popular image of the latter and, in particular, the inner workings of court politics.

Endymion is an allegory that is informed by different particular genres. Its division into scenes and acts, its constant mythological references and its Plautinian characters (such as Tophas, an example of *Miles Gloriosus*) reveal the influence of classical comedy. At the same time, the play's principal male character pursues a path toward self-knowledge and maturity, shunning worldly temptations along the way (those represented by Tellus) and following instead the virtuous way that Cynthia offers him, in a way that bears the mark of the moral allegories of medieval times. However, the plot is secular, taking on political tones when it implicitly alludes to the complex relationship between the artists of the court – Lyly – and the sovereign.

The dramatic action focuses on the loyalty of Endymion to Moon, who, because of a curse placed upon her by Tellus and the witch Dipsas, is sceptical of her vassal's honesty. Endymion is a victim of the jealousy of Tellus, who, with the help of the witch, makes him fall into a deep sleep from which he may only be awakened in his old age by a kiss from Cynthia. Once this treachery and those responsible for the curse are discovered, the queen dispenses justice. The play ends with the queen pardoning Dipsas and Tellus, who confess their deeds and declare their repentance, and with order being restored at court.

The adoration of Cynthia, representing Elizabeth I, is the main theme of the work, and neoplatonic language is the chief instrument that transforms her into a synonym of perfection:[104] "[EUMENIDES:] She, whose figure of all is the perfectest and never to be measured, always one yet never the same, still inconstant yet never wavering"; "[GERON:] And is not Cynthia of all circles the most absolute? . . . Then who can it be but Cynthia, whose virtues, being all divine, must needs bring things to pass that be miraculous?" (III, iv, 165–169, 179, 190–191). The use of juxtaposed negations to describe the character highlights her divine nature; this was a discursive strategy that was characteristic of mystical writers, when they attempted to explain the process of the soul's coming nearer to God.

The association of Cynthia with the truth – "They are thrice fortunate that live in your palace where truth is not in colours but life, virtues not in imagination but execution" (IV, iii, 52–54) – and the continual references to God's endorsement of her government – "Cynthia, being placed for light on earth, is also protected by the powers of heaven" (V, iv, 9–11) – also point to Elizabeth's commitment to the values of the Reformation and her opposition to Catholicism: "I have always studied to have rather living virtues than painted gods, the body of truth than the tomb" (IV, iii, 55–56). Her role as victim within Endymion's dream emphasizes another of the recurrent themes of Elizabethan anti-Catholicism:

> [ENDYMION:] I beheld many wolves barking at thee, Cynthia, who, having ground their teeth to bite, did with striving bleed themselves to death. There might I see Ingratitude with an hundred eyes, gazing for benefits, and with a thousand teeth gnawing on the bowels wherein she was bred. Treachery stood all clothed in white, with a smiling countenance but both her hands bathed in blood. Envy, with a pale and meagre face, whose body was so lean that one might tell all her bones, and whose garment was so tattered that it was easy to number every thread, stood shooting at stars, whose darts fell down again on her own face. There might I behold drones or beetles, I know not how to term them, creeping under the wings of a princely eagle, who, being carried into her nest, sought there to suck that vein that would have killed the eagle. I mused that things so base should attempt a fact so barbarous or durst imagine a thing so bloody. (V, i, 132–148)

These images revolve around symbolic and iconographic themes and images that were widely known at the time. The characters Ingratitude, Treachery and Envy refer to the iconological constructs of the same names.[105] The vision of bees and scarabs reproduces Alciatus's emblem CLXIX, *A minimis quoque timendum* (One ought to fear even the tiniest creatures), in which the admonition is to beware your enemies, though they be of little strength or courage. Cynthia emerges victorious from all the attacks against her, calling to mind Elizabeth's triumph over the plots against her by the followers of the pope throughout her reign. The many obstacles and dangers that must be overcome stress her characterization as a Protestant martyr in the reformist literature of the period, an image further enhanced by the opposition of Tellus and Dipsas.

In many ways, Tellus embodies the characteristics of the Catholic stereotype: She is cruel (I, ii, 57–60; II, iii, 41–45), irrational (I, ii, 60–67), envious (V, iv, 87–91), tyrannical (II, iii, 41–45) and insincere (IV, i, 29–31; IV, iii, 116–118; V, iv, 55–58). Despite all this, at times in the play her character presents serious ambiguities. On the one hand, her virginity (I, ii, 9–10) and constancy in her love for Endymion (III, iii, 30–32) are revealed, which draws parallels with the character of Cynthia, especially in her role as victim:

> [TELLUS:] Corsites, Cynthia may restrain the liberty of my body; of my thoughts she cannot. And therefore do I esteem myself most free, though I am in greatest bondage. [CORSITES:] Can you then feed on fancy, and subdue the malice of envy by the sweetness of imagination? [TELLUS:] Corsites, there is no sweeter music to the miserable than despair; and therefore the more bitterness I feel, the more sweetness I find. For so vain were liberty, and so unwelcome the following of higher fortune, that I choose rather to pine in this castle than to be a prince in any other court.[106] (III, iii, 6–16)

Tellus is a victim of her own desire and of her beloved's deceit – "[TELLUS:] When he saw the depth of my affections, he swore that mine in respect of his were as fumes to Etna, valleys to Alps, ants to eagles, and nothing could be compared to my beauty but his love and eternity" (V, iv, 96–100).[107] Her only culpable trait is her weakness (compared to Cynthia's spiritual strength), a fault that could often be seen as a result of Endymion's hypocritical dealings with her. Tellus ultimately has compassion for Endymion and repents her actions, the result of jealousy and desperation (IV, i, 9–20). Therefore, hers is not such a negative character as one might expect given her association with Catholicism; instead, the audience might experience a certain sympathy for this character, and even reject her manipulation by Endymion. Hence there is still room for doubt over Lyly's intentions.[108]

The punishment of Dipsas is, in contrast, much clearer, since her association with acts of witchcraft and superstition (I, iv, 28–31) link her directly with the Catholic stereotype. The playwright draws a clear parallel between this character and Rome when he refers to the threat the latter has posed to the Protestant government since the reign of Henry VIII:

> [CYNTHIA:] Dipsas, thy years are not so many as thy vices, yet more in number than commonly nature doth afford or justice should permit. Hast thou *almost these fifty years* practised that detested wickedness of witch-

craft? ... *Thou hast threatened to turn my course awry and alter by thy damnable art the government that I now possess by the eternal gods.* (V. iv. 1–8) (My emphasis)

Dipsas and, by extension, Catholicism are responsible for the social instability of the kingdom and for acts of sedition against the monarchy. Her deceitful and manipulative character explains why Tophas, a naive and vain soldier who is the butt of all sorts of jokes and humiliations, falls in love with her, reinforcing one of the main reformist arguments on the ignorance of Catholics.

At the same time, the witch's behaviour justifies the wish felt by many of the subjects of the kingdom to do away with her and thus neutralize the danger she represents: "That heaviness argueth a malice unremovable in the enchantress, and that no power can end it till she die that did it or the heavens show some means more than miraculous" (IV, iii, 154–157). These words reflect a widely-held opinion within Protestant circles, which supported the idea of making punishments against Catholics more severe as the only means of eliminating the threat they posed. Perhaps, as Bevington notes, this could also be related to Elizabeth's initial refusal to execute Mary Queen of Scots, a position that had exasperated many English Protestants:[109] "[ZONTES:] For how can it be that she that is unwilling to punish her deadliest foes with disgrace will revenge injuries of her train with death?" (V, iv, 10–13). One senses here a degree of disagreement with and opposition to the policy of the monarchy, at least as regards religious dissidents.

Cynthia's opposition to such persons, along with the praise heaped upon her imperial and Christian virtues, does not prevent an at times contradictory portrayal of the figure of the queen. The first such paradox is seen in the idea of mobility and instability that is symbolized by the moon (I, i, 35–45; III, iv, 184–185). This is inconsistent, which draws into question the character's stability and trustworthiness, above all with regard to decision making; in addition, her inaccessible nature (I, i, 23–24; II, iii, 18–20) points to the queen's arguably capricious nature and the many obstacles that the courtiers have to face in order to satisfy her. The worship of the queen reaches the point of seeming ridiculous or absurd, as Eumenides points out when he speaks of Endymion's declaration of love for Moon: "Without doubt Endymion is bewitched; otherwise in a man of such rare virtues there could not harbour a mind of such extreme madness. I will follow him, lest in this Fancy of the moon he deprive himself of the sight of the sun" (I, ii, 88–92). The neoplatonic discourse directed at the queen is interpreted as false and artificial, and is articulated through the use of terms often associated with the margins of normal behaviour, such as magic, madness and ignorance. Thus the author questions the panegyrics around the figure of Elizabeth I, which in the 1590s reached levels that made many of her subjects uncomfortable.[110]

Comments on her eternal beauty and youth (I, ii, 59–66; II, ii, 89–98), therefore, hide a profound disquiet about the queen's age, the passage of time, and the inevitable problem of succession. The fact that Endymion admits having deceived Tellus (V, iv, 106) also underscores his insincerity and thus questions his loyalty to Cynthia.

The play concludes with the repentance (perhaps too spontaneous and mechanical) of the negative characters, and a royal pardon. Nevertheless, the many paradoxes in the presentation and the actions of some of the characters seem to question these attitudes. At the time the text was written (1585–1588), conspiracies, foreign threats, the queen's benevolent but unpredictable attitude, and the loss of all hope of her producing an heir, could only have provoked serious concern among her subjects. John Lyly, in a delicate position in the Queen's court after years of unsuccessfully competing for an official post, seems to express the very feeling of doubt and frustration that must have been present in many segments of English society.

Midas, published in 1592, at first glance lacks the critical tone of the previous play. The playwright's change of attitude is probably due to the predominating spirit of England when he wrote the play; that is, not long after the victory over the Spanish Armada. This would explain the triumphant tone of the play's first performances, first in St. Paul's in November of 1589 and later in January of 1590 in the court.[111] The play is, in principle, a celebration of England's victory over the Spanish Empire, and ratifies the imperial rights of Elizabeth against the supposed weakness of Spain.

Midas follows the same allegorical format as *Endymion*, although in this case the presence of classical elements is more accentuated, since the play is a re-elaboration of two episodes of Ovid's *Metamorfosis* that were well known to a Renaissance audience.[112] Arthur Golding's contemporary translation of the first of these makes clear the personality of the main character: "In Midas of a covetous wretch the image we may see/ Whose riches iustly to himself a hellish torment bee / And of a foole whom neyther proof nor warning can ament,/ Untill he feele the shame and smart that folly doth him send".[113] Midas is a cruel, ambitious and tyrannical monarch, traits that are made manifest by the punishments he is forced to endure: the curse of the golden touch emphasizes his greed, while the donkey ears underscore his stupidity through reference to Alciatus's emblem VII, *Non tibi sed religioni* (Not for you, but for religion) and Ripa's emblem *Ignorance of all things*.[114] These were all associated with the Catholic-Spanish stereotype and, in turn, formed part of the general iconography of the tyrant-king that was current in the sixteenth century.

His tyranny also explains his love of boundless pleasures, as we see in the description by Martius, one of the King's counselors, of Midas's court:

> Since this unsatiable thirst of gold and untemperate humour of lust crept into

the king's court, soldiers have begged alms of artificers, and with their helmet on their head been glad to follow a lover with a glove in his hat; which so much abateth the courage of true captains, that they must account it more honorable in the court to be a coward so rich and amorous, than in a camp to be valiant if poor and maimed. He is more favored that pricks his finger with his mistress' needle, than he that breaks his lance on his enemy's face; and he that hath his mouth full of fair words, than he that hath his body full of deep scars. (p. 292)

The effeminate court of King Midas is a focal point of corruption, where moral values are inverted in favour of material pleasures and social and political irresponsibility.

Following the victory over the Armada, in England the ambitious figure of Midas could have alluded to no one else but Philip II, with whom numerous parallels are established in the play: the alleged tyranny of his foreign policies, through allusions to his fleet – "Have I not made the sea to groan under the number of my ships?" (p. 123) – his many conquests, by reference to the exploitation of American lands – "I accounted pirates, and myself that suppressed whole fleets, a conqueror; as though robberies of Midas might mask under the names of triumphs, and the traffic of other nations be called treachery . . . I have written my laws in blood and made my gods of gold" (pp. 212–213) – his network of spies in foreign courts – "Have not I enticed the subjects of my neighbour princes to destroy their natural Kings" (p. 213) – and the supposed usurpation of other kingdoms, a clear reference to Portugal – "To what Kingdom have not I pretended claim, as though I had been by the gods created heir apparent to the world, making every triffle a title?" (p. 213). The degeneration of Midas is, ultimately, the cause of the confusion and chaos that exists in his kingdom: "Our King hath no ears to hear, or no care to consider, both in what state we stand being his subjects, and what danger he is in being our King. Duty is not regarded, courage contemned, altogether careless of us and his own safety" (p. 228).

The presence of commercial and trading motives displaces considerations of religion and doctrine to a position of secondary importance, and they do not conceal the evident economic thrust of the plot. The new Elizabethan empire, represented by the figure of Lesbos and her king, should replace Spain as the principal European power. Nevertheless, the struggle for commercial monopolies in Europe and America was not exclusive to Spain; Elizabeth had for years backed all manner of activities, mostly illegal, with the goal of capturing Spanish lands and ships. One appears to see, therefore, the emergence of a discourse that disguised economic interests beneath the sheep's clothing of patriotism.[115]

The apparently conciliatory ending of the play is thus deceptive. Lesbos –England – adopts, yet again, a defensive position in the conflict and so avoids its political responsibilities.[116] Lyly portrays, and implicitly criticizes, the typical behaviour of Elizabeth, in that she never accepted any active involvement in the European conflicts of the 1580s. In the matter of Mary Queen of Scots, of the Low Countries, of France or Spain, the queen had held herself to be obliged to act not of her own volition but, instead, by circumstance. Lyly ponders this and seems to question the position and image of the queen by giving a clearly active role to Midas who, in spite of his tyranny – a consequence of the influence of his counsellors'[117] – ultimately arouses the audience's sympathy. Thus, the feeling of triumphalism one seems to feel on a first reading is obscured. It would only be a couple of years until this paradoxical image of the queen as imperial goddess and victim would come to be discussed more explicitly.

Anti-Catholic discourse in public theatres

The stages of public theatres constituted one of the principal fora where anti-Catholic discourse was elaborated during the final phase of the reign of Elizabeth. The reason for this resides perhaps in the social and ideological diversity among the spectators who attended them. This diversity defined these public spaces as centers for the shaping of attitudes, perceptions, and models of social intercourse. The difficulty of controlling such arenas also ensured the maximum freedom of reaction for the spectators, who not only saw themselves as represented onstage, but could echo these principles and messages beyond the limits of the theatre. Playwrights did not fail to take advantage of such an opportunity to fan the flames of contempt that, in some cases, were already burning and, in others, to question the discourses that had provoked such hatred.

Historical drama was the principal genre employed on the public stage to foster anti-Catholic sentiment, since it appealed to the spectators' interest in history and, especially, to their restlessness and concerns over contemporary politics.[118] In general, the events referred to occurred in the very recent past, which made the Catholic-Spanish threat seem all the more real. The works selected here are similarly situated: *The Massacre at Paris* (1594?) by Christopher Marlowe and the anonymous *A Larum for London* (1602) are probably the two most representative anti-Catholic works in this genre. *The Life of Sir John Oldcastle* (1600) distinguishes itself from these two since it depicts a much more distant past, and was one of the first examples of the tragedies around Protestant martyrs. Finally, *The Spanish Tragedy* (1592) forms part of the genre of revenge tragedies, although it also utilized historical material that doubtless influenced its enormous popularity.

According to J. B. Steane, the date of composition of *The Massacre at Paris* had to be after the death of Henry III of France in August of 1589 – and perhaps after the death of Pope Sixtus V on 27 August 1590 – and before its first documented performance, in January of 1593.[119] The play enjoyed one of the greatest public successes of the last decades of Elizabeth's reign, with a total of eleven performances in the span of only two years (1593 and 1594).[120] The preeminent status of The Queen's Men, the only performing company with sponsorship prior to 1574, had been assumed by The Admiral's Men, and beginning in 1591 or 1592 the latter troupe led in the number of dramatic productions in public theatres and, at times, in the court.[121] This was the company responsible for the repeated performances of Marlowe's play at the Rose Theatre, which was highly popular at the time.

One of the main reasons for the unanimously positive reception of this play was probably the degree to which it caused spectators to identify with it. It portrayed one of the most tragic episodes in the history of European Protestantism: the massacre of Huguenots in France in 1572 by order of Catherine de' Medici and the Guise family, an event that came to be known as the Night of St. Bartholomew. Marlowe thus refers to events which, although they were very recent, already formed part of the collective memory of Protestant England due to their having been mentioned so often in the pamphlet literature of the period.[122]

The play is divided into two distinct parts. The first begins with the wedding of Princess Margaret to Navarre, one of the principal defenders of the Huguenot movement in France. From the very beginning of the play, religious conflict and problems of succession are seen as of paramount importance, which explains the conspiracies that are hatched within the faction led by members of the Guise family (Ramus, Condé), to eliminate the Protestants who could pose an obstacle to their political ambitions (vi, 20–30; xi, 1–57). These plots end in the killing of the Huguenots on the Night of St. Bartholomew (vi-ix). The second part of the play focuses on the question of succession, and on the desires of the Guise family and Queen Catherine to ensure that their candidate should gain the French throne. This unleashes a new civil war between King Henry III and his chief rival – Guise – that ends with the deaths of both of them, and the victory of the legitimate successor, Henry IV, the erstwhile Navarre.

Although, at the beginning, the play makes an appeal to English Protestantism's collective memory as a warning against the persistent Catholic menace, the playwright also uses this motif to frame a deeper debate on political tyranny that transcends matters of religion. At first glance, the play seems to focus on the dualism between Navarre and Guise. However, the way they are portrayed does not avoid sowing the seeds of doubt within the minds of the audience.

Guise fits the mold of the Machiavellian character that began to gain popularity in the theatres of England during this time.[123] As Douglas Cole points out, at the end of the sixteenth century, Machiavelli's writings were interpreted as recommending treachery, cunning, hypocrisy, or any immoral act as a means of gaining and holding power.[124] The figure of

Guise, in effect, is characterized by obsessive ambition, extreme cruelty and lack of scruples in carrying out his secret plans:

> [GUISE:] Now, Guise, begins those deep-engend'red thoughts/ To burst abroad those never-dying flames/ Which cannot be extinguis'd but by blood . . . / For this I wake, when others think I sleep . . . / For this, my quenchless thirst whereon I build,/ Hath often pleaded kindred to the king;/ For this, this head, this heart, this hand and sword,/ Contrives, imagines, and fully executes,/ Matters of import aimed at by many, / Yet understood by none./ For this, hath heaven engend'red me of earth. (ii, 34–35, 48, 50–56)

His seditious nature is perhaps this character's most disquieting trait; his ultimate aim is to occupy the Throne of France, but to achieve this he must ally himself with Rome and Spain:

> For this, this earth sustains my body's weight,/ And with this weight I'll counterpoise a crown,/ Or with sedition weary all the world./ For this, from Spain the stately Catholic/ Sends Indian gold to coin me French écus;/ For this have I largess from the Pope,/ A pension and dispensation too. (ii, 57–63)

Connecting Spain and the pope with this Machiavellian personage broadens his characterization. Guise becomes a point of inflection of the various forms of the "other" that began to converge in England during this period. In fact, the Italian stereotype as a compendium of the vices soon melded together with the pre-existing prejudices against the Spanish, to such a degree that the two were considered by the Elizabethan public to be one and the same.[125] No doubt the main link between the two national stereotypes was their supposed connection to Rome, which enabled Italy, Spain, and the Holy See to form part of a single, antagonistic bloc against which the forces of good were set, represented here by Navarre.

To these accusations of ambition and cruelty is added a third element, which completes the process of denigration of Guise and his followers: atheism. "[GUISE:] My policy hath fram'd religion" (ii, 65).[126] Guise's words echo one of the primary reasons for attacks on the ideas of Machiavelli, who states in his *Discourse on the First Ten Books of Titus Livy* that

> "[I]t can be seen, by closely analyzing Roman history, how useful religion was in commanding armies, in comforting the working class, in keeping good men in their place and in shaming the bad . . . And truly, there never has been a legislator who made excellent laws for the people without referring to God, for the laws would not be accepted otherwise; because there are many good things that, though known to a prudent man, are not convincing to everyone else. This is why wise men, wishing to avoid this difficulty, refer to God.[127]

Machiavelli's thoughts on the practical uses of religion were heavily criticized in Catholic sectors – among them, in Spain – and by Protestants,[128] who saw their theocratic conception of royal power imperiled. Machiavellian scepticism could lead to a deep mistrust of the monarch's divine authority and, with that, a serious destabilization of the political order. The progressive advance of atheist currents in England, especially during the final two decades of Elizabeth's reign, highlighted the crisis of authority from which the regime seemed to be suffering. Although critics such as David Riggs blame the Protestant educational system for the proliferation of these ideas,[129] Machiavelli represented the perfect scapegoat for the existence of these new trends. Guise's statement in *The Massacre at Paris* echoes them, which in turn characterizes him as a subversive character who is a danger to the monarchy.[130]

His dissimulating and hypocritical nature accentuates the menace posed by his actions, and accounts for the manipulation he undertakes of King Charles and Queen Catherine in order to carry out his plans. The dynamism of this character – compared to Charles's naiveté, Henry III's irresponsibility and Navarre's commitment – makes him the center of the dramatic action. Guise keeps the others on a secondary plane while he remains onstage, which may have complicated his reception by an audience who perhaps saw the attraction in such a restless, energetic character. Marlowe avoids homogeneous depictions of his characters, exploring their other possible dramatic aspects. For example, Guise is the butt of a joke when it is discovered that he has been betrayed by his wife, in love with Epernoun, a Huguenot counsellor to Henry III:

> [HENRY:] So kindly, cousin of Guise, you and your wife/ Do both salute our lovely minions (*He makes horns at the Guise*)/ [GUISE:] How now, my lord, faith, this is more than need./ And I thus to be jested at and scorn'd? . . . / And here by all the saints in heaven I swear, / That villain for whom I bear this deep disgrace,/ Even for your words that have incens'd me so,/ Shall buy that strumpet's favour with his blood,/ Whether he have dishonoured me or no./ *Par la mort Dieu, il mourra!*/ [HENRY:] Believe me, this jest bites sore./ [EPERNOUN:] My lord, 'twere good to make them friends,/ For his oaths are seldom spent in vain. (xvii, 10–11, 15–16, 23–31)

Although, ironically, Guise's promise is carried out, its comical presentation softens, in principle, the danger the character represents, in a way that also reflects the already common dramatic practice of transforming menacing characters through the use of humour.[131]

Nor does his attitude just prior to his murder lack in buffoonery: although one of the servants warns him that the killers are lying in wait for him, the Duke makes one last display of vanity and feigned bravery that results in his death, and undoubtedly gives a comical nuance to a moment that might have been a climactic point in the play. The playwright's approach thus borders on sarcasm, through the burlesque representation of one of the figures most despised and feared by European Protestants. Often accused of atheism himself, Marlowe seems to eschew the extremist tendencies of one faction or the other by questioning on stage the demoniacal descriptions which were the domain of the most radical reformist literature.

Queen Catherine is another character open to debate. Her most distinctive trait is an irrationality that discredits all of her political decisions. Her lack of control and excessive passion for Guise recalls the misogynous literature that attacked the government of the Queen-Regent in France. The author of *The Contre-Guyse* (1589) was happy, for example, that France is "freed from the womens gouerment . . . through the benefite of the Salike Lawe, a lawe that is the onely oracle of France . . . a lawe that preserveth us from the dominion of strangers, and that cutteth off all forraine fashions and kindes of life" (sig. D2v). The pamphleteer Michael Hurault softened his attack, though he pointed to the female-led governments of France and England as the principal cause of the growing power of Philip II:

> Philip at this day King of Spaine hath beene favoured with such fortune as had never interruption. But that is more to bee atributed, to that which tell out about him, then to himselfe. France in this time hath beene ruled by a woman, and by children, or so toyled by civill warres, that they alwaies found woorke enough within themselves. England likewise ruled by a woman, who following the nature of her kinde, hath wisely contented her selfe with mainteining her subiectes in peace, and defendeing her state from her neighbours attempts, not enterprising anything against them . . . . so that we must not say, that he had good lucke everie where, but that hee founde no where any bodie that might breede him any evill lucke. (p. 39)

The association between the two queens confuses the perception that the audience might have of Catherine, who possesses the very characteristics described in the misogynistic literature of the Renaissance. She is weak and passionate, fickle and easily manipulated by Guise, as he himself states: "The Mother Queen works wonders for my sake,/ And in my love entombs the hope of France,/ Rifling the bowels of her treasury,/ To supply my wants and necessity" (ii, 76–79). Her dependence on the Duke leads her to sacrifice her kingdom's well-being and to put her lover's life before that of her own children: "I cannot speak for grief. When thou wast born,/ I would that I had murdered thee, my son./ My son? Thou art a changeling, not my son" (xxiii, 144–146). Her anti-natural character condemns her and explains her extreme cruelty and ambition, as a result of her lack of self-control:[132]

> Ay, but my lord, let me alone for that,/ For Catherine must have her will in

Gloriana and the Victory of Protestantism

France/ As I do live, so surely shall he die,/ And Henry then shall wear the diadem;/ And if he grudge or cross his mother's will,/ I'll disinherit him and all the rest;/ For I'll rule France, but they shall wear the crown,/ And if they storm, I then may pull them down. (xi, 38–45)

In Guise, Catherine finds a mirror in which to observe herself; she projects herself onto the person of the Duke to such a point that his death foreshadows her own:

Sweet Guise, would he [Henry] had died, so thou wert here!/ To whom shall I bewray my secrets now,/ Or who will help to build religion?/ The Protestants will glory and insult;/ Wicked Navarre will get the crown of France;/ The Popedom cannot stand; all goes to wrack,/ And all for thee, my Guise; what may I do?/ But sorrow seize upon my toiling soul,/ For since the Guise is dead, I will not live. (xxii, 154–162)

A government led by a woman is thus portrayed as a perversion that could only bring about the nation's decline. Catherine's description as a foreigner, a Catholic, and a woman underscores her marginal position and recalls the Protestant portrayal of Mary I and Mary Queen of Scots. Even so, this does not prevent the criticism from reaching as far as the current Queen Elizabeth I. The political implications of the character would not go unnoticed by the audiences of public theatres, many of them weary of and disillusioned with the ageing Queen, who avoided the controversial question of succession and whose public image was further and further away from reality.

Also, the association of women with political tyranny was a common motif of the period. Rebecca Bushnell explains how the two most popular female stereotypes during the Renaissance – the whore, the deceitful and sexually insatiable woman, and the shrew, the obstinate, capricious and domineering woman – often came together, especially when feminine sexuality was linked to the power that it exercises over men.[133] The character of Catherine in *The Massacre at Paris* refers, in a broad sense, to these cultural concepts. As whore, the queen submits to Guise's desires; as shrew, she manipulates her two children, both of them kings, who sacrifice the good of the nation because of their mother's counsel (iv, 23–27).

The powerful influence of the Queen-Regent feminizes both these rulers, so that they forget their commitment to their people.[134] This is the case, especially, with Henry III, who is the clearest example of the tyrannical monarch, since he unites the three defining and fundamental traits of this character type in the sixteenth century: a bestial nature, theatricality and femininity.[135] The reduction of the king to an animal level occurs as a result of his lack of self-restraint and his love of pleasure; his immoderation brings him close to the irrationality traditionally associated with women, which discredits his power and accentuates his political irresponsibility: "Our solemn rites of coronation done,/ What now remains but for a while to feast,/ And spends some days in barriers, tourney, tilt,/ And like disports, such as do fit the court?" (xiv, 39–42).[136] Finally, allusions to the king's preference for the young boys of the court (xiv, 46; xvii, 1–3; xix, 13) emphasize his unnatural femininity and, therefore, his hypocrisy, particularly when he orders Guise's murder (xxi, 62–79). His amoral ways and submission to the desires of his favorite darken the portrayal of the character and give credence to the description of him given by the Duke who, unlike Henry III, finds favour with the people. Guise controls his public image and so wins the support of the people of Paris by following the dictates of Machiavelli:

> So, it is not necessary that a prince truly possess all these qualities, but it is quite necessary that he appears to. Furthermore, I daresay that to possess them and to observe them is always detrimental, while pretending to possess them is useful; it is like seeming to be pious, loyal, humane, honest, religious, and to truly be thus; but, at the same time, to have the willingness of spirit to be able to and to know how to change to the opposite quality if it be necessary.[137]

One therefore sees the possibility of a positive response to Guise's actions in the face of the king's incompetence. On the other hand, an indirect reference to the skillfulness of Elizabeth I herself in the management of her own image could have been suggested; such an implicit association with Machiavellian theory would, though, have been disquieting to an attentive public.

In addition, Henry III acts outside legal boundaries. The death of Guise, which should have been the result of his public condemnation for sedition, is a direct consequence of the monarch's desire for vengeance. Henry disobeys the civil and religious laws that punish such crimes, and thus brings into question the legal apparatus and his authority as king. His submission to the desires of Epernoun underlines his weakness, although this could be a strategy to avoid a too-direct attack on the monarchy, whose mistaken decisions were blamed on its counsellors.[138] The criticisms that many French authors, both Protestant and Catholic, leveled against King Henry III of France between 1588 and 1589[139] were no doubt influential in the production of this puzzling character, who encourages distrust in the monarchy as an institution. The question of succession and the possibility of a change in religion under the rule of a new sovereign were constant sources of concern for the French writers, who thus indirectly alluded to one of the biggest fears in Elizabethan England. Although, in contrast to Henry III, Elizabeth had forbidden any debate on her succession, this did little more than add to her subjects' discomfort. In this way, then, Marlowe utilizes the figure of the French king to revive the discussion.

The playwright makes use of one of the principal historical incidents for European anti-Catholicism to question on stage the most radical reformist perspectives and debate certain aspects of monarchical politics. The frequent association made between Catholicism and political tyranny in reformist discourse was not seamless, leaving gaps that no amount of pious characterization of the Protestant hero – in this case, Navarre – could hide.[140]

The Spanish Tragedy (1592) by Thomas Kyd was one of the most popular plays in the closing years of the century, with almost thirty performances between 1592 and 1597 by various companies of actors – Lord Strange's Men, The Admiral's Men, Pembroke's Men and, perhaps, The Chamberlain's Men – who staged the play in several public theatres: The Rose, The Fortune, probably The Cross Keys Inn, Newington Butts, The Curtain, and the first Globe.[141] There is a record of its receiving a broadly positive reception by audiences in London, surpassing that of the also-successful *The Massacre at Paris*. It is quite likely that the same factors that led to the favourable reception of Marlow's play were repeated with Kyd's work. In effect, there are two fundamental elements that would have had an influence on its reception: first, the new dramatic genre that it represented, the revenge tragedy, full of political intrigues and mysteries, violence and sensationalism, seemed to hold a great appeal for this type of audience; secondly, recent historical events were once again employed to attract the spectators' attention.[142]

In addition to utilizing the existing prejudices toward Spain and Catholicism in England, Thomas Kyd exploits the popularity of Machiavelli during the second part of Elizabeth's reign as a means of analysing the grave consequences of the process of Italianization that, in the eyes of many of Kyd's contemporaries, England appeared to be undergoing.[143] In reality, the general fear of foreign influences only revealed England's internal weaknesses. The work by William Rankins, *The English Ape* (1588) is a clear exponent of these deep feelings of xenophobia:

> Howe hatefull will it hereafter seeme to ourselves . . . our condition then to be so altered, our manners transformed, our estates so estranged, and our dueties so disguised with the spotted imitation of other Nations . . . Such is the contemptuous condition of these Imitators: that there is not any vice particularly noted in any Countrey, but the Englishman will be therein as exquisite, as if he had Nature at commaunde for every enormity. If it be in *Creete*, he can lye, in *Italy*, flatter, if in *Fraunce*, boast, if in *Scotland* cloake the treachery of pretended treason . . . He lovingly bringeth his merchandize into his native Country, and there storeth with instructions the false affectors of this tedious trash.[144]

Italy and Spain were the main focus of the attack. In the 1560s, Robert

Ascham had already counselled against the young people of England traveling to Italy, since many of them, "who partyng out of England fervent in the love of Christes doctrine, and well furnished with the feare of God, returned out of Italie worse transformed, than ever was any in Circes Court" (*The Scholemaster*, p. 24). The figure of the "Italianate Englishman" was shown as a serious foreign threat, which rather highlighted the deep-seated immaturity of English national identity.

Kyd dramatizes these concerns in *The Spanish Tragedy* by placing the dramatic action in the Spanish court, a scenario for the actions of several Machiavellian characters. In some cases, however, their characterization is not uniform, and once again questions the cultural base that underlies it. Nevertheless, only by placing the action in a far-away country, disparaged by many of the English, could such politically incorrect questions as tyranny and sedition be examined onstage.

In principle, the Spanish court as shown by Kyd displays an exemplary character, contrary to the many prejudices of the day. The play begins with an air of optimism following military victories that, curiously, are interpreted as being the result of Providence (I, ii, 10–11). The general describes one such battle in chivalrous terms, particularly because of the courtesy with which the Spaniards treat their enemy, who is never debased (I, ii, 22–84). The Spanish monarch is fair and caring toward the people, rewards his soldiers (I, ii, 129–130) and behaves equitably toward Horatio and Lorenzo, who ask for their respective rewards for having defeated Balthazar and taken him prisoner. In spite of Portugal's having broken its treaty with Spain by declaring war on her (I, iii, 46–47), the Spanish king rejects any idea of vengefulness (I, iii, 48), and instead treats his prisoner with respect, assuring his Portuguese rival of his friendship. The character of the king thus unites the main characteristics of the biblical monarchs that sustained the royal models of the sixteenth century: "But that I know your grace for just and wise" (I, ii, 166).

His behaviour stands in contrast to that of the Viceroy of Portugal who, in the light of suspicions surrounding the death of his son, loses his mind and acts unfairly toward Alexandro[145] (I, iii). His words reveal him to be a tyrannical ruler who acts for his own gain:

My late ambition hath disdained my faith,/ My breach of faith occasioned bloody wars,/ Those bloodie wars have spent my treasure,/ And with my treasure my people's blood,/ And with their blood, my joy and best beloved,/ My best beloved, my sweet and only son./ O wherefore went I not to war myself?/ The cause was mine, I might have died for both. (I, iii, 33–40)

The Viceroy becomes an irrational and violent being, incapable of controlling his actions, and therefore easily manipulated – in this case, by Viluppo. Also, his speech, brusque and forceful, discredits his royal authority by not allowing the accused to defend himself:

> Ay, ay, my nightly dreams have told me this./ Thou false, unkind, unthankful, traitorous beast,/ Wherein had Balthazar offended thee,/ That thou shouldst thus betray him to our foes?/ Was't Spanish gold that bleared so thine eyes/ That thou couldst see no part of our deserts?/ Perchance because thou art Terceira's lord, / Thou hadst some hope to wear this diadem,/ If first my son and then myself were slain: / But thy ambitious thought shall break thy neck./ Ay, this was it that made thee spill his blood, (*Take the crown and put it on again*)/ But I'll now wear it till thy blood be spilt. (I, iii, 76–87)

The character thus places his pain as a father before his duty as ruler, since he chooses revenge over any peaceful resolution. Only the good news that later arrives from Spain (III, i, 60–108) can keep him from violence. From the outset, therefore, vengeance is set in contraposition to reason and as a parallel to tyrannical attitudes.

The clearest example of vengeance/irrationality/tyranny is Hieronimo. Although the pathos that surrounds the presentation of the character may at times arouse the audience's sympathy, the attitude that he adopts after Horatio's murder diminishes him in the eyes of the spectators. On one hand, his excessive love for his son might be interpreted as a sin of vanity and rebellion against God.[146] His mistrust of divine and earthly justice is, in fact, apparent from the moment Horatio's body is discovered. Though the Spanish king does not refuse to hear him, it is Hieronimo who will not give him the chance to punish the guilty, and he simply flees at the moment of truth (III, xii, 25–110; III, xiv, 40–169).[147]

On the other hand, and in spite of receiving the help of Providence in the shape of the letters of Bel-Imperia and Pedingrano,[148] Hieronimo never abandons his violent intentions. Thus he is set in opposition to the entire legal system which he, as marshal of the court, should represent. His rebellious and seditious attitude threatens the legal and political apparatus of the court, which is destabilized, and foreshadows the future destruction of the *status quo*. His secretiveness and premeditation (II, i, 60–63) reveal him as a typical Machiavellian character.

The influence that Bel-Imperia and Isabella exercise over him is also meaningful, since he carries out his vengeance largely provoked by the demands of the two women, who assume – especially the former – the role of the shrew of the misogynist literature of the Renaissance. The young woman twice disobeys her father's wishes by continuing her relationship with Andrea and Horatio, both of a lower social class. Her longings for vengeance are explicit from the moment she receives news of the death of her first love, and she decides to set in motion her own plans to punish Balthazar. Her manipulation of Horatio is obvious; it puts the authenticity of her love for him in doubt, as he is transformed into a mere pawn. She herself points out: "But how can love find harbour in my breast,/ Till I revenge the death of my beloved?/ Yes, second love shall further my revenge./ I'll love Horatio, my Andrea's friend./ The more to spite the prince that wrought his end" (I, iv, 64–68).

Horatio's death is, ultimately, the result of Bel-Imperia's vengefulness, and is the root of the tragedy. The refusal on the part of the king's niece to marry Balthazar in order to secure peace and stability in the kingdom can be read as an act of political irresponsibility on the part of the young woman and, indirectly, of her father and the king, both of them ignorant of her machinations. The king's words underline the consequences of her seditious behavior:

> Now, brother, you must take some little pains/ To win fair Bel-imperia from her will:/ Young virgins must be ruled by their friends./ The prince is amiable, and loves her well,/ If she neglect him and forgo his love,/ She both will wrong her own estate and ours. (II, iii, 41–46)

As had occurred with the Viceroy of Portugal, placing one's individual desires before the good of the nation bears unfortunate consequences. Both the letter that Bel-Imperia writes to Hieronimo (III, ii, 24–31) and the pressure that she exerts upon him (IV, i, 1–52) to avenge the death of his son heighten his state of madness.

Isabella's demented state and later suicide also reveal her weakness and her desire to carry out her plan for vengeance. She accuses Hieronimo of shirking his responsibilities as a father (IV, ii, 29–34) and decides to take his place – symbolically[149] – in order to avenge Horatio's death. Her influence on her husband's final decision is beyond question:

> [HIERONIMO:] Bethink thyself, Hieronimo,/ Recall thy wits, recompt thy former wrongs/ Thou has received by murder of thy son;/ And lastly, not least, how Isabel,/ Once his mother and thy dearest wife,/ All goe-begone for him, hath slain herself./ Behoves thee then, Hieronimo, to be revenged./ The plot is laid of dire revenge:/ On then, Hieronimo, pursue revenge. (IV, iii, 21-29)

Hieronimo is thus caught in a spiral of violence from which he cannot escape. His attitude as magistrate in the trial that takes place in III, xiii, 51–75 highlights his unjust nature: far from arriving at any positive conclusion for the parties involved, Hieronimo abandons his impartiality when he sees himself reflected in the character of the old man who rushes in, seeking help after the death of his son. The judge does not listen to him but interrupts the people, who look on in amazement as the law defends violence and vengeance (III, xiii, 86–89). His speech is forceful and poignant, arousing both pity and distrust of a man incapable of administering justice. The moment in which he tears the legal documents into a thousand pieces (III, xiii, 124–128) foreshadows the rupture of political order.

The equating of the Spanish court with Babel and Babylon (IV, i, 172–181; 195–198) inevitably alludes to anti-Catholic discourse, in which Rome – and by extension Spain – were synonymous with corruption and chaos. Hieronimo's words presage the fall of the Spanish court, and would probably have brought up a complete cultural construct – that of anti-Catholic and anti-Spanish sentiment – within the collective mind of the public. Nonetheless, the character's lack of both reason and political responsibility would have been disquieting, leaving a bitter taste in the mouths of an audience pondering a system that at no time in the play is described as corrupt or pernicious.

The three small performances that are prepared within the play for the Portuguese ambassador (I, iv, 138–179) indicate this same idea. As this scene unfolds, Horatio has not yet died, and Hieronimo is an important figure in the court, recognized by his king. The three English victories over Spanish and Portuguese forces that are shown in the pageants do not, then, appear to have much meaning. The attitude of the magistrate Hieronimo is incomprehensible, and seems to reveal an underlying desire to break off peaceful relations between the two countries. Aside from advancing the plot toward its conclusion and pointing out its providential nature, these spectacles emphasize Hieronimo's possible disloyalty, even before his son's murder. The danger that he poses is manifest at the end of the performance, when he succeeds in deceiving the villain Lorenzo, considered to be one of the first Machiavellian characters of the English stage.

Lorenzo is hypocritical and ambitious, and his character would probably have aroused the suspicions of an audience predisposed by contemporary anti-Machiavellian literature against any amoral behaviour in the pursuit of political interests: "Where words prevail not, violence prevails; / But gold doth more than either of them both" (II, ii, 108–109). Lorenzo fuels disloyal attitudes, and defends a kind of extreme individualism that challenges the validity and honesty of all social relationships:

> Thus must we work that will avoid distrust,/ Thus must we practice to prevent mishap,/ And thus one ill another must expulse./ This sly enquiry of Hieronimo/ For Bel-Imperia breeds suspicion./ And this suspicion bodes a further ill./ As for myself, I know my secret fault;/ And so do they, but I have dealt for them./ They that for coin their souls endangered,/ To save my life, for coin shall venture theirs:/ And better it's that base companions die,/ Than by their life, for me to fear their faith:/ I'll trust myself, myself shall be my friend,/ For die they shall, slaves are ordained to no other end. (III, ii, 105–119)

His constant betrayals – of Hieronimo, of his family, of his king – mark him out as the principal disruptor of order, together with Hieronimo.[150] The Spanish court becomes the focal point of disputes between two forces

(Hieronimo and Lorenzo) that are equally subversive and destabilizing. The harmony seen at the play's beginning is destroyed in favour of chaos. The Machiavellian attitudes of many of the characters result in the decay of a solid and fair political system and therefore nullify any hope for the nation. The lack of an heir exacerbates the disquiet felt at the prospect of the end both of a reign and of a dynasty. There is no doubt that audiences would have seen the parallels to the English court, a setting for political struggles and seditious attitudes stemming, according to contemporary opinions, from growing foreign influence:

> The courte of princes, which is the piller of vertue, the sword to cut vice, the stay of justice, and the axe to hewe downe each start uppe stemme, should (by the inferiour mindes of some suffered underminers) bee made the author of all pryde and ambition. These spyders than convert so sweete a flower to poison, turne honney to gall, would be shaken from the stately pillers of a Princes dominion, not be suffered to build their Netts under their Noses. (Rankins, *The English Ape*, pp. 10–11)

Kyd utilizes the common prejudices against Spain and, to a lesser degree, against Rome as a device to attract a receptive audience. The anti-Spanish discourse not only guaranteed him success at the box office, it also afforded him a scapegoat which he could use in order to discuss thorny political questions. In addition, he establishes an ongoing dialogue with various contemporary "others" – Machiavelli, the atheist, the Italian, the tyrant – which highlights the crisis that the identity of Protestant England was experiencing. The different processes of alterity, "otherness", come together, and produce a multiple and complex "other" that nevertheless always possesses the same basic element: loyalty to Rome.

A Larum for London (1602), by an anonymous author, refers to another recent historical event, the fall of Antwerp to Spanish troops in 1576. In this case, the primary source was a pamphlet entitled *The Spoyle of Antwerpe Faithfully Reported by a True Englishman Who was Present at the Same* (Gascoigne, 1576). As the title indicates, Gascoigne had fought at Antwerp, and was witness to the mutiny there by Spanish troops, which lent credibility and authority both to the pamphlet and to the later drama before their respective audiences. According to William Maltby, this tragic incident stemmed from Philip II's problems in maintaining his troops; they were poorly paid and poorly fed, which caused deep discontent among the soldiers. In the spring of 1576, after the King had declared himself bankrupt, when their pay had been owing for twenty-two months, and in the absence of any authority who could control them, the Spanish troops sacked the city of Antwerp, subjecting its people to all manner of humiliations.[151]

The play centres on a detailed description of the atrocities that the citizens of Antwerp suffered during the several days that the siege lasted. Scenes of indiscriminate brutality occur at the hands of the Spanish characters; as one citizen declares, a blind father of two sons who, with his wife and the rest of his family, is murdered by the Spanish soldiers:

> (Weeping) Hard harted Soldiers, where have you bin bred?/ Get honour on the proude resisting foe,/ My selfe have bin a Soldier as you are,/ Now blinde with age:/ Olde men, weake women, and poore wretched infants/ Should be respected in the heate of slaughter. (sig. E2v)[152]

Maltby indicates, however, that of the 54,300 soldiers in the Spanish armies in the Low Countries, only 7,900 were Spanish; the rest were locally recruited.[153] Despite this, the play groups them all under the same nationality, and automatically imbues them with the principal characteristic of the Spanish stereotype: cruelty.

The author appears to make reference to the origin of this trait by means of the character of Van End, who betrays his fellow citizens and works as a spy for Spain. His goal, as it is for the rest of the negative characters, is to get money (sig. C1r). This objective emerges, in fact, as the main motor of the dramatic conflict, since almost all the characters struggle in pursuit of economic interests, including the citizens of Antwerp. The treatment of this latter group is far from a simple portrayal of them as victims. Instead, they are seen as guilty of the city's decadence:

> [MARQUES D'HAUURYE:] Count Egmont, surelie Antwerpe is bewitcht,/ Securitie hath slaine their providence,/ And riches makes them retchles of their friends;/ We must assume the charge upon our selves,/ And pray the Prince and States to beare the pay;/ Or else their private avarice, will pull/ Publicke destruction on this flower of townes,/ To the disgrace of all the Netherlands.[154] (sig. B3v)

The criticism leveled at the citizens of Antwerp explains the fruitless labors of the Dutch noblemen, followers of William of Orange and, by extension, of Elizabeth I herself. The queen, transformed into the protector of Protestants in France and the Low Countries, could scarcely carry out this task, given the profound dissensions and incoherencies of religious politics in the two countries. The citizens of Antwerp are, in fact, described as cowards, prone to sacrificing their honour in extreme situations. One of them, for example, does not hesitate to give his money or even sacrifice his own daughter's virginity and her life in order that he himself might escape death (sigs D3v-E1r); others choose to endure continuous torture rather than surrender their wealth (sig. F3v). Theirs are merely material values, which causes Danila, the Spanish general who is the principal antagonistic character in the play, to describe the citizens' punishment as being the result of their extreme attachment to worldly goods: "But they were wanton and lascivious,/ Too much addicted to their private lust:/ And that concludes their Martirdoome was iust" (sig. G1v). It is also significant that the play's only English characters – the governor, his servant Gofrey, and Factor – quickly succumb to the threat of Danila and Alva without putting up a fight (sigs D3v-D4r-v).

Money and survival are placed before honour, and the latter concept is nearly rendered meaningless within the chaotic situation that arises. Only Stumpe, a disabled soldier in the Prince of Orange's forces, and the captain of the foreign troops attempting to protect the city from the Spaniards remain steadfast in the face of the threat and die for their principles. Although they appear at times as the protagonists of the play (especially Stumpe), their function lies in establishing a stark contrast between Spain's tyranny and Antwerp's cowardice and irresponsibility; hence, they merely serve to highlight the faults of the other opposing characters. Danila in fact praises their bravery at the end of the play, decides to bury them with military honors (sigs F4v-G2r), and shows signs of regret: "Oh in remorse of humaine clemency,/ My heart (me thinkes) could sigh, my eyes shed teares,/ To call to minde and see their misery" (sig. G1v).

The same happens to Alva, the subject of the most disparaging portrayal in the play, in which his thirst for violence is emphasized, as well as his irresponsibility toward the citizens and the hatred that he inspires in them (sigs B2v, B4v-C4r, E3v). In the final battle, Count Egmont, another nobleman who defends the city, falls wounded at his feet; Alva, surprisingly, recognizes his bravery and decides to protect him:

> [DANILA:] Why stands thou then to guard an enemie?/ [ALVA:] Because I will, honor encites me to it,/ The honor of this worthie Noble-man,/ And his high spirit even in the face of death,/Yeeld thee brave Egmont, Alva doth intreate thee,/ In pitie of thy bolde adventurous youth,/ And hopefull Fortunes shining in thine eyes,/ Thou seest these slaine, yet will I save thy life:/ Thou seest me wounded to preserve thy life./ I that was never pitifull before,/ Am forc't to pitty thee, what wouldst thou more? (sig. C4r)

These utterances complicate the iconographic construction of Alva himself, who regains his humanity, even if only briefly – Egmont rejects his enemy's compassion, and so is taken as a prisoner. The play thus points out the hidden aspects of the antagonists, and questions the legitimacy of the Black Legend that had already begun to take shape around the figure of the Spanish general the Duke of Alba.

This text represents one more step in the condemnation of the Spanish enemy, but Rome is never mentioned. However, there are certain ambiguities in the work that might contradict this discursive process and even compromise the audience's reaction. Given its date of publication (1602) and the relative calm in Anglo-Spanish relations at that time, the play seems to transcend a mere rehashing of the Spanish stereotype as the cause of the tragedies of Europe, and points to the responsibility of other participants in these conflicts. Perhaps the playwright is showing the necessity of being alert not only to the Spanish threat but also to the problems presented by English society itself – more urban, more commercial, and with money as its new structuring element: If the citizens of Antwerp had fallen as a result of their own vanity, it was possible that London might still suffer a new Spanish invasion as punishment for its growing interest in material wealth. Audiences – many of them from the newly enriched middle class – would not have remained dispassionate in the light of the playwright's message. Danila's positive disposition at the play's end is consistent with the closing message of the chorus: learn from these mistakes and avoid future massacres:

> His [Time's] care is fruitefull, and doth wish to see/ No heavie or disastrous chance befall/ The sonnes of men if they will warned be;/ But when they spurne against my discipline/ Wasting the treasure of my precious houre/ No marvayle then like misery catch holde/ On them, did fasten oh this wofull towne/ Whose bleeding fortune, whose lamenting cries/ Whose streetes besmear'd with bloud, whose blubred eyes/ Whose totter'd walls, whose buildings overthrone/ May be a meane all Cities to affright / How they in sinne and pleasure take delight. (sig. G2r)

The Life of Sir John Oldcastle (1600) stands somewhat apart from the works considered previously, since contemporary historical events are replaced by the tradition of reformist martyrs. Its authorship is uncertain, and, although at first glance it appears to be an anonymous text, critics such as Margot Heinemann maintain that it was the result of a collaboration between Michael Drayton, Anthony Munday and Robert Wilson.[155] The dates of the play's composition and of its first performance are also unknown, although there is a record of it having been registered on 11 August 1600 under the title *The Second and Last Parte of the History of Sir John Oldcastle*,[156] which suggests the existence of a first part, which has not been preserved.

The revival of the tradition of Protestant martyrs and the emphasis on the perpetual struggle of English reformers against Catholicism refer us to the City of London's rejection of a possible succession by a Spanish princess – an idea that was defended by the Jesuits and their protectors – or even by James VI, the son of the controversial Mary Queen of Scots. Like John Bale before him, the writer of the play combines historical drama with politico-religious allegory in order to deliver various messages that could allude to contemporary reality without the fear of censure.[157] Once again, the combination of the two genres forms one of the principal instruments of Protestant propaganda.

The dramatic action unfolds around the figure of Sir John Oldcastle,[158] head of the new reform movement in England at the end of the fourteenth and beginning of the fifteenth centuries. His connections to Lollardism are thus inevitable, which appears to suggest a return to the early years of the schism, when the English Reformation had stressed its ties to this earlier movement in an effort to offset the accusations of seeking a rupture with tradition that were aimed at them by the Catholic Church. Oldcastle is described as a model of Christian virtue and, especially, of loyalty to the Crown (sig. A2r). He is charitable (sig. B4v), humble (sig. B4v), and openly attacks papal supremacy (sig. D2v) in favour of the power of Scripture (sig. D3r). His courage and willingness to sacrifice himself are constantly emphasized through the many persecutions of which he is a victim, perpetrated by the country's Catholic hierarchy, particularly the Bishop of Rochester. This figure combines the main characteristics of the Catholic stereotype, especially cruelty (sigs G4r, H1v), corruption (sigs K2r, H2r) and deceit (sig. D3v), and thus is associated with similar figures from other periods, such as the Bishops Gardiner and Bonner.[159]

Oldcastle manages to escape his opponent's many traps, demonstrating his innocence when he is accused of having relations with groups disloyal to the king (among them a reformist group who were attempting to overthrow the Catholic monarch) and the French faction within the court, who were plotting to depose the king with the help of that country. The play concludes with a demonstration of Oldcastle's loyalty and the punishment of the traitors. Nevertheless, the character of Rochester, still in power, represents a serious threat to the protagonist, who has to continue his flight to escape the bishop's tyranny.

This revives, therefore, the tradition of Protestant victimhood of another age; but, above all, it stresses the need for obedience to the institution of the monarchy, perhaps one of the text's most problematic aspects. The role of the king – Henry IV – is, in fact, very passive, and on many occasions he appears to be manipulated by the chief motivating force of the drama, Rochester, who leads him to doubt Oldcastle's honesty. The king's irresponsibility in the face of the attempts at rebellion by many of his subjects is another point of debate, presented as a fundamental reason for the conspiracies that are taking shape around him, as he himself recognizes: "The King's asleep, wake not his maiestie,/ . . . hee's at rest in bed,/ Kings do not use to watch themselves, they sleep,/ And let rebellion and conspiracie,/ Revel and hauocke in the common wealth" (sig. F3r-v).

Regicide is a recurring theme throughout the drama. One of the rebels debunks the figure of the king in this manner: "[TOM:] What if ye should kill the King?/ [MURRAY:] Then weele make another" (sig. E4r);[160] in other cases, his deposition is only accepted when tyranny rears its head:

[BEVERLY:] We meant no hurt unto your maiesty,/ But reformation of Religion./ [HARRY:] Reforme religion? Was it that you sought?/ I pray who gave you that authority?/ Belike then we hold the scepter up,/ And sit within the throne but for a cipher;/ Time was, good subiects would make knowne their griefe,/ And *pray amendment, not inforce the same,/ Unless their King were tyrant*, which I hope/ You cannot iustly say that Harry is. (sig. G2r)

Although the playwright makes it clear that this is not the case and at times praises the king,[161] the spectre of regicide is ever present and continues to be an option, valid or not, in the face of particular problems.

Given the state of confusion in which England found itself at the end of Elizabeth's reign, this type of discourse heightened social and political tensions. Neither did the economic crisis in which the reign came to an end do anything to remedy the climate of instability, something that the playwright points out as he establishes a clear link between these various aspects:

(Enter three or foure poore people, some souldiers, some old men) 1: God help, God help, *there's law for punishing, but theres no law for our necessity*: there be more stockes to set poore soldiers in, than there be houses to releeve them at./ [OLDMAN:] Faith, *housekeeping decayes in every place*, even as Saint Peter writ, still worse and worse:/ 4: Maister maior of Rochester has given commaundment, that none shall goe abroad out of the Parish, and they have set and *order downe forsooth, what every poore householder must give towards our reliefe: where they be some ceased I may say to you, had almost as much neede to beg as we*./ 1: It is a hard world the while./ [OLD MAN]: *If a poore man come to a doore to aske for Gods sake, they aske him for a licence, or a certificate from a Iustice*./ 2: Faith we have none, but what we beare upon our bodies, our maimed limbs, God help us./ 4: And yet, as lame as I am, Ile with the king into France, If I can crawle but a ship-boorde, I hadde rather be slaine in France, than starve in England. (sig. B3v) (My emphasis)

Social and economic crisis is suggested as the principal causative agent of political conflicts. War, poor harvests and large commercial monopolies eroded the citizens' hopes for the *status quo* as installed by Elizabeth I. Although the programme to create employment that was introduced by Robert Cecil was a great novelty and had positive effects for the poorest among the population, in 1600 it was still too early to judge its effect. The playwright merely stresses the dangers that these conditions of scarcity bring, and he sounds one last alarm to the authorities, who are seriously threatened by the public's dissatisfaction: "[JUDGE:] You maister Maior, looke to your citizens,/ You maister Sherife unto your shire . . . / There be no meetings, When *the vulgar sort/* Sit on their Ale-bench, with their cups and kannes,/ *Matters of State be not their common talke,/ Nor pure religion by their lips prophande*" (sig. B1r) (my emphasis).[162]

The play demonstrates a suspicion of monarchical politics, and suggests a return to reformist values as a response – one that had been forgotten by the queen, according to the most radical sectors. The fact that a character associated with Lollardism is selected as protagonist seems to emphasize exactly that need for revival and a return to the origins of English Protestantism. On the other hand, the audience gets a glimpse of a profound criticism of the queen's shortcomings, and the possible disastrous consequences of them for her subjects. Thus the two pillars of the foundation of Elizabeth's iconographic construction as queen are brought into question: her commitment to the Reformation and her imperial character.

Despite the monarchy's many attempts to control dramatic activity – the royal proclamation of 1559 prohibiting any play dealing with religion or state politics was followed by successive proclamations in 1574, 1586 and 1589[163] – playwrights were still able to place the political questions that most concerned their audiences on the stage and still escape censure. Anti-Catholic discourse once again served as a tool to establish an identification with the audience and, most especially, to conceal dangerous criticism of the ruling system. The different responses that the various plays put forward interacted with the opinions of those who went to see them, a public who were also conditioned by the growing pamphlet and sermonizing literature of the moment.

An example of anti-Catholic discourse in the private theatre

The final text belongs to a different type of stage than those already considered, which determines the demands it makes and the tone in which it presents them. The play is *The Three Lords and the Three Ladies of London* (1590) by Robert Wilson, probably performed by The Queen's Men in a private theatre.[164] There is no documentary evidence of this performance, although the dramatic genre that was utilized, the allegorical drama, and its extensive use of the symbolic leads one to imagine a mainly educated audience. The author in fact indicates the nobility as his play's natural audience (h. sig. 14r) and, although the context in which the dramatic action unfolds is the City of London and many of the elements introduced are peculiar to it, there is an explicit criticism of its citizens who attempt to advance themselves socially. This posture reveals a deep conservatism, a recurrent theme in private theatre, where the values of the upper classes were usually reaffirmed:

> [SIMPLICITY:] I forgot to ask you whither your three Lords of London be Courtiers or Cittiners?/ [WIT:] Citizens borne and courtiers brought up: Is this all? Farewell./ [SIMPLICITY:] Citizens borne and Courtiers brought up, I thinke so, for they that be borne in London are false Courtiers before they see the Court. (sig. C3r)

Although the protagonists correspond to symbolic types, the play departs from the particular structure of the moral allegory and introduces elements that point to the future form of the city comedies, since it is set in an urban milieu and depicts the corruption of the citizens in their love of money. Hence it is a hybrid type of text, at a liminal point in the evolution of English Renaissance drama. It describes the courting of the three main female characters (Love, Lucre and Conscience) by three lords of London (Pollicie, Pompe and Pleasure). The three women are under the care of an old man, Nemo, who attempts to protect their honour so that they might be married and become good wives (sig. C3v). The three English lords must struggle against the four gallants (Fraud, Usury, Dissimulation and Simony) who have won over the women in the past, and against three suitors who arrive from Spain (Pride, Ambition and Tiranny) with the intention of invading the city and winning the ladies' favour:

> DILIGENCE:] The Spanish forces Lordings are prepar'd,/ In braverie and boast, beyond all boundes/ T'invade, to win, to conquer all this land./ They chieflie aime at Londons stately pompe,/ At Londons pleasure, wealth and pollicy./ Intending to dispoile her of them all,/ And over all those lovelie Ladies three,/ Love, Lucre, Conscience, peerlesse of the rarest price,/ To tyrannize and carie hardest hand,/ From Spain they come with Engine and intent/ To slay, subdue, to triumph and torment. (sig. F1v)

The Spanish characters fulfill the main characteristics of the Spanish stereotype and seem, in the beginning, to establish themselves as the antagonists of the story, in clear opposition to the supposed virtues of the three protagonists. However, and even though the performance ends with the victory of Pollicie, Pompe and Lucre over their enemies, the writer does not direct the nationalistic spirit against Spain alone; instead, the position taken in the text underscores a general xenophobia directed against many nationalities, as is demonstrated by the association established between such nations and the gallants, very similar to the characterization of the vices in the moral allegories:

> [SIMONY:] Tis not our native countrie [England], thou knowest, I Simony am a Roman, Dissimulation a Mongrel, half an Italian, halfe a Dutchman, Fraud too, halfe French, and halfe Scottish: and thy parentes were both Jewes, though thou wert borne in London, and here Usury thou art cried out against by the preachers: ioine with us man to better thy state, for in Spain preaching toucheth us not. (sig. F4r)

Their foreign origin explains both their lack of scruples in allying themselves with the Spaniards and the impossibility of their living in London: "[FRAUD:] Here is no living for us in London, men are growen so full of conscience and religion, that Fraud, Dissimulation and Simony are disciphered, and being disciphered are also dispised" (sig. F4r). Economic considerations remain hidden behind a nationalistic and patriotic pretext, which highlights the uncorrupted nature of London and by extension of the English nation, inheritor of the virtues of the great empires:

> [LONDON:] All England is, and so preseved hath bene,/ Not by mans strength, his pollicie and wit,/ But by a power and providence unseene./ Even for the love wherwith God loves our Queen:/ In whome, for whom, by whom we do possess/ More grace, more good, than London can expresse./ And that hath bred our plenty and our peace. (sig. A2v)

The design on the shield of the English herald suggests the same idea. It is a drawing of an olive tree, which Felty interprets in this way: "London lives in peace,/ Your [Spaniards'] native fruit dooth wither on your soile,/ And prospers where it never planted was" (sig. G4r). The motif of the olive tree was also seen in portraits of the queen; the most well-known example is *The Ermine Portrait*, in which she appears as the symbol of peace and justice, represented as an olive branch that she carries in her hand, as well as a sword.[165] The identification of the herald with the queen refers to the speech, already discussed, made by Elizabeth at Tilbury, and specifically to the union of the queen and her subjects against the Spanish enemy.

The characterization of the two camps is carried out chiefly through the use of national stereotypes, and relegates the religious debate to a secondary plane. There are only a few references to the differences between the Protestant and Catholic faiths (sigs G3r, G4r), and at no time is either Rome or the figure of the pope mentioned. The play eschews any doctrinal teachings and focuses instead on strictly moral questions.

Although the play's xenophobic message runs deep, at other times the playwright presents an internal critique that goes beyond simple nationalism by not portraying the English characters as models of virtue.[166] At the play's beginning, all three lords want to marry Lucre, an indication of their greed:

> [NEMO:] Thus Lordes you showe your imperfections:/ Subiect to passions, straining honours boundes,/ Be wel advisde, you promised to be rulde,/ And have those Dames, by me disposed to you,/ But since I see that humaine humours oft/ Makes men forgetfull of their greater good. (sigs E4r-v)

The fact that, even after they have defeated the Spaniards, the three ladies continue to distrust the men is not without significance, and implies possible dubious intentions on the part of the three protagonists:

> [LUCRE:] Prepare would we garlands of Laurell greene,/ To welcome them,

more for the common good,/ Than for affection private that we beare./ [LOVE:] To meet them comming will not be amisse,/ But what know we how they will take such work,/ [CONSCIENCE:] Report may be much more than there is cause,/ We may them meete and greet with iofull heartes,/ And make them garlands when we know their mindes. (sig. H1v)

Their portrayal is thus not a positive one: they barely catch on to the tricks of the gallants, who consistently outwit them and manage to escape unpunished. The final scene perhaps best represents this dynamic, since it reveals the stupidity and irresponsibility of the three English lords, particularly Pleasure, who, instead of accepting the obligations of his rank delegates to the clownish Simplicity the punishment of Fraud. Simplicity decides to put a blindfold over his own eyes when he burns out the vice's tongue, but in the process, Fraud is set free by Dissimulation, and both escape before anyone can stop them (sigs I3v-I4r).

The play ends in a state of confusion and uncertainty, as the threat remains. The alternative that the three gentlemen present is not acceptable, and seems to underline the impossibility of such men serving as a model for the country's nobility. The City and its inhabitants do not meet expectations, and in spite of the appeals made to nationalistic sentiments and imperial goals, there remains a wide margin of doubt that these can be achieved in a nation with growing social mobility. The text reveals, therefore, a profound conservatism, by reaffirming the *status quo* and the values of the upper classes, whose ranks are suspicious of the growing power of the bourgeoisie. The anti-Spanish discourse is blurred behind a general xenophobia that manifests the same fear of being "corrupted" by agents from outside certain circles of power, the boundaries of which were ever less strictly defined.

The many political and socioeconomic changes in England in the Elizabethan era resulted in a situation that influenced essential features of accepted ideas of the individual and of society. Elizabeth I attempted to relieve these uncertainties by means of a complex and excessive iconography that invoked Providence and the special status of the queen and the English nation as having been chosen and favoured by it, at the same time as it emphasized the need for loyalty, hope and patience on the part of her subjects. On the other hand, it also stressed a series of imperial virtues that reaffirmed the power of the queen and her international policies, especially those related to colonial imperialism; in this way, xenophobic behaviours and discourse could be justified – particularly against Spain – as were the profits gained by certain individuals in the name of the national interest.

Such discourses no doubt did not receive the unanimous approval of the English people, who considered the theatre as a place of relative freedom, where they could see their doubts and fears dramatized. Playwrights were aware of that, and in many cases attempted to respond to the public's demands, which explains the box-office success of certain plays with an anti-Catholic tone. Nevertheless, perhaps most important was the function that the dramatic stage acquired as a medium for channeling all kinds of political messages, which many times managed to avoid censure. The anti-Catholic and anti-Spanish discourse thus constituted a basic element in criticism of the established system, at the same time as it also served to fuel hatreds and to create unity in a deeply divided society. It equally reaffirmed political and ecclesiastical authority, indispensable in a period of crisis and transition that marked the end of a reign. Not only did anti-Catholicism not disappear, it continued to assimilate new elements, features, and even characters – the Jesuit – that made it one of England's most relevant culturual constructs of the sixteenth and seventeenth centuries.

EPILOGUE

Nostalgia for Elizabeth and Anti-Catholic Discourse

It is not easy to draw definitive conclusions when one studies a phenomenon that continued to operate beyond the time frame that is the focus of research; therefore, instead of setting out on a final summary that is limited to the material that has been covered, I believe it to be more in keeping with the objectives and method of this study to give an account of the final significant contribution that was made to anti-Catholic discourse: nostalgia for Elizabeth.

By 1603 a cultural stereotype of Catholicism had been consolidated that would be essential in the later configuration of English national identity. A series of dramatic works that were performed and published after Elizabeth's death will be useful to us in exploring the way the figure of the queen acted as a metonymical vehicle capable, by its mere presence, of evoking – and substituting for – the entire body of anti-Catholicism. The death of Elizabeth I, then, can be seen as a point of inflection that allows us to review the elements that had been incorporated in anti-Catholic discourse from its beginnings and to point out its lines of evolution through the seventeenth century.

Following her death, the image of a deified Elizabeth, as an icon both of national identity and of English Protestantism, became a symbol that rendered the detailed accusations and rationalizations of anti-Catholicism redundant. Such an unconscious mechanism of identification can be seen in Freud's comments explaining the relation between the masses and their leader:

> The conditions required for the members of a multitude of human beings grouped together by chance to form something resembling a mass, in a psychological sense, is that those persons have something in common, a shared interest in an object, a matching affective orientation in a certain situation, and (I am tempted to say "as a consequence") a certain level of capacity to mutually influence each other ... The stronger these links of commonality ... the more readily do these individuals form a psychological mass.[1]

The degree of identification of the individual with the object is proportionate to the "reciprocal bond" with other members of the mass,[2] which explains why anti-Catholic discourse reached its maximum expression under Elizabeth, since she represented the most effective object of identification for the reformist community. Thus, the Tudor queen became a defining element of Protestantism in England both during and after her reign, which explains the later invocation of her memory during difficult times that jeopardized the unity of English Protestants. The reign of King James I was one such period.

Despite the doubts that were raised over his claim to the throne, it seems that James was largely well received by the English people, who saw in him the hope of change. The words of some members of the House of Commons at the end of the first session of Parliament in 1604 are significant:

> A general hope was raised in the minds of all your people that under your Majesty's reign religion, peace, justice, and all virtues should renew again and flourish; that the better sort should be cherished, the bad reformed or repressed, and some moderate ease should be given us of those burdens and sore oppressions under which the whole land did groan.[3]

Disillusion was not long in coming. In 1604 peace was signed with Spain, and the following year conversations were begun regarding a marriage of the heir to the Throne of England, Prince Henry, with a Spanish Princess.

While peace could, at least theoretically, ease the country's economic difficulties, radical Protestant sectors soon opposed the policy of tolerance toward Catholics that was initiated as a result of the new diplomatic relations. Aware of the strength of anti-Catholic prejudices, King James introduced several laws in the years between 1603 and 1606 that were aimed at appeasing Protestant discontent. However, these laws were not enforced strictly, which allowed Catholics to practice their faith in private and even to grow in number.[4]

The many disputes with Parliament, mounting economic crisis and disagreement with many of the reforms demanded by the Puritans contributed to the creation of a climate of hostility toward the new king. The court's corrupt and licentious character did not go unnoticed by many, who also disapproved of the monarch's favouritism toward Scottish noblemen, as well as his supposed pro-Catholic tendencies and lack of interest in affairs of state.[5] Comparisons to his predecessor were inevitable. Bishop Godfrey Goodman, a monarchist and an Anglican, had this to say in the 1650s about the transition from the reign of Elizabeth to that of James:

> For the Queen, she was ever hard of access, and grew to be very covetous in her old days . . . that the court was very much neglected, and in effect the people were very generally weary of an old woman's government . . . But after a few years, when we had experience of the Scottish government,

then in disparagement of the Scots, and in hate and detestation of them, the Queen did seem to revive; then was her memory much magnified, such ringing of bells, such public joy and sermons in commemoration of her, the picture of her tomb painted in many churches, and in effect more solemnity and joy in memory of her coronation than was for the coming in of King James.[6]

A statue of the queen that stood before her tomb from 1606 was the object of worship by the people, who also continued to celebrate her birthday.[7] The many anti-Catholic and anti-Spanish pamphlets and sermons served as an intertext for a complete cultural reproduction of the former monarch with a clear purpose that was, if not critical of the new system, then at least admonitory. Although Curtis Perry admits the possibility that many of the texts eulogizing the Elizabethan government stressed the continuity between the reigns of Elizabeth and James and thus endorsed the Stuart king,[8] this general discontent makes it impossible not to view the comparison between the two reigns with a certain amount of irony. The insistent memories of the queen could only be seen as a heavy burden for her successor, who stated before parliament in 1621: "I will not say I have governed so well as she did".[9] The queen had become a central element in anti-Catholic rhetoric, and a symbol of the defence of England's autonomy in the face of foreign threats. True or not, this image had transcended the discursive plane and proved an effective vehicle for criticism of the tolerant attitude towards Spain and Rome of the new *rex pacificus*.[10]

The Whore of Babylon (1607) by Thomas Dekker, and the first and second part of *If You Know not Me You Know Nobody* (1605–1606) by Thomas Heywood, exemplify the use of both cultural constructs – anti-Catholicism and nostalgia for Elizabeth – as instruments to criticize the Stuart monarch. They serve, therefore, to summarize the dynamic process of the construction of anti-Catholic and anti-Spanish sentiment in England. These works reiterate many of the anti-Catholic arguments of earlier times, so that they represent a compendium of many of the elements discussed in this research. They serve to demonstrate, then, the manner in which anti-Catholic discourse was the result of a constant process of accumulation of facts, images and personalities, which remained etched in the collective memory of English Protestants[11]

The Whore of Babylon (1607) was probably written in 1606, or just after the Gunpowder Plot of 5 November 1605.[12] This conspiracy against the king served notice that the Catholic threat was still very much alive: its principal instigators – Robert Catesby,[13] Thomas Percy,[14] Jack Wright and John Winter – all came from noble families of recusants, and had been joined by Guy Fawkes, a mercenary soldier born in Yorkshire who had fought for the Catholic cause in the Low Countries. The Jesuits John Gerald, Oswald Tesmond and especially Henry Garnett[15] were also implicated. Although neither the pope[16] nor their superior in the Society, Robert Persons,[17] knew of the plan to kill the king, Protestant public opinion was quick to hold all Catholics responsible for this treason against the crown. The governing elite also used this conspiracy to strengthen King James's identification with his predecessor, in that they were both protected by Providence against Catholic intrigues. John Watkins explains that according to this myth, the discovery of the conspiracy against James was on a par with Elizabeth's victory over the Spanish Armada.[18]

The king's attitude, nevertheless, was unsettling to his Protestant subjects, who looked on as Rome and Spain were exonerated of any involvement in the plot. The court did not favour investigating the disposition of the accused, and the monarch himself seemed to be first in suggesting that the whole thing be forgotten, as was apparent in his speech to Parliament shortly after the plot was discovered:[19]

> I wish you to consider, that I would bee sorry that any being innocent of this practice, either domestical or foraine, should receive blame or harme for the same. For although it cannot bee denied, that it was the onely blind superstition of their errors in Religion, that led them to this desperate devise; *yet doeth it not follow, that all professing that Romish religion were guilty of the same* ... And therefore do we iustly confesse, that many Papists, especially our forefathers, laying their onely trust upon Christ and his Merits at their last breath, may be & oftentimes are saved, *detesting in that point, and thinking the cruelty of Puritanes worthy of fire, that will admit no salvation to any Papist. I therefore thus doe conclude this point, That as upon the one part many honest men, seduced with some errors of Popery, may yet remaine good and faithfull Subiects* ... And for the part of sorraine Princes and States ... *That no King nor Prince of Honor wil ever abase himselfe so much, as to thinke a good thought of so base and dishonorable a Teachery* wishing you therefore, that as God hath given me an happy Peace and amitie, with all other Christian Princes my neighbours ... that so you will reverently iudge and speake of them in this case ... *for then might you all see no alteration in my minde for this accident.*[20] (My emphasis)

The confirmation of the threat, together with the king's behaviour, heightened the discontent of the radical reformers, who saw a golden opportunity slip through their fingers to demand a tougher stance against Catholicism. Thomas Dekker, who was also the author of political pamphlets during this period, questioned the monarchy's approach in *The Whore of Babylon*,[21] written in the middle of this debate. Heywood, on the other hand, had written the two parts of *If You Know not Me You Know Nobody* before the assassination attempt – probably between 1604 and 1605[22] – and although critical of the Catholic sector it does not contain the explicitly hard edge of Dekker's work,[23] which obviously conforms to the characteristic fear of conspiracies that was the hallmark of anti-Catholic literature.

The dominant dramatic genres continued to be moral allegory and historical drama. Although somewhat old-fashioned by the early years of the seventeenth century, these were the most useful formats for displaying the universe of opposites upon which anti-Catholic dramatic literature was sustained. Also, the historical play formed one of the principal modes of expression of the new English national consciousness. Using figures from the past as a mirror in which to ponder rulers had been a key resource in works such as *King Johan* (1558) by John Bale, or the anonymous *The Life of Sir John Oldcastle* (1600), which had substituted the saints of the Christian tradition with the Protestant martyrs popularized after the publication of *Actes and Monuments* (1563).

The works of Dekker and Heywood can therefore be placed within the Protestant literary tradition, and dramatize distinct moments in the life of Elizabeth I, who becomes the main heroine of the Reformation in England.[24] Both plays stress the ongoing Catholic menace that had existed even before Elizabeth's reign, as well as the strength that she manifested to overcome it. Anti-Catholic language continues as the principal vehicle for describing the Elizabethan government's virtues as a model for its successors.[25] The queen's characterization perpetuates her image as martyr in Protestant literature,[26] and the appeal to her imperial power recalls one of the main themes of the dramatic and pamphlet literature of the previous reign.

The Whore of Babylon is the clearest example of the use of anti-Catholic rhetoric to pose questions about imperialism on stage. The play dramatizes the Protestant interpretation of the Book of Revelation, mainly focused on the confrontation between the true Church of Christ – Titania – and the Whore of Babylon – the Empress, who allies herself with the forces of Catholicism (the pope, Spain, and France) in order to overthrow the queen. The play is structured in three acts, separated by the introduction of various dumb shows that summarize the dramatic action.[27] The first of these[28] alludes to Whitney's emblem *Veritas Temporis*[29] and to Ripa's emblems of Time and Truth[30] and identifies the character Titania with the restoration of the Word of God. Dekker evokes the symbolic representation that had taken place during Elizabeth's entry into London in 1558, and emphasizes the queen's commitment to Protestantism from the very beginning of her reign. In the play, as happened in real life, the queen kisses a book (symbolizing the Bible), a gesture that associates the text with the reformist principles defended in the royal entry.[31] Before the play begins, the audience can already identify the heroine as Queen Elizabeth I and her opponents as the representatives of the Church of Rome.

The description of the Whore of Babylon and her followers includes all the elements of the Catholic stereotype. Her portrayal makes reference to one of Dekker's sources, *The Faerie Queene* by Edmund Spenser, the most prominent exponent of the cult of the queen in the late sixteenth century. His argument and objective – the celebration of Elizabeth's reign as the culmination of a divine (and imperial) plan for England – are repeated in *The Whore of Babylon*,[32] which retraces the main elements of this encomiastic tradition and portrays Titania as the legitimate inheritor of her ancestors, responsible for a new Golden Age:

> [FIDELI:] [May she guide Fairie Land] Even Till stooping time/ Cut for her (downe) long yeres that shee may climbe/ (With ease) the highest hill old age goes o'er,/ Or till her Fairie subiects (that adore/ Her birth-day as their beeing) shall complaine,/ They are weary of a peacefull, golden raigne. (sig. B4v)

Her link with Protestantism is set forth clearly by means of an indirect connection with Una, a paragon of purity in *The Faerie Queene*: "And on her now a garment she did weare,/ All lilly white, withoutten spot, or pride,/ That seemd like silke and silver woven neare" (I, xii, 22). Dekker's protagonist is described in similar terms: "[TITANIA:] How? Feare? Why should *white* bosomes / Feare a Tyrants Arme" (my emphasis) (sig. I3r); "Enough it is for me, if with a hand, / (*Unstaind* and *un-ambitious*) fairy Land / I Crowned with *Olive*-branches" (sig. B4r) (my emphasis); she thus assumes the same connotations as Spenser's heroine. Helen Hackett draws a parallel between Una as an "unstaind" character and the bride in *The Song of Songs*, symbol of the Protestant Church in the Geneva Bible. According to Hackett, the absence of stain upon this biblical character may be an allusion to Una's/Elizabeth's/the Church of England's saintliness, purity and truth, as opposed to the duplicity of Duessa/Mary Stuart/the Church of Rome.[33] The same meaning can be applied to the pairing of Titania/Whore, which neatly summarizes the Protestant theory of the Two Churches.

The religious glorification of the monarch (Una/Titania) implies, conversely, Rome's wickedness, as well as that of its complex network of political agents: the three kings (France, Rome and Spain), the clergy, the Jesuits (Campion), and also the English Catholic courtiers and subjects,[34] all like-minded collaborators in the plot.[35] They are shown as uniting against the sovereign in the third dumb show, in which Falsehood appears dressed as Truth and is defended by the Friar Campeius and other noblemen. In addition to pointing out the collaboration between the Jesuits, the clergy and the nobility in the projects of English Catholicism, Falsehood's depiction alludes to the figure of Duessa in *The Faerie Queene*, also associated with the Whore of Babylon in the poem:

> What man so wise, what earthly wit so ware,/ As to descry the *crafty cunning traine*,/ By which deceipt doth maske in visour faire,/ And cast her colours

dyed deepe in graine,/ To seeme like Truth, whose shape she well can faine,/ And fitting gestures to her purpose frame;/ The guiltless man with guile to entertaine?/ Great maistresse of her art was that false Dame,/ The false Duessa, cloked with Fidessaes name. (I, vii, 1)

Nonetheless, the characterization of this negative element is complex, and implies a critical attitude that goes beyond the Catholic community. In principle, the theatricality of the antagonists and their frequent use (like Duessa) of masks, paint and disguises to achieve their purposes, not only link them to the ideas of falseness and hypocrisy (integral to the Catholic stereotype), but also make reference to the format of the moral allegory, in which the vices – in this case, the Spanish King – stand out because of their versatility and capacity for deception.[36] This emphasis on the theatrical and opulent nature of the enemy guaranteed a difficult reception by the audience, who were aware of King James's love of the splendour of masquerades and other courtly entertainments. A comment made by one of the king's chaplains on the nobility's excesses hints at an indirect parallel with the Catholic community, attacked in the play: "To what an immense riches in his time did the merchandise of England rise to above former ages! What buildings! What sumptuousness! What feastings! What gorgeous attire! What massy plate and jewels! What prodigal marriage portions were grown in fashion among the nobility and gentry, as if the skies had rained plenty!"[37]

In addition, the aesthetics of the Jacobean monarchy also satisfied the classical canon, which gave the monarchical image a genuinely absolutist character. Far from awakening an identification of the people with imperial ambitions (as had been the case with Elizabeth), the new king stressed his absolute authority and the English people's subordination to it, a message that was made very clear at the time of his entry into London for his coronation.[38]

The theatre echoed contemporary perceptions of the images of the two monarchs, indirectly contrasting the king's absolutist tendencies with the populism of Elizabeth I, who was depicted as having been adored by her people,[39] who remained forever loyal before her merciful and protective attitude.[40] This mutuality of interests was seen as showing the way to avoiding internal divisions. The fact that in *If You Know not Me* (I) Elizabeth's popularity is held up in contrast to the tyrannical attitude of Mary I and her counsellors also presents problems in connection with the absolutist image of James, since he, again, is associated with Catholics. Hence, a debate is joined on stage regarding different models of monarchy, which touches on contemporary concern at the mounting influence of European absolutism on the English political system.[41]

Heywood introduces this question at the beginning of the first part of the play, when he describes the breaking of the pact between Mary I and her subjects, who had supported her during Wyatt's rebellion. The Queen does not grant them the freedom of conscience that they had agreed upon (sigs A3v-A4v) and insists, as she is advised by Winchester, upon freely exercising her will above the wishes of her people (sigs A4v-B1r).[42] In contrast, in *The Whore of Babylon*, Titania listens to all the members of her council before making decisions. While she is always the person ultimately responsible – a fact she makes very clear (sig. C4v) – this is still evidence of a more conciliatory government. The two systems that are suggested – power as the result of a contract with the people, as opposed to the absolute power of the monarch – are the subject of the debate, which sends a clear message to the new sovereign, whose tendencies had very likely already begun to make many citizens uncomfortable. The relationship between this type of government and Catholic tyranny suggested a criticism not only of the allegedly pro-Catholic policy of James I but also of the model of monarchy that he was attempting to install.[43]

The references to Elizabeth's compassionate attitude, however, do not fail to arouse some suspicions. The behaviour of the Queen in the play towards Dr. Parry[44] underlines the danger that, according to some reformists, went with pardoning Catholics, since they would never stop conspiring against Protestant monarchs.[45] The most representative example is in the enactment of the trial of Mary Queen of Scots, which takes place in the last part of *The Whore of Babylon*. Titania's words highlight her merciful nature – "Must we then,/ Strike those whom we have lov'd? Albeit the children,/ Whom we have nourist at our princely breast,/ Set daggers to it, we could be content/ To chide, not beat them (might we use our will,)/ Our hand was made to saue, but not to kill" (sig. G4r) – and also replicate Mercilla's stance in the trial of Duessa in Spenser's poem:

> But she, whose Princely breast was touched nere/ With piteous ruth of her so wretched plight,/ Though plaine she saw by all, that she did heare,/ That she of death was guiltie found by right,/ Yet would not let iust vengeance on her light;/ But rather let in stead thereof to fall/ Few perling drops from her faire lampes of light. (V, ix, 50)

Hackett stresses the possible dire consequences of this behaviour, considering such excessive mercy to be effeminate and improper,[46] an opinion also shared by Thomas H. Cain, who alludes to the impossibility of combining this concept of justice and mercy with political action in the iconographic representation of Elizabeth.[47] Thus, Dekker revives the polemic that had begun among radical Protestants during the last decade of the reign of Elizabeth I. In this way, a parallel is established between the queen's attitude in the 1590s and James's peaceful – and for some, excessively tolerant – policy towards Catholics. The playwright, in order to denounce the "effeminate" – and therefore, tyrannical – policies of the new king, recalls the anxiety that at times of crisis was aroused by

Elizabeth's government. In the play, Titania, like Mercilla in *The Faerie Queene* (V, x, 4), reconsiders and imposes justice (sig. G4r). Elizabeth and James, however, did not change their views, despite what many of their English subjects demanded.

The militaristic and patriotic tone with which *The Whore of Babylon* concludes, like that of the second part of *If You Know* . . . , emphasizes the same idea. References to the Armada reappear strongly in the early Jacobean period to indicate – or arouse – suspicion of any treaty with Spain. On the other hand, repeated references to dynastic continuity and the ancestry of Elizabeth I in both texts voice doubts that had been awakened by the question of succession and the arrival of a new dynasty on the throne of England. The association of the last of the Tudors with Protestantism and the imperial ideal might cast doubts upon the capability of the Stuarts to continue with the same objectives. Only a glimmer of hope is revealed in the final scene of *The Whore of Babylon*, when a baby boy is born on the battlefield on which the Spaniards are defeated (sig. K2v). The continuity of the military spirit symbolized by the baby could be a reference to the only Stuart who represented the future of English Protestantism in those years: Prince Henry.[48] Even so, the possible reference to the future heir as a counterpoint to his father could only have had a destabilizing effect on the newly-crowned king.

The second part of Heywood's text also makes use of the imperial question to discuss the king's policies. Unlike the previous scenes, it does without many elements of anti-Catholic rhetoric[49] and instead focuses on the justification of the City of London and its inhabitants as the cornerstone of imperial expansion. It thus moves away from the customary dramatic tradition and adopts an original position by linking the interests of London to Elizabeth I's colonial designs. The queen only appears on three occasions: when she inaugurates the Royal Exchange, in the part of the play when Dr. Parry's stratagems to assassinate her are discovered, and in the episode of the Armada. Although these scenes seem to break up the flow of the dramatic action, they have a very definite function. In the light of traditional prejudices against the city's corruption and the growing and pernicious power of money, the playwright attempts to reconcile virtue with mercantile profits and, in so doing, to justify a fast-developing economic system.

The figure of Gresham is honest (sig. A2r), charitable toward the poor (sigs F2v, H2r) and committed to the city's progress, to which end he has financed the construction of a college of science (sigs F2v-F3r) and the Royal Exchange. The description of the latter makes reference to the greatness of Elizabeth's reign:

[LORD:] You have travel'd Sir, how do you like this building?/ Trust me it is the goodliest thing that I have seene,/ England afford not such./ [LORD:] Nor Christendome:/ I might say all the world has not his fellow./ I have been in Turkies great Constantinople,/ The Marchants there meet in a goodly temple,/ But have no common Burse in Rome, but Rome's/ Built after the manner of Franckeford, and Emden . . . / This Gresham hath much grac't your Cittie London,/ His fame will long out-live him. (sig. E4r)

The parallel between the Royal Exchange and the Elizabethan empire is almost inevitable, underscoring the importance of trade in its development. Hobson, another London merchant, mentions several times the loans he has made to the crown (sigs E1r, H1v), probably to finance expeditions and wars in which it found itself involved, illustrating the crown's dependence on the wealth generated by the city for the implementation of its military ambitions. On the other hand, the presence in the building of portraits of the various English monarchs (sigs E4r-F2r) reveals the approval given to the project by Elizabeth (as a character in the play). The merchants' activities are therefore justified by their commitment to the people of London and to their queen. With this emphasis on the need to make virtuous use of wealth,[50] the pursuit of wealth is legitimized, and individual interests are equated with those of the nation.[51]

The presence of the queen at City events and this relationship of mutual need that she establishes with the people of London also points to a new demand put forward by the playwright, who thus refers indirectly to the citizens' discontent at the lack of interest shown in them by James I. Thomas Dekker alludes to this uneasiness in *The Dead Tearme* (1608), a pamphlet composed in the form of a dialogue between the characters Westminster and London, who discuss the advantages and disadvantages of living in one place or the other. London's words concerning King James I are quite meaningful:

> I begin to growe jealous of thee [Westminster], that thou seekest to rob me of my best, my most worthy, most Princely, and my most desired Lover, to enioy him solely to thy selfe: else wherefore dost thou repine that either I, or any other of our Sister citties, should be made happy by his company? It shewes that thy heart is stufte with a rancke and boyling envie, thou greedest that any should prosper but thy selfe. It condemnes thee of ambition (which sinne thou thinkest becomes thee, because thou art a Courtier) . . . I esteeme my selfe the most fortunate of all my neighbour Citties in this large kingdome, if that Royall Maister of us both (nay of us all) doe but vouchsafe to passe by mee, not but so much as to cast hys eie upon me, and dost thou cry out Thou art undone, when after his embracings of thee so many whole moneths (of tentimes) together, after his bestowing so many dignities, and so much wealth upon thee: yea, and when hee gives thee his Royal word, not to be absent from thee long? Cannot this content thee, and satisfie the flame of thy desyres, but that thou must wish to have him fonde over thee, and that the beams of this most princely and free affection, should have all their points meete in thy bosome, as their onelie true Obiect? (sig. E3v)

In this context, and through his re-creation of Elizabeth, Heywood fashions a wake-up call for the king with regard to his relationship with his capital city. The promotion of London's commercial activities is posed as fundamental to the queen's imperial program, an idea that the play attempts to transmit to the Stuart monarch, who had supplanted the search for new markets with a politics that was both centralist – as was evident from the union of England and Scotland, as well as from the settlement of Ulster – and pacific, with little regard for foreign trade.

Finally, the scene representing the events surrounding the Armada confirms the relationship between the imperial cause and the Exchange. The parallels made between the brave English soldiers and London's merchants are almost unavoidable, and place both groups on a similar footing with regard to the achievement of a common goal: the power and enrichment of their country. The messenger's words to the queen – "England nere bred/ Men that at sea fight better managed" (sig. I4v) – could be applied to both groups, even outside court circles. The value of the city to the state's interests prevails at the end of the play, and thus it upholds the principles of those of the ample and powerful middle class that attended public theatres.

As we have attempted to show, the functions of anti-Catholic discourse in England became more diverse as it was becoming consolidated. The pejorative connotations associated with this stereotype allowed Catholics to be identified with all sorts of activities dangerous to the stability of government. Sedition, tyranny and absolute rule began to be viewed through the prism of anti-Catholicism, which demonstrates the visibility this construct had attained at the beginning of the seventeenth century, as well as its assimilation by a large section of English society. The strength of this discourse and the dangers it implied explains why many English monarchs – including Elizabeth I – attempted to distance themselves from it, and why it would come to be associated with radical Protestant groups who would use it as an instrument to exert pressure on the religious and foreign policies of different sovereigns. Nevertheless, the parallels between this discourse and other cultural constructs, such as the imperial discourse or the nostalgia for Elizabeth, made such a complete disassociation from anti-Catholic propositions impossible for the crown, since they legitimized its power with regard to the pope and strengthened the nation's autonomy in the face of possible foreign intervention.

James's conciliatory position and his reluctance to allow himself to be carried along by anti-Catholic prejudices were in fact attacked by a broad sector of English society, who had come to accept the seditious nature of the followers of Rome as doctrine. The king's foreign origins – another cause for concern among his subjects – were seen as the reason for his benevolence towards the Catholic community, which once again confirmed the link between religion and nationalism. Elizabeth had understood how to hold the two together, for the purpose of achieving stability and, especially, filling the state's coffers. This was not the case with James I, who could not nor would not understand the extent of anti-Catholic feeling and rhetoric. This apparent naiveté dogged his dynasty like a black cloud, which set the stage for, among other things, the execution of Charles I, and the dethronement of James II following the restoration of the monarchy in the second half of the century.

The role played by pamphlet and dramatic literatures was fundamental in the origin and development of anti-Catholic rhetoric and ideas. The power of the printed word and the stage combined to create a political force out of what, at the beginning, had been merely a political expedient contrived by the crown. The two media certainly became an exceptional propaganda tool, an instrument by means of which a great variety of political and religious actors moulded public opinion via the transmission of all sorts of messages, both in favour of and in opposition to the *status quo*. Reformist drama assumed the mantle of heir to medieval religious and allegorical theatre, and adapted its format to the evolving needs of a new Protestant England. The allegories became more flexible, and broadened their thematic scope to include moral issues that, in many cases, concealed clear political and socioeconomic criticism.

The doctrinal character of the Reformation's first phase in England gradually gave way to a steady development of the Catholic stereotype which, during the reign of Mary I, and especially after 1580, merged with the Spanish stereotype. Playwrights adopted and expanded upon aspects of the character types on stage and, by so doing, enriched the uniform and monolithic nature of the medieval vices. These, in turn, were seen as influenced by the buffoonish types inherited from the classical period, such as the *miles gloriosus* or the *parasitus*. The confluence of these distinct traditions – medieval anticlericalism, classical comedy, and even the new Italian *commedia erudita* – engendered a portrayal of Catholic characters that, in some cases, replaced a threatening demeanour with one that was merely comical. The influence of other genres, such as the historical or biblical drama and the saints' tragedy, enriched the allegorical works, which were able to remain popular even with the commercial expansion that the theatre experienced after 1576. Not only was anti-Catholicism not diminished by this expansion, it became a guarantee of box-office success. The interests of playwrights, as those of their patrons and theatre impresarios, thus extended beyond mere political or religious protest.

Most of all, the appeal to national unity in the face of the danger posed by Rome and Spain was the sole means by which Protestant England achieved a measure of stability amid deep religious divisions. Even so, such unity consistently revealed another truth: the exclusion of many of their Catholic countrymen, who were denied their English identity in spite of their continuous declarations of loyalty to the crown. The dualist rhetoric of anti-Catholicism was a stratagem that did not go unnoticed by many playwrights, who questioned it onstage and revealed to their audiences the many contradictions hidden within it. In contrast to the one-dimensional nature of the pamphlet literature, the theatre showed the many and varied faces of the conflict. The arguments of one faction or another were expounded before the spectators, who at times must have had conflicting feelings toward particular heroes[52] and their antagonists. Whether intentionally or not, the dramatists appealed to the people's prejudices and fears, and challenged their attitudes towards these persecuted groups, Catholic or Puritan. Many of these plays analysed the reasons for such behaviours, and proposed a variety of responses. They represented, therefore, an opportunity for reflection on the religious, political and socioeconomic changes in the country, concealed within the facade of anti-Catholic attacks. The discourse of anti-Catholicism served, hence, as a tool for debate in the new Protestant England which, because of its break with Rome and the Tudors' affirmation of empire, also used it to construct its religious and national identity, even if at the expense of many of its subjects.

Notes

Prologue

1. Anne McLaren "Gender, Religion, and Early Modern Nationalism: Elizabeth I, Mary Queen of Scots, and the Genesis of English Anti-Catholicism", *American Historical Review* 2002, 107.3: 739–767, p. 740.
2. As an example, historians such as Peter Lake, Christopher Haigh, Eamon Duffy, Anthony Milton, Peter Holmes, Arnold Pritchard, Christopher Hill and John Bossy stand out. Noteworthy among literary critics are Carol Z. Wiener, Arthur Marotti, Alison Shell, Frances E. Dolan, Huston Diehl, Paul Christianson, C. A. Patrides and Joseph Wittreich.
3. These were usually members of the middle class, educated in universities or Inns of Court; on the other hand, the social distribution of the readers of such writings included everything from apprentices, artisans or merchants, to members of the nobility. See Joad Raymond, *Pamphlets and Pamphleteering in Early Modern England*, Cambridge, Cambridge University Press, 2002, pp. 58–59.
4. As the market for printed texts developed, these became more autonomous and independent of their authors, a fact that favoured anonymity and the use of pseudonyms. Raymond, *Pamphlets and Pamphleteering*, p. 97.
5. Alexandra Halasz, *The Marketplace of Print. Pamphlets and the Public Sphere in Early Modern England*, Cambridge, Cambridge University Press, 1997, pp. 14–15.
6. Frances E. Dolan, *Whores of Babylon. Catholicism, Gender and Seventeenth Century Print Culture*, Ithaca, Cornell University Press, 1999, p. 26.
7. Joy Wiltenburg, *Disorderly Women and Female Power in the Street Literature of Early Modern England and Germany*, Charlottesville, University of Virginia Press, 1992, p. 30.
8. Dolan, *Whores of Babylon*, p. 29.
9. Peter Matheson, *The Rhetoric of the Reformation*, Edinburgh, T&T Clark, 1998, p. 6.
10. Marco Tulio Cicerón, *El Orador*, Translated by Antonio Tovar and Aurelio R. Bujaldón, Madrid, CSIC, 1992, p. 35. Cited in José Luis Sánchez Lora, "Retórica, oralidad y lectura en la Edad Moderna", *Cuadernos de Historia Moderna Anejos*, 2002, I, 65–84, p. 76.
11. Umberto Eco, *Obra abierta*, Barcelona, Ariel, 1984, p. 67.
12. Halasz, *The Marketplace of Print*, p. 79.
13. John King, *English Reformation Literature. The Tudor Origins of the Protestant Tradition*, Princeton, Princeton University Press, 1982, p. 285.
14. John Gillis, *The Geography of Difference*, Cambridge, Cambridge University Press, 1994, p. 9.

15 Fustel de Coulanges, "Religion as the Constituent Principle of the Ancient Family and City", *Sociology and Religion. A Book of Readings*, Norman Birnbaum & Gertrud Lenzer (Eds), New Jersey, Prentice Hall, 1969, 110–126, pp. 117–119.
16 Karl Ulrich Syndram, "The Aesthetics of Alterity", *National Identity - Symbol and Representation*, J. Th. Leerssen & M. Spiering (Eds), Amsterdam, Rodopi, 1991, 177–190, pp. 188–189.
17 Sigmund Freud, *Psicología de las masas. Obras Completas*, James Strachey (Ed.), Paraguay, Amorrotu Editores, 1995, vol. XVIII, 65–136, pp. 74–75.
18 Nigel Fabb defines intertextuality as a relationship between texts, whether literary or not, and whether they belong to the same or different eras. Intersubjectivity, on the other hand, includes the relationship of any text with other spheres of knowledge that the reader should bear in mind in order to interpret the text correctly. See Nigel Fabb, *Linguistics and Literature*, Oxford, Blackwell, 1997, pp. 259–260.
19 Four basic works of Renaissance emblem literature and iconology in England have been considered: the *Emblematum Liber* (1531) or *Emblemas* by Andrea Alciatus; *A Choice of Emblemes* (1586) by Geoffrey Whitney, a translation and adaptation of Alciatus's emblems into English; the *Iconologia* (1603) by Cesare Ripa; and *Minerva Britanna* (1612) by Henry Peacham. Although only the first work is contemporary with the period covered in this research, the remainder constitute a compilation of the total iconographic tradition begun in classical antiquity, such that, although they were published after many of the works analysed here, they may still be useful in their study.

CHAPTER ONE Anti-Catholic Discourse during the Reigns of Henry VIII (1509–1547) and Edward VI (1547–1553)

1 These were known as "The Pilgrimage of Grace", and originated in various parts of the northwest and east of England. Their apparent religious motives and the hatred shown towards the principal agents of the new regime (Cranmer, Cromwell and Rich) did not hide the socioeconomic causes of these protests, which were provoked by changes introduced in property laws, the distribution of lands expropriated from the Church, and new royal taxes. See Claire Cross, *Church and the People 1450–1660. The Triumph of the Laity in the English Church*, Atlantic Highlands, New Jersey, Humanities Press Inc., 1976, pp. 65–69.
2 In Brewer et al. (Eds), *Letters and Papers, Foreign and Domestic of the Reign of Henry VIII, 1509–1547*, London, 1862–1910, 1920, vol. III, doc. 1772. References in this work are listed by document number rather than page number.
3 In fact, Luther responded quickly to the first German translations of the *Assertio* in 1522, an attack that received the support of other Lutherans, such as Thomas Murner, and was criticized by English Catholic authors such as John Fisher, Thomas More and John Eck. See E. Doenberg, *Henry VIII and Luther*, Stanford, Stanford University Press, 1961, pp. 35 and ff.
4 Philip Erlanger, *Enrique VIII*, Barcelona, Salvat, 1986, pp. 94–95.

5 Juan Luis Vives, John Fisher, Thomas de Vio, Cardinal Cayetano, Belarmino, Vitoria, Thomas Abel, Fernando de Loazes and Bartolomeo de Spinia, among others. For more information on the support that these figures offered to Queen Catherine by means of the works they wrote in her defence, see J. J. Scarisbrick, *Henry VIII*, Eyre & Spottiswoode, 1968, pp. 166–167.
6 *A Glasse of the Truthe*, London, 1532, sigs B1v-B2r.
7 In Edward Hall, *Hall's Chronicle; Containing the History of England, during the Reign of Henry the Fourth, and the Succeeding Monarchs, the End of the Reign of Henry the Eighth in which are Particularly Described the Manners and Customs of those Periods*, London, 1809, pp. 754 and ff.
8 Italian cardinal, lawyer and humanist, he was nuncio to five popes between 1511 and 1539, ambassador of Emperor Maximilian between 1511 and 1513, and spoke at the assemblies of Regensburg (1524) and Augsburg (1530). He was made Bishop of Salisbury in 1524, and in 1528 acted as co-legate with Cardinal Wolsey in the dispute about the marriage of Henry and Catherine of Aragon.
9 It continues, "to God's great displeasure . . . These be the sores that vex my mind, these be the pangs that trouble my conscience and fore these griefes I seek a remedy." Edward Hall, *Hall's Chronicle*, pp. 754 and ff.
10 The text focuses on a precept of the Hebrew religion known as the levirate (from the Latin *levir*: brother-in-law).
11 The problem of reconciling two such disparate texts as these passages from Leviticus and Deuteronomy had been discussed on many occasions prior to the debate over Henry's divorce. Almost all theologians had treated the subject of marriage and its impediments, some even posing the same questions as Henry VIII. Of course, the opinions differed on almost every point. Scarisbrick analyses some of them and their relationship to the problem (pp. 167–173).
12 It was said that the bull was the result of a misunderstanding between diplomats of the two countries, who tried to seal an alliance with the marriage, when the two countries were already allies. Henry VIII's youth was also offered as proof, in that the bull had been invalidated by the time it was used (some six years after it was procured).
13 See David Loades, *Enrique VIII y sus reinas*, Barcelona, Plaza y Janés, 1999, pp. 97–98.
14 Thus it was stated that no English citizen could be called to appear before the court of Rome, as the former privileges and traditions of the Realm of England did not permit its citizens to be subject to foreign laws. See Brewer et al. *Letters and Paper*, vol. IV, doc. 6667.
15 Scarisbrick, *Henry VIII*, p. 261.
16 The complete title is *Articles Devisid by the Holle Consent of the Kynges moste Honourable Counsayle, his Gracis Licence Opteined therto, not only to Exhorte but also to Enfourme his Louynge Subiectis of the Trouthe*.
17 Thomas F. Mayer examines this confrontation between the king and Rome in his article "On the Road to 1534: the Occupation of Tournai and Henry VIII's Theory of Sovereignty," included in the work by Dale Hoak, *Tudor Political Culture*, Cambridge, Cambridge University Press, 1995, 11–30.

18 Alfonso de Valdés, *Diálogo de las cosas acaecidas en Roma*, Rosa Navarro Durán (Ed.), Madrid, Cátedra, 1992, p. 95.
19 In *A Glasse of the Truthe*, numerous references are made to England's internal conflicts, where a high proportion of the people did not accept the new changes. Blame for them is placed on those subjects who allow themselves to be led by Rome's supposed machinations and who neither listen to nor value the king's words and actions (sigs B2v, B3r, B8r, C2v-C6r).
20 The pope's disregard for the decisions made in the general councils justifies this disobedience. In the Elizabethan period, the reasoning is of another kind, and is based on the subordination of religious power to the absolute authority of the prince.
21 A. F. Pollard, *Henry VIII*, London, Longmans, 1930, pp. 298–299.
22 Brewer, *Letters and Papers*, vol. VI, docs 451, 487, 653, 807.
23 This idea is strengthened by enumerating several cases in which saints came to disobey papal power. See *A Glasse of the Truthe*, sigs E1r-v.
24 Cross, *Church and the People*, pp. 31–80.
25 Richard Grafton, *Abridgement of the Chronicles of Englande*, London, 1589, p. 164.
26 R. Whiting, "Abominable Idols: Images and Image-Breaking under Henry VIII", *Journal of Ecclesiastical History*, 1982, 33, 30–47, p. 33.
27 Ibid; p. 55.
28 Margaret Aston, "Iconoclasm in England: Official and Clandestine", *Iconoclasm vs Art and Drama*, Clifford Davidson & Ann Eljenholm Nichols (Eds), Michigan, Western Michigan University, 1989, 47–91, pp. 65–72.
29 Cited in J. R. Dasent (Ed.), *Acts of the Privy Council of England*, London, Eyre and Spottiswoode, 1890–1907, vol. II, p. 29.
30 Cited in John Strype, (Ed.), *Memorials of the Most Reverend Father in God Thomas Cranmer Sometime Lord Archbishop of Canterbury*, Oxford, Clarendon Press, 1840, vol. I, p. 206.
31 Cross, *Church and the People*, p. 82.
32 Ibid., pp. 88–90, 100
33 This phenomenon was not exclusive to England, since similar denunciations had already been heard in other parts of Europe. Perhaps the most visible exponent was Marsilius of Padua, who, in his *Defensor Pacis* (1324) spoke of the need to return to evangelical poverty and attacked clerical ambition and power. The Italian scholar described Rome as a cradle of vice and corruption: "[T]he faithful [. . .] will clearly see for themselves that it has become the refuge of almost every villain and huckster, both spiritual and temporal; while those who have kept away from it will learn the same thing from the tales of a large number of trustworthy faithful. For what else is to be found there except a concourse of simoniacs from all parts? What else but the din of lawyers for hire, insults of slanderers and affronts to just men? There justice for innocents is either endangered or – if they cannot buy it for a price – deferred so long that they are ultimately forced to relinquish their just and pitiable suits from exhaustion, worn out with countless efforts. For there the laws of men thunder from on high while divine teachings are silent or all too rarely make a sound[.]" *The Defender of the Peace*,

34 *The Lantern of Lizt*, L. M. Swimburg (Ed.), London, K. Paul Trench, Trübner & Co. Lld., 1917, p. 41.
35 Ibid; p. 16.
36 *The Holy Bible . . . in the Earliest Version Made from the Latin Vulgate by John Wicliffe and his Followers*, J. Forshall & F. Madden (Eds), Oxford, 1850, vol. I, p. 34.
37 J. F. Davis, "Lollards, Reformers, and St. Thomas of Canterbury", *University of Birmingham Historical Journal*, 1963, 9, 1–15, pp. 9, 13.
38 Walter Lynne, *The Beginning and Endyng of all Popery*, London, 1548, sig. C4r. This pamphlet is based on the German translation of the *Vaticinia* of Joachim de Fiore (1130–1201), an Italian mystic theologian of strongly apocalyptic tendencies, whose prophecies were greatly influential among a broad range of religious groups and communities until well into the sixteenth century.
39 John Bale, *The Three Laws*, London, 1547, sigs F1v-F2r.
40 See also John Bale, *King Johan* (1539). *The Complete Plays of John Bale*, Peter Happé (Ed.), Suffolk, St. Edmundsbury Press, 1985, vol. I, I, 370 (the quote belongs to the first part of the work; it refers to the verse line, not the page).
41 *The Beginning and Endyng*, sig. C3r; *King Johan*, I, 469, 1355–1357; II, 2399, 2540–2541; *The Three Laws*, sigs F3r-I3v. See also the references in the two anonymous pamphlets *A Treatise wherin Christ and his Teachinges are Compared with the Pope and his Doinges*, London, 1534, pp. 12r, 13r-v, 19r; and *The Hunting and Finding out of the Romish Fox*, London, 1543, sigs A8r. B5v, B7v, B8r.
42 The song ridicules Catholic vestments and rituals, and once again their lack of concern for God's message, lost in their attempts to hoard wealth. Bale makes use of rhyme, alliteration and repetition in order to provoke the audience's laughter: "[Sedicyon:] For I perceve welle the Pope is a joyle fellawe,/ A trymme fellawe, a ryche fellawe, yea, and myry fellawe./ [Imperyall Majestye:] A jolye fellawe how dost thu prove the Pope?/ [Sedicyon:] For he hath cross keyes with a tryple crowne and a cope, Trymme as a trencher, havynge hys shoes of golde, Ryche in his ryalte and angelyck to beholde./ [Imperyall Majestye:] How dost thu prove hym to be a fellawe myrye?/ [Sedicyon:] He hath pypes and belles, with kyrye, kyrye, kyrye./ Of hym ye maye bye both salt, creame, oyle and waxe./ And after hygh masse ye maye learne to beare the paxe./ [Imperyall Majestye:] Yea, and nothynge heare of the Pystle and the Gospell?/ [Sedicyon:] No, sir, by the masse; he will gyve no suche counsell" (II, 2557–2568).
43 The use of Latin in religious services was according to the reformers one of the main means by which the Church of Rome kept its followers in ignorance, another idea that they inherited from the Lollards, which explains these authors' insistence on the need to use the vernacular for the reading of biblical texts and in church ceremonies.
44 *King Johan*, I, 415–427; II, 1550–1555, 1841–1842; *The Three Laws*, sigs F3r-v. The comparison that is made between them and the figure of the

donkey (Ibid; sig. F3r), the Renaissance emblem of ignorance, emphasizes the supposed stupidity of Catholics.
45 "We hold still hallowyng of chirches and of vestementes and that a prest may not say masse but in a hallowed place with out a superaltare" (*The Hunting and Finding*, sig. A7r).
46 Although written in 1537, it was not published until 1565, in the middle of the reign of Elizabeth I, so it portrays the conflicts that were of concern in both periods.
47 *Albion Knight*, London, 1565, 27–34 (the number of lines is given; there is no division into acts and scenes). In the quote there may be a reference to the emblems and iconologies of False Religion – *Religione Finta* – in which a woman appears adorned with magnificent jewels and ornaments of gold. See Cesare Ripa, *Iconología*, Juan Yago Barja (Ed. and Tran.), Madrid, Akal, 1987, vol. II, p. 263. Alciatus's emblem VI, *Ficta Religio*, is also very revealing. See Santiago Sebastián's edition of Alciatus's emblems (Madrid, Akal, 1993). In contrast, Justice is associated with True Religion, which, like this character in the play, appears dressed in white in Ripa's *Iconología* (vol. II, p. 262). This figure is portrayed in contrast to Slander and Injury, the names of its antagonists.
48 Margaret Aston, *England Iconoclasts. Laws against Images*, Oxford, Clarendon Press, 1988, p. 7.
49 See Gillis, *The Geography of Difference*, p. 29. A number of authors accuse the pope of becoming an idol that believers worship, thus emphasizing his blasphemous character, since he attempts to substitute himself for God: "He [the Pope] calleth hym here ydoll, not for his unhappy worshipping of ydols, but bicause he wolle be worshypped of the people as he were god" (*A Treatise*, p. 22).
50 The meanings associated with this type of animal figures underlines the use of this metaphor. The fox, for example, was considered to be symbolic of the devil during the Middle Ages, and was associated with cunning and falsity in the symbolic literature of the Renaissance, as is seen in the emblems used by Peacham, *In dilapidantes sibi credita aliena*, where it represents a false and traitorous friend (p. 70) and *Dolis minime fidendum*, where it appears as a symbol of pride and vanity (p. 138). The dog, on the other hand, although it usually represented obedience, could also suggest very negative references to falsehood and envy. See the emblem of *Persuasion* (Ripa, *Iconología*, vol. II, p. 203) and the emblems 44 (*Desiderium spe vacuum*) and 184 (*Nec sibi nec alteri*) by Whitney, an author who also considered them symbolic of stupidity (emblem 213, *Inanis impetus*) and greed (emblem 39, *Mediocribus utere partis*).
51 This same image appears in *King Johan*, wherein Henry VIII is presented as a new David (I, 1114) who will liberate England from the Catholic yoke. Comparisons to other biblical characters such as Moses and Joshua (I, 1107–1113) also stress his character as guide and liberator of his people. The Reformation, in fact, revived the nationalism of the Old Testament, and adopted as its own the three traits that defined it: the idea of the elect, that of historical national consciousness, and national messianism. See Hans Kohn, *Historia del nacionalismo*, Samuel Cosío

Villegas (Trad.), Ciudad de México, Fondo de Cultura Económica, 1949, p. 44.

52 Margaret Aston, *The King's Bedpost, Reformation and Iconography in Tudor or Group Portrait*, Cambridge, Cambridge University Press, 1993, p. 43.

53 This took place following Cromwell's downfall in 1540, when the king's conservative policies intensified. He was exiled for the second time after Mary I's accession to the throne.

54 White points out other spaces used by such companies, such as abbeys and universities, which would indicate a wide variety of spectators. See Paul W. White, *Theatre and Reformation. Protestantism, Patronage, and Playing in Tudor England*, Cambridge, Cambridge University Press, 1993, p. 25.

55 See T. W. Craik (Ed.), *The Revels History of Drama in English*. 1500–1576, London, New York, Methuen, 1980, vol. II, p. 183.

56 The work is divided into two acts, united by the character of Interpretour, a narrator who serves as a link between the two parts, which portray two time periods separated by a span of seven years. The first act begins with a description of the desolation of the country, represented allegorically by the character Englande, who goes to the king in search of help. After listening to her complaint, in which the clergy is blamed for social and political chaos, the king decides to consult representatives of the church and the nobility. This dialogue alternates with the comings and goings of Sedicyon, the play's antagonist, who informs the king of the corruption of all the kingdom's estates, especially the ecclesiastical. This leads to the first confrontation between Johan and these estates which, at first, acknowledge their guilt and swear obedience to the monarch. Nevertheless, their oath is false, and soon the clergy's true intentions are discovered, which is to maintain their position of privilege and their allegiance to the Holy See. Though they are reluctant to do so, the nobility are finally convinced to overthrow the king. The conversation between Sedicyon and Dissymulacyon confirms these plans. The two promise to bring together the remaining vices (Private Wealth and Usurpid Powre) to provoke the country's spiritual decline and end Johan's life. For seven years the king attempts to reform the nation, but all his efforts are in vain. The second act begins with the king cornered by the forces of Catholicism – seen now as represented in every group in society, including the people (Communalty) – and unable to stop the war that is destroying the country. In the face of imminent foreign invasion, Johan surrenders himself and the crown to his adversaries. The pathos of the play reaches its peak when Johan is poisoned by Dissymulacyon. At the end, order is restored following the speeches of Veritas and Imperyall Majestye, who decide to grant forgiveness after hearing the repentance and promises of obedience from the nobility, the clergy and the English people.

57 These eliminate the abstract aspect of allegory and stress the real nature of the danger that threatens them.

58 Refers to Pandulfo, legate of the pope, although in reality he was never a cardinal (Happé, p. 12).

59 Happé, p. 95.

60 Infidelitas looks for Idolatria and Sodomismus so that they might corrupt

the Law of Nature; the former will try to poison the heart of the nobility, while the latter will focus on the clergy. Infidelitas continues in his mission, giving a new tandem formed by Ambicio and Avaritia the job of destroying the Law of Moses. To do this, they will have to deceive the rulers and the people so that they seek only profits and good social and economic position. The final law to overthrow is the Gospel, or the Law of Christ, a mission that Hypocrisie and Pseudodoctrina take on. They focus their efforts on imposing the pope's authority, and with it, all the traditions and ceremonies of the Church of Rome. Therefore, the action takes shape gradually. Each pair of characters destroys one of God's laws, in ascending order, since the laws are organized as to their importance, as are those who defend them – Nature, Moses, Christ – and the punishments that they receive, which get tougher as the action progresses. At the end, and faced with the decline of the three laws, divine vengeance falls upon Infidelitas and his allies. Vindicta Dei, guided by God, returns to establish the Kingdom of God and spread the true principles of God's doctrine throughout the world.

61 Son of Henry II, who, upon the death of his brother, Richard the Lionheart, murdered his nephew Arthur in Rouen in 1203; summoned by Philip Augustus to answer for the crime in France, he refused to appear and was declared a traitor and stripped of his French lands. Following a conflict with the Holy See, which provoked yet another intervention by the King of France and a revolt among the English barons and prelates, he was defeated at Bouvines (1214) and forced to concede to the barons the famous *Magna Carta* of English liberties (1215). See *Encyclopaedia Britannica* and Kenneth Morgan, *The Oxford Illustrated History of Britain*, Oxford, Oxford University Press, 1984, pp. 129–133.

62 Happé, p. 99.

63 C. A. Patrides & Joseph Wittreich (Eds.), *The Apocalypse in English Renaissance Thought and Literature. Patterns, Antecedents and Repercussions*, Ithaca, New York, Cornell University Press, 1984, p. 94. Other reformist groups outside England also made use of this idea. The most relevant example was that of the *Magdeburg Centuries* (1556–1587). Originally proposed by the Lutheran Flacius Illyricus (Mathias Francowitz, 1520–1575), their aim was to bestow a historical tradition upon the Protestant Church that began in the Primitive Church. A team of nearly fifteen authors participated in the project and alternated during the various stages of the work's composition. Although the book had little influence in the reformed world, it encountered an ample response in the Catholic sphere by generating controversy and giving rise to numerous works of rebuttal. José L. De Orella and Unzúe have carried out a detailed study of the Catholic reception of the Magdeburg Centuries in *Respuestas católicas a las Centurias de Magdeburgo* (1559–1588), Madrid, Fundación Universitaria Española, 1976.

64 The main vice in *King Johan* is Sedicyon, a political term that directly refers to the seditious activities of English subjects that were caused, according to the reformers, by the influence of the pope in the country.

65 The pamphlets stressed the danger that was represented by the ambitions

of the Bishop of Rome, whom they blamed for causing wars between Christian kingdoms in an attempt to weaken their power (*A Treatise*, pp. 11–25; *The Beginning and Endyng*, sigs C2r-C4v). According to the authors, the pontiff obeyed no laws whatsoever (*A Treatise*, pp. 14–15) and used all kinds of devices to usurp the power of rulers, from excommunication of those monarchs who failed to comply with his wishes (*A Treatise*, pp. 14–15) to provoking internal divisions that encouraged civil disobedience. These accusations are presented by the use of metaphors that underscore the pope's cruelty. On numerous occasions, he is compared with animals, such as the wolf (*The Three Laws*, sig. I2v; *The Beginning*, sigs F1r, H1v), the bear (Ibid; sig. D1r) and all sorts of mythical beasts and monsters (*King Johan*, II, 2425-2430; *The Three Laws*, sigs F3r, G1). All of these are synonymous with violence and aggression in Renaissance emblem literature.

66 Cross, *Church and the People*, pp. 17–18.
67 Scarisbrick, *Enrique VIII*, pp. 358–364.
68 The play is incomplete and lacks evidence of its performance either in a prologue or epilogue, as they have not been preserved. Despite being produced during the reign of Henry VIII, it did not emerge onto the record until the Elizabethan period, specifically, August 1565.
69 See Ripa, *Iconología*, vol. II, p. 183.
70 Refers to the line number
71 Cross, *Church and the People,* pp. 64–65.
72 This is the symbol of ignorance and vulgarity in Alciatus' emblem CXXXIX.
73 It is likely that the work was performed by the Lord Protector's Men before a general audience. See King, *English Reformation Literature*, p. 274.
74 Refers to the line number.
75 Conscience's accusation against this character doubtless signals the corruption of the high-ranking leaders who had used the expropriated lands for dishonest ends: "Restore soche goodes as ye have gotten/ wrongefully by oppressyon" (342–343) or "God forfende that shoulde be/ Howe shall men doo that be of greate reputacyon/ Whyche kepte theyr goodes on this same fashyon/ By ususry, dysceypte, and by extorcyon" (334–336).
76 All those related to characteristics of the Catholic stereotype, such as corruption, simony, lust and dissimulation
77 The author's attitude toward Catholicism is sometimes paradoxical. The association of the character Peace with the Catholic community, for example, seems not to be accidental, as his indirect defence of the doctrine of merits as a mode of salvation demonstrated: "Everi man shulde folowe his trace/ That in heaven wyl clayme a place" (99–100).
78 White suggests the possibility that William Hunnis (a nobleman connected to the choir of the Royal Chapel during the reigns of Edward VI and Mary I) wrote it. For further information on the debate regarding Hunnis's possible authorship, see White, *Theatre and Reformation*, pp. 118–119.
79 In this case, the epilogue would have been added in the 1568 edition.
80 Medieval biblical plays continued to enjoy great popularity in England until the 1550s. After that time, they diminish in number due to the persistent

work of the censors on material touching on religious themes. Even so, in some cases dramatists managed to avoid the censor by making use of the temporal and geographical distance between these plays and contemporary reality. See Louis B. Wright, "The Scriptures and the Elizabethan Stage," *Modern Philology*, 1928, 26, 47–56, pp. 47–56.

81 The character of Rebecca is not without controversy: not only does she drive the dramatic action and take an active position despite being a woman, but the methods that she makes use of are Machiavellian (secrecy, lies, and cunning), closer to the behavior of a villain than a virtuous person. Her rejection of her own son (Esau) highlights her anti-natural character and, with that, puts all her actions in question: "I deede syr, I can not love Esau so well/ As I doe Iacob, the plaine truth to you I tell" (I, iv, 99–100).

82 See Ripa, *Iconología*, vol. I, pp. 475–476.

83 In Nordic mythology, for example, the wolf was considered the prince of evil. See Juan E. Cirlot, *Diccionario de símbolos tradicionales*, Barcelona; Ediciones Luis Miracles, 1958, p. 268. Ripa uses this image repeatedly in the iconologies of Greed (vol I, pp. 122–123), Mischief (vol. II, p. 198) and Plague (vol. II, p. 205).

84 The tough theatrical legislation of 1549 would not have permitted it, since it punished harshly those plays that opposed the regime's official doctrine. See Craik, *The Revels History*, pp. 26–27.

85 The play which celebrated the new king's coronation was a deliberate anti-Catholic attack, as it can be assumed from the inventory listing the actors' wardrobe, which included the vestments of friars, priests and cardinals, in addition to a tiara and a cross for the part of the pope. See Anglo, *Spectacle Pageantry*, p. 295. Other sources suggest that Edward VI himself played some of the roles in this play, among them that of the priest. See Albert Feuillerat, *Documents Relating to the Revels at Court in the Time of King Edward VI and Queen Mary*, Louvain, A. Uystruyst, 1914, pp. 3–8, 255–258. This author also adds references to the performance of *The Tower of Babylon* during the Christmas of 1547 and a play in which there appeared priests, hermits, and a dragon with seven heads, in February 1549. Finally, it seems possible that various performances featuring hermits, monks and pilgrims were prepared during Christmas of the same year. See pp. 26, 39–43, 266–267, 269–270.

CHAPTER TWO Mary I (1553–1558) and the Discourse of Victimhood

1 S. T. Bindoff, *Tudor England*, London, Penguin Books, 1950, pp. 147–166.

2 Many of them, such as John Hooper, John Royers, Hugh Latimer and Nicholas Ridley, defied the royal decree and were arrested. Archbishop Cranmer was also jailed for criticizing Catholic Mass. Reformist literature was confiscated, and fears of a revival of the anti-heresy laws were renewed. See Alison Weir, *Children of England. The Heirs of King Henry VIII*, London, Pimlico, 1996, p. 206.

3 See Cristina H. Garret, *The Marian Exiles: A Study in the Origins of Elizabethan Puritanism*, Cambridge, Cambridge University Press, 1938.

4 For more information on these negotiations, see E. H. Harbison, *Rival*

Ambassadors at the Court of Queen Mary. London, Oxford University Press, 1940.

5 Cited in Weir, *Children of England*, p. 282. Nevertheless, Mary was not always disposed to accept this subordinate position with regard to her husband, one of the main reasons for Philip's failure to be satisfied with their marriage.

6 The words of Queen Mary to the Imperial Ambassador shortly before being crowned were quite explicit in this regard: "After God, I desire to obey no one but the Emperor, whom I have always looked upon as a father; I am determined to follow his Majesty's advice and choose whomsoever he might recommend". Cited in Weir, *Children of England*, p. 187.

7 Bindoff, *Tudor England*, p. 172.

8 The portrait that the Jacobean chronicler John Stow paints of the Tudor queen once the rebellion was quelled is quite significant, contrasting with the image of her as cruel and bloodthirsty that would later be forged. Stow describes her as a compassionate and merciful monarch, capable of pardoning subjects who had before risen against her: "The 22 of February, certaine of Wiats faction to the number of 400 and more, were led to Westminster, coupled together with halters about their neckes, and there in the Ciltyard, the Quene . . . pardoned them". See John Stow, *The Abridgement of the English Chronicle*, London, 1618, p. 269. The majority of those implicated in Wyatt's revolt were able to return to their homes without charges, and only those nobles suspected of complicity were jailed.

9 See James A. Williamson, *The Tudor Age*, London, Longman, 1979, pp. 227–229.

10 Nevertheless, the opulence of the pageantry is interpreted by John Foxe in his *Book of Martyrs* in a contrary sense, as one more example of the Catholic love of ornament and ostentation. Foxe describes the indignation of Cranmer – the Protestant Archbishop who would be executed a year later – throughout the ceremony: "They came into the church with great solemnity and pomp, the kyng first, then every estate in order . . . The Cardinal did execute with muche singing and organe playing: The people stode with great devotion and silence, praying, looking, kneeling, and knocking, theyr mindes beyng fully bend and set (as it is the manner) upon the externall sacrament. It cannot be spoken how grevously these thynges dyd pricke and move this young man's minde, partly to beholde the miserable absurditie of those thynges, partly to see the foly of the common people: not onely of the common people, but specially when he saw the King himselfe, and the Kinges counsayle with so many sage and wise men so seduced with like Idolatrie". See John Foxe, *Actes and Monuments of these Latter and Perillous Dayes Touching Matters of the Church wherin Are Comprehended and Described the Great Persecutions & Horrible Troubles that Have Been Wrought and Practised by the Romishe Prelates, Specially in this Realme of England and Scotland, from the Yeare of our Lorde a Thousand, unto the Tyme Now Present*, London, 1563, fol. 876.

11 Elder's chronicle, entitled *John Elder's Letter Describing the Arrival and Marriage of King Philip, his Triumphal Entry into London, the Legation of Cardinal Pole, &c*, is included as an appendix in the work by John

Gough Nichols (Ed.), *The Chronicle of Queen Jane, and of the Two Years of Queen Mary, and especially of the Rebellion of Sir Thomas Wyatt*, London, Candem Society, 1850. The electronic version (www.tudorhistory.org/ primary/janemary/title.html) is cited herein.

12 The intervention of authors such as Richard Grafton, the King's Printer under Edward VI, when he had shown clear reformist tendencies, confirms the difficulty of the task, which represented a complete turnaround from the objectives of similar pageants in other times and thus obstructed an entirely coherent productions. For more information on the various individuals involved in the production of the royal entry, see Anglo, *Spectacle Pageantry*, p. 326.

13 According to *The History of the Kings of Britain* by Geoffrey of Monmouth (1155), two Trojans, Corineus and Brutus, the great-grandson of Aeneas, conquered England after exterminating the giants who lived there. Corineus, the founder of Cornwall, destroyed the giant Gogmagog and so restored order and peace, thus opening the way for the foundation of England – New Troy. According to this myth, the Tudors were of Welsh or British ancestry; therefore, when the Tudor dynasty occupied the English throne, the former race of Trojan-British kings had returned to assume imperial power, inaugurating a Golden Age for England. See Frances A. Yates, *Astraea. The Imperial Theme in the Sixteenth Century*, London, Boston, Routledge, Kegan Paul, 1975, pp. 5–23, 50.

14 See Arthur Kinney, *Renaissance Drama: An Anthology of Plays and Entertainments*, Oxford, Blackwell, 1999, pp. 22, 31, 33, 34.

15 This idea is repeated on the second stage, which relates the Spanish prince to King Philip of Macedon, the father of Alexander the Great, founder of the Alexandrian empire.

16 See the 1597 edition of Foxe's work: *The Seconde Volume of the Ecclesiasticall Historie Conteyning the Acts and Monuments of Martyrs, with a Generall Discourse of these Latter Persecutions, Horrible Troubles and Tumulte, Stirred up by Romish Prelates in the Church, with Divers Other Things Incident, Especially to this Realme of England and Scotland, as Partly Also to All Other Forreine Nations Appertaining, from the Time of King Henry the VIII to Quene Elizabeth our Gracious Ladie Now Raigning. Newly Recognised and Inlarged by the author Iohn Foxe.* London, fol. 1338.

17 See emblem CLXXX of Alciatus, *Eloquentia Fortitudine Praestantior* (Eloquence, surpassing strength).

18 Weir, *Children of England*, p. 162

19 *An Act for the Renewing of Three Statutes Made for the Punishment of Heresies.*

20 Williamson, *The Tudor Age*, pp. 234–235.

21 Weir, *Children of England*, p. 293.

22 John Old, *A Short Description of Antichrist unto the Nobilitie of England, and to all my Brethen and Countreymen Borne and Dwelling therin, with a Warnyng to See that They Be not Deceaved by the Hypocritical and Crafty Conveyaunce of the Clergie*, Emden, 1555, sig. E3r.

23 Ibid; sig. E7r.

24 Grafton, *Abridgement of the Chronicles of England*, p. 186.
25 The English people are described as the immediate victims of their rulers' decisions. Their Catholic beliefs are seen as be result of the supposed deception to which they have been subjected by their Catholic leaders.
26 *An Apology or Defence against the Calumnations of Certayne Men, which Preferring Wylfull Wyll and Carnal Reason before the Playn Trueth of Gods Gospel Do Slaunder those Men, which for the Better Servinge of God with a More Pure Conscience, according to his Holy Word Have Abandonned theyr Livings and Vocation, Abydinge as Exyles in Poore Estate oute of theyr Natyve Countrye*, The location of its printing is unknown.
27 Nicholas Ridley, *Certein Godly, Learned and Comfortable Conferences between the Two Reverend Fathers and Holy Martyrs of Christe Dr. Nicholas Ridley Late Bishoppe of London and M. Hughe Latymer Sometyme Bishoppe of Worcester during the Tyme of theyre Emprysonments*, Emden, 1556.
28 See John Hooper, *Whether Christian Faith May Be Kepte in Secret in the Heart, without Confession thereof Openly*, Roane, 1555, p. 7.
29 See other examples in Ridley, *Certein Godly*, sig. B7v; *An Apology or Defence*, sig. A5v; Thomas Cranmer, *A Confutation of that Popishe and Antichristian Doctryne which Mainteineth the Ministry on and Receiving of the Sacrament under one Kind*, Wesel?, 1555?, sigs A2r-v; Thomas Becon, *An Answer to a Certaine Godly Mannes Lettres Desiring his Frendes Iudgement whether it be Lawfull for a Christian Man to be Present at the Popishe Masse, and other Supersticious Churche Services*, Strasburgh, 1557, sigs A2r-A4r, A7r-A9r.
30 Bartolomew Traheron, *A Warning to England to Repente and to Turne to God from Idolatrie and Poperie*, Wesel, 1558, sig. B3v. See also sigs B4v, B5r-v and B7r in the same work, and other examples in Ridley, *Certein, Godly*, sig. A4v and Turner, *The Hunting of the Fox*, sig. A8r.
31 See examples in Cranmer, *A Confutation of that Popishe*, sigs A3v, A4r; Becon, *An Answer*, sig. A6r; Philip Melanchthon, *A Faithful Admonition of a Certeyne True Pastor and Prophete Sent vnto the Germanes at such a Time as Certain Great Princes Went about to Bryng Alienes into Germany, [and] to Restore the Papacy; the Kingdom of Antichrist. [Et]c Now Tra[n]slated into English for a like Admonicion vnto all true Englyshe Harts; wherby They may Learn and Know how to Consider [and] Receiue the Procedinges of the English Magistrates and Bishops*, London, 1554, sig. A5v.
32 See Grafton, *Abridgement of the Chronicles of England*, p. 184, and Stow, *The Abridgement of the English Chronicle*, p. 270.
33 See Ridley, *Certein, Godly*, sig. D3r and *An Apology or Defence*, sigs A7r, B2v.
34 See Stow, *An Abridgement of the English Chronicle*, pp. 272, 277, and Grafton, *An Abridgement of the Chronicles of England*, pp. 183, 189.
35 Years later, Foxe would include Lady Jane in his list of Protestant martyrs. This is how he describes in the abridged version of *Actes and Monuments* the moment of her execution: "The 12 of February the Lady Jane was

beheaded: to whom two dais before her death was sent M. Fecknam, to reduce her to the Popish religion; whom she constantly and with great power of Gods spirit resisted". See John Foxe, *An Abridgement of the Booke of Actes and Monuments of the Church*, London, 1589, X, 106. Nevertheless, the Queen had initially refused to put to death Lady Jane and her husband, Guilford Dudley, as she considered them to be victims of the ambitious schemes of their parents. However, Wyatt's rebellion was the detonating factor that led her to give in to the pressures of power. See Weir, *Children of England*, pp. 195–200, 249.

36 This pamphlet may have been a new edition of *The Hunting and Finding out of the Romish Fox* (1543), which indicates the similarity of the arguments used by the most radical reformers against the regimes of Henry VIII and Mary Tudor.

37 The mythological dog that guarded the gates of hell.

38 Foxe also portrays Bonner as a cruel and unbalanced character: "nature's worke is thus deformed now/ with belly blowen, and head so swolne, for I shal tel you how:/ This Cannibal in three yeares space/ three hundred martyrs slew:/ they were his food, he loved so blood,/ he spared none he knew." See the 1563 edition of *Actes and Monuments*, fol. 1689.

39 See Weir, *Children of England*, pp. 293–294.

40 See Weir, *Children of England*, pp. 294, 297.

41 The complete title is *Antichrist, that is to Say: A True Report that Antichrist is Come*, Southwarke [Emden], 1556. See pp. 49, 50–53. In one of the letters he wrote to the Queen before his execution, Cranmer argued that to accept the pope's power would be to betray not only the Law of God, but those of England as well. He openly criticized Queen Mary's attitude, and directly accused her of responsibility for her people's misfortune: "I do not beleve that either the kyng or Queenes Maiestie or the nobles of this Realme, or the commons of the same wold ever have consented to receave agayne suche a forrain auctoritie, so iniurious, hurtful and prejudicial as well to the crowne as to the lawes and customes and state of this Realme: as wherby they muste nede acknowledge themselves to be accursed ... That by his [the Pope's] autoritie he subverteth not only the lawes of this Realme, but also the lawes of God." See Thomas Cranmer, *The Copy of Certain Letters Sent to the Quene*, Emden, 1556, sigs A6r, A7v. Similar denunciations appear in sigs B2v, B3r and B7r.

42 Years later John Foxe would add to these negative qualities the extreme seriousness of the Spaniards, in addition to the allegedly authoritarian and disrespectful character of their monarch, an image that he captures in his account of an incident that seems to have taken place during Philip's arrival in England on 20 July 1554: "As he [Philip] set foot upon the land, drewe out his sword and caried it naked in his hand a good pretty way. Then met him ... the Maior of Southampton, with certain commoners, who delivered the keyes of the towne unto the prince, who removed his sword (naked as it was) out of his right hand, into his left hand and so received the keyes of the Maior without any word speaking, or countenance of thankfulnes, after a while delivered the keyes to the Maior againe". See the 1597 edition of *Actes and Monuments*, fol. 1337.

43 Williamson, *The Tudor Age*, p. 237.
44 Weir, *Children of England*, p. 297.
45 See Geoffrey Parker, *La gran estrategia de Felipe II*, Madrid, Alianza Editorial, 1998, pp. 149–150.
46 One of the principal leaders of the Presbyterian movement in Scotland, in 1549 Knox went to England, where he soon rose to prominence in reformist circles. The accession of Mary Tudor to the throne forced him to flee to France and then to Geneva (1554), where he was one of the translators of the Geneva Bible into English. In 1559 he returned to Scotland and helped to establish Presbyterianism. Following the death of the regent Marie de Guise, he contributed to abolishing Catholic worship at the court of Mary Queen of Scots, contributed to her fall, and organized the Protestant Church in Scotland. He died in 1572. See Teófanes Egido López, *Las reformas protestantes*, Madrid, Síntesis, 1992, pp. 135–137 and E. D. Moreau, *La crisis religiosa del siglo XVI*, Valencia, Edicep, 1978, pp. 559–562.
47 The text is found at www.swrb.com/newslett/actualnls/FirBlast.htm. The page numbers are those of the web site.
48 This idea is emphasized by numerous analogies and comparisons to prophetic figures, such as Jeremiah, Ezekiel and Daniel, and to the apostles, charged with preaching repentance as the sole means of achieving salvation (pp. 2–3).
49 Other works that took the same line of attack were *An Humble Suplicacioun unto God for the Restoring of his Holye Woorde unto the Churche of England* (1554) by Thomas Becon, *How Superior Powers be Obeyed* (1558) by Christopher Goodman, and *An Admonition to England and Scotland* (Geneva, 1558) by Anthony Gilby. For more information on the debate on female rule and its projection in pamphlet literature of the day, see Constance Jordan, "Woman's Rule in Sixteenth-Century British Political Thought", *Renaissance Quarterly*, 1987, 40:3, 421–451.
50 Circe is one of the characters in Homer's *Odyssey*, who changed the companions of Ulysses into pigs. This figure is the subject of Alciatus's emblem LXXVI *Cavendum a Meretricibus* (One ought to beware of prostitutes). The explanation of this emblem given by the publisher of this edition of Alciatus summarizes the negative meanings linked to her: "Circe is the great whore who changes men to wild beasts, those who are not led by reason and turn to brutish and dishonest ways." See Andrea Alciatus, *Emblemas*, Santiago Sebastián (Ed.), Madrid, Akal, 1993, p. 112. It also appears in the same sense in the emblem 82 by Geffrey Whitney, *Homines Voluptatibus Transformantur* (Men are transformed by pleasures). See Peter M. Daly et al. (Eds), *The English Emblem Tradition*, Toronto, University of Toronto Press, 1988, vol. I, p. 178.
51 Nicholas Udall, *Respublica. Tudor Interludes*, Peter Happé (Ed.), Harmondsworth, Middlessex, Penguin Books, 1972, 221–270, p. 223.
52 The group formed by the virtues reminds one of the stages that had featured in the pageant given for the monarchs as part of their ceremonial entry following their wedding. They formed part of the iconographic programme to legitimize Mary, her government and her faith.

Notes to pp. 56–63

53 These vices represent the reformists as a body, as is demonstrated by the name taken by Oppression: Reformation (I, iv, 36–38). The reference to Edward VI's reign is explicit at other points in the performance, as can be seen in the words of Respublica: "Insolence, Oppression, Adulation./ O lorde, howe have I been used these five yeres past?" (V, ix, 113–114).
54 This is made possible through a discursive strategy that employs a fixed set of images, episodes and characters which, independent of their historical or biblical meaning, had come to symbolize the True Church against the False Church.
55 The first coins that were minted during her reign contained, in fact, this same *motto*, underlining her miraculous victory over Northumberland. See Weir, *Children of England*, p. 199.
56 Avarice is brought before the Constable by People, while Insolence and Oppression are taken to jail to await judgment.
57 The prologue also associates the queen with this character, who was considered a symbol of divine vengeance in Renaissance emblem literature. See Alciatus's emblems XXVII and XLIV, *Nec Verbo, Nec Facto Qvendam Laedendum* (Harm no one, by word or deed) and *In Simulacrum Spei* (On an image of hope).
58 "To hance" meant to raise, especially prices, so its use as a name here suggests a possible reference to the growing enrichment of certain foreign merchants. The threatening sense of the term is significant from the beginning.
59 Prince Philip could say only a few words of English, so this could be a clear satire and criticism of the future king.
60 See Craik, *The Revels History*, p. xxx.

CHAPTER THREE   Elizabeth (1558–1579): A Failed Attempt at Reconciliation

1 Included in Kinney, *Renaissance Drama: An Anthology of Plays and Entertainment*, pp. 17–34.
2 The author was probably Richard Mulcaster, headmaster of Merchant Taylor's School in London, and a Member of Parliament, which would explain the clear political orientation of this supposedly objective description of the ceremony.
3 The people's function as plaintiffs in these events seemed to form part of a rhetorical strategy directed from the highest levels of power. See Judith Richards, "Love and a Female Monarch: The Case of Elizabeth Tudor", *The Journal of British Studies*, 1999, 38:2, 133–160, p. 148.
4 Anglo, *Spectacle Pageantry*, p. 346.
5 Helen Hackett, *Virgin Mother, Maiden Queen. Elizabeth I and the Cult of the Virgin Mary*, London, MacMillan Press, 1995, p. 48.
6 Ibid., p. 48. For more on the politics of affection between the queen and her subjects, see Richards, "Love and a Female Monarch", pp. 135–140.
7 The same problem that had been seen in Edward VI's coronation is repeated.
8 See Hackett, *Virgin* Mother, pp. 11, 19, and Jean Wilson, *England's Eliza*, New York, Octagon, 1966, pp. 207, 219 y 226.

9 Quoted in David M. Bergeron, *English Civic Pageantry, 1558–1642*, Columbia, University of South Carolina Press, 1971, p. 14. For more details of the reception this character received during the royal passage, see David M. Bergeron, "Venetian State Papers and English Civic Pageantry, 1558–1642", *Renaissance Quarterly*, 1970, 23, 37–47.
10 Ripa, *Iconología*, vol. II, p. 35.
11 Ibid., p. 428.
12 See Marina Warner, *Alone of All her Sex: The Myth and the Cult of the Virgin Mary*, London, Pan-Picador, 1985, pp. 92–94.
13 See Colin Burrow, "The Sixteenth Century", in *The Cambridge Companion to English Literature* 1500–1600, Arthur F. Kinney (Ed.), Cambridge, Cambridge University Press, 2000, pp. 11–63, p. 14. For a more in-depth look at the political involvement of Grafton and Mulcaster in the royal entry, see Roy Strong, *The Tudor and Stuart Monarchy: Pageantry, Painting, Iconography*, Woodbridge, The Boydell Press, 1995, pp. 38–40.
14 The city of London had been identified with reformist values since the reign of Edward VI. See Huston Diehl, *Staging Reform, Reforming the Stage. Protestantism and Popular Theatre in Early Modern England*, Ithaca, London, Cornell University Press, 1997, p. 1.
15 Elizabeth, however, seemed at first to pursue the line of her father, who had never completely broken with Catholicism. In fact, the queen considered that the use of ceremony would be necessary for discipline, and shared with Henry VIII his rejection of married clergy. The use she made of the symbols of Catholic worship, such as the cross or candles, was also a cause of debate among her detractors (see Margaret Aston, *England's Iconoclasts. Laws against Images*, Oxford, Clarendon Press, 1988, pp. 243, 306–313, and by the same author, *The King's Bedpost*, pp. 110–112). The presence of numerous vestiges of Catholicism in certain areas of England was a constant during the first years of her reign. A study on Yorkshire has demonstrated the existence and expansion of a certain religious conservatism in the first stage of Elizabeth's reign, since many traditional practices (such as the use of holy water, images, and other religious objects) continued to be present in many communities. See A. G. Dickens, "The First Stages of Romanist Recusancy in Yorkshire, 1500–1590", *Yorkshire Archaeological Journal*, 1943, 35, 157–181, pp. 161–163). Arnold Pritchard states, in fact, that the hostility between the Protestant and Catholic communities was very weak during these first years, since the dividing line that separated them was unclear (See *Catholic Loyalism in Elizabethan England*, Chapel Hill, The University of North Carolina Press, 1979, p. 3).
16 As Gómez Lara points out, this trio of characters may also represent a new version of the iconographic opposition of the Woman Clothed with the Sun of the Revelation – Pure Religion – and the Whore of Babylon – Superstition. See M. J. Gómez Lara, "Apocalyptic Iconographies and Elizabethan Political Propaganda in *The Quenes Maiesties Passage through the Citie of London to Westminster the Daye before her Coronacion*", in *Gloriana's Rule. Literature, Religion and Power in the Age of Elizabeth*,

Rui Carvalho and Fátima Vieira (Eds), O Porto, Editora da Universidade do Porto, 2006, 83–103, p. 90. This last figure appears in this sense in Alciatus's emblem VI, *Ficta Religio* (False religion), and is reinforced by the following one, *Non Tibi, sed Religioni* (Not for you, but for religion), in which a donkey carrying an image of a goddess shows his foolishness by thinking that it is he who is being worshipped. Geoffrey Whitney includes the second of these in his work *Index Emblematicus* (1586). See Daly, *The English Emblem Tradition*, p. 97.

17 This message was repeated in the slogans that decorated the throne of the monarch. They stressed the seditious character of the followers of Rome, a common accusation against them especially after 1570.

18 The passage is from Matt. 5:3–10.

19 From a letter sent by Knox to William Cecil on 10 April 1559, included in David Laing, *The Works of John Knox*, Edinburgh, 1864, p. 19.

20 See Hackett, *Virgin Mother*, p. 43.

21 See Ripa, *Iconología*, vol. II, pp. 360–361; 393; Alciatus, *Emblemas*, p. 39 and the emblem by Geoffrey Whitney, *Veritas Temporis Filia* in Daly, *The English Emblem Tradition*, p. 93. Although the only image that Ripa includes about Truth does not appear with such a timepiece, it is referred to in the various descriptions that are made of the figure.

22 The dramatist probably thought it unwise to attack Mary I, since that might be interpreted as a failure to obey the queen, so the denunciations of the previous regime are merely insinuations directed to a knowing audience.

23 Hackett, *Virgin Mother*, p. 44.

24 Knighted in 1547, he was rumoured to have been the illegitimate son of Henry VIII.

25 Gómez Lara, "Apocalyptic Iconographies", p. 96.

26 Hackett, *Virgin Mother*, p. 44.

27 This idea, however, was nothing new to English political thought. In fact, the concept of government that existed throughout the entire sixteenth and seventeenth centuries in England oscillated between the idea of a holy and imperial monarchy and one restrained by Parliament and the Royal Council. See Kinney, *The Cambridge Companion to English Literature 1500–1600*, p. 13.

28 The insistence on presenting the queen as continuing Henry VIII's work already appears in Elizabeth's Act of Proclamation as Queen of England. Nicolas Heath, her Lord Chancellor, identified her as *Defensor Fidei*, a title that her father had obtained for the Tudor dynasty. It had been denied to her sister Mary, which is a patent demonstration of the Protestant character of the new government, and which could be interpreted as a warning to those who failed to conform. See Arthur F. Kinney, *Elizabethan Backgrounds: Historical Documents of the Age of Elizabeth I*, Hamden, Conn., Anchor, 1990, pp. 4–5.

29 See Paul Christianson, *Reformers and Babylon: English Apocalyptic Visions from the Reformation to the Eve of the Civil War*, Toronto, University of Toronto Press, 1978, pp. 48–49.

30 Cited in Christianson, *Reformers and Babylon*, p. 52.

31 Cited in Albert Peel (Ed.), *The Seconde Parte of a Register Being a Calendar*

of Manuscripts under that Title Intended for Publication by the Puritans about 1593, Cambridge, 1915, vol. I, p. 561.
32 See Alexandra Walsham, *Church Papists. Catholicism, Conformity and Confessional Polemic in Early Modern England*, New York, The Boydell Press, 1993, pp. 10–11.
33 See A. C. F. Beales, *Education under Penalty: English Catholic Education from the Reformation to the Fall of James II 1547–1689*, London, The Athlone Press, 1963, pp. 29–30.
34 See Charles G. Bayne, *Anglo-Roman Relations, 1558–1565*, Oxford, Clarendon Press, 1913, pp. 163–181.
35 Williamson, *The Tudor Age*, pp. 264–265.
36 Ibid., p. 277.
37 Williamson, *The Tudor Age*, pp. 288–290.
38 Papal Bull Regnans in Excelsis (1570). Included in the work of William Camden, *The Historie of the Life and the Reigne of the Most Renowned and Victorious Princess Elizabeth, Late Queen of England Contayning the Most Important and Remarkeable Passages of State, during her Happy, Long and Prosperous Raigne*, London, 1563.
39 See Patrick McGrath, *Papists and Puritans under Elizabeth I*, London, Blandford Press, 1967, pp. 104–105.
40 The government did not hesitate to harden the punishments for Catholics. An act of parliament of 1571 ruled Catholicism to be high treason and ordered the confiscation of the property of all those who disobeyed the laws of the Anglican Church. Fines were levied against the laity, and they could also be jailed or, for the worst infractions, executed. This produced a mass exodus to other countries in Europe. The Catholic clergy was the target of harsher persecutions, frequently resulting in their imprisonment or death (Pritchard, *Catholic Loyalism*, p. 7). The *Encyclopaedia Britannica* points to the execution of 183 English Catholics between 1577 and 1603, some for offenses as trivial as obtaining licenses to get married from the pope.
41 Pejorative term for Catholics who attended Anglican services
42 A college founded by Cardinal William Allen in 1568, where Catholic priests were prepared for the evangelizing mission in England. Lay students were not excluded, however, and although at the beginning Allen was not politically involved, Douai would become one of the prominent European centres of Catholic resistance of the period. See Beales, *Education under Penalty*, pp. 40–41.
43 This explains the queen's interest in controlling the production of pamphlets and dramatic texts in England. The stationers, who had existed as one of the City of London's companies since 1403 and had been given license to print by Mary I, continued to hold a monopoly over all printed works in the country after 1559. In exchange, a strict control over published material was exercised. In this way, the queen attempted to restrict the subversive power of pamphlet literature and to limit or eliminate possible attacks on her government. It was no easy task, and soon new publications and vendors sprouted up, circulating texts without a license to do so. For more information, see Halasz, *The Marketplace of Print*, pp. 23–27, 53–54, and Raymond, *Pamphlets and Pamphleteering*, pp. 66–67.

44 The pamphlets of the second decade of the Elizabethan period offer most examples of the Catholic stereotype. Outstanding among its features are, for instance, their pride, falseness, hypocrisy, lust, blasphemy and ignorance, themes which permeated dramatic works, such as *New Custom* (III, i, 161–163); the character Ignorance in *Enough is as Good as a Feast* might represent the priests of the northeast part of the country who, far from the city, continued to practice the Catholic faith in their parishes. The fact that the character is drunk and speaks in Latin connects him to the stereotype of the Catholic clergy which dominated Protestant literature. William Wager, the author, ridicules him and shows his incapacity to be a spiritual guide. There are also many accusations of corruption, as William Fulke summarizes in *An Answer of a True Christian to a Counterfait Catholike* (London, 1577): "You shall never be able to charge us with such ryot, whordom, adulterie, incest, sodomity, bestiality, murther, poysoning, necromancie, apostasie, blasphemie, &. As both the worlde seeth to overflowe in your Prelates at this daye" (p. 94). Within the same text, this list is appended with comparisons with the Whore of Babylon (pp. 33, 57, 75, 79, 100), Sodom (p. 100) and Egypt (p. 100).

45 The writing of Thomas Norton, *A Warning agaynst the Dangerous Practices of Papistes* (London, 1569) is a clear exponent. See, as examples, sigs B1r-v, B2r-v, C2r-v, C4v-E1v.

46 Ibid; sig. B2r.

47 John Phillips, *A Frendly Larum or Faithful Warnynge to the True Harted Subiectes of England Discovering the Actes, and Malicious Myndes of those Obstinate and Rebellious Papistes that Hope (as they Terme it) to Have their Golden Day*, London, 1569, sig. A4v.

48 This point of view is very similar to that which the queen had adopted toward Catholics, whom she was inclined to tolerate as long as they presented no threat to the regime.

49 Skinner also emphasizes the queen's possible irresponsibility by not completely doing away with the Catholics. See Vincent Skinner, *A Discovery and Playne Declaration of Sundry Subtill Practices of the Holy Inquisition of Spayne*, London, 1569, sigs A4r, A7r-v, A8r.

50 J. S., *The Serpent of Division, Whych hath Ever Bene Yet the Chefest Undoer of any Region or Citie. London*, 1559, sig. C3v.

51 For more information, see H. J. Schroeder, *Canons and Decrees of the Council of Trent*, St. Louis, London, Mo, B. Hender Book Co., 1941, p. 216.

52 Regarding ambition, see examples in H. Bullinger, *Confutation of the Popes Bull against Elizabeth Queen of England*, London, 1572, pp. 32, 36, and P. Melanchthon, *Of the Two Wonderful Popish Monsters to Wyt, of a Popish Asse which was Found at Rome in the River of Tyber, and of a Monkish Calfe, Calved at Friberge in Misne, translated to English by John Brook*, London, 1579, p. 4. The clearest exponent is the character of Covetous in *Enough is as Good*. Attacks on Catholic ambition are usually associated with criticism of papal pride, which will later comprise one of the inevitable links with the Spanish stereotype. Regarding tyranny, see examples in Bullinger, *A Confutation*, pp. 22–23, 32; T. Naogeorg, *The*

Popish Kingdome, or Reigne of Antichrist, London, 1570, pp. 2–6, 11, and Fulke, *An Answer of a True Christian*, p. 28. The character of Policy in *Enough is as Good* might refer to the same attack. In fact, the *Oxford English Dictionary* defines the term "policy" as political cunning, craftiness and dissimulation, ideas which will later be associated with the Society of Jesus. This group, according to reformists, was at the service of the pope's imperial aspirations. Bernard Spivak confirms these meanings, pointing out that around 1550 the word had clearly pejorative connotations derived from its association with Machiavelli and his pragmatic and amoral conception of politics. See his work *Shakespeare and the Allegory of Evil*, New York, Columbia University Press, 1958, pp. 373–376.

53 Naogeorg, *The Popish Kingdome*, p. 3. See other examples in Melanchthon's *Of the Two Wonderful Popish Monsters*, p. 3; Bullinger, *A Confutation*, pp. 24, 36, and Fulke, *An Answer of a True Christian*, p. 94.

54 Melanchthon, *Of the Two Wonderful Popish Monsters*, p. 7.

55 Bullinger, *A Confutation*, p. 36.

56 See Claire Mceachern & Debora Shuger (Eds), *Religion and Culture in Renaissance England*, Cambridge, Cambridge University Press, 1997, pp. 69–70.

57 See Yates, *Astraea*, p. 43.

58 Cited in M. A. S. Hume (Ed.), *State Papers Relating to English Affairs, Preserved Principally in the Archives of Simancas*, London, 1892–1899, vol. I, p. 247. Roy Strong points out the performance at court of numerous anti-Catholic pieces in the season between 1558 and 1559. Generally, these took the form of strong satires against Mary's regime and signalled the continuity between the new queen and her predecessors, Henry VIII and Edward VI. See his work *The Tudor and Stuart Monarchy*, p. 35.

59 Editions of the two works by Mark R. Benbow (Lincoln, University of Nebraska Press, 1967) have been used.

60 For example, see the reference that the character Piety makes at the end of *The Longer Thou Livest* to the "magistrates of this region" (1976). Only the line number is given, since there is no division into acts and scenes.

61 "We have ridden and gone many sundry waies" (25). Again, the line number is indicated.

62 The vices, particularly Infidelity, frequently address the audience, which suggests a certain proximity between the actors and spectators, who would thus be made part of the dramatic action. This proximity was usually found when plays were performed in the towns, where often there a stage barely existed. Ibid; 7, 989.

63 There is no record of the location of the performance, nor textual references to the type of audience at which it was aimed.

64 Neither is there information about its production, although (given the topics it touched on) it would not have been staged for a general audience.

65 Its date of composition is not known exactly, although it is thought to have been written during the first decade of Elizabeth's reign (1559–1570). There is no consensus about the year in which it was published, since the official record does not include entries made between 22 July 1571 and 17 July 1576. It is therefore believed that the work was registered within this

time period, though the documents have been lost. In fact, William Jackson places it in about 1570 in the Short Title Catalogue.
66 Published in 1578, its date of composition oscillates between 1559 and 1577.
67 See Robert Potter, *The English Morality Play. Origins, History and Influence of a Dramatic Tradition*, London, Boston, Routledge, Kegan Paul, 1975, p. 117.
68 See Craik, *The Revels History*, p. 202.
69 The character Money is Pleasure's father and Sin's grandfather, and has a son named Endless Damnation. Satan, on the other hand, is a relative of Gluttony and Pride, Adulation's friend, and Endless Damnation's master.
70 The concept of social class is an anachronism in this era, but the changes that were taking place in the economic and social pyramid, as well as the mobility between the different social groups that had begun to manifest itself might justify its use.
71 The progressive increase in the population was not matched by the growth of food production, which caused persistent price increases that failed to translate into wage increases. This was accompanied by periods of poor harvests, military spending by the government, and frequent devaluation of the currency. See Brian Gibbons, *Jacobean City Comedy*, London, New York, Methuen, 1980, p. 22.
72 See A. G. Dickens, *The English Reformation*, Oxford, Clarendon Press, 1964, pp. 235–236.
73 The cult of money was part of a long tradition of religious satires (invectives) that arose in the Middle Ages against wealth and its abuse.
74 Benbow points out in the aforementioned edition of *Enough is as Good* the parallel between this play and *The Exposition upon the Fifth, Sixth and Seventh Chapters of Matthew* (1532) by William Tyndale, reformist and translator of the first English Bible (1535) (x–xi). Both explain that the problem of wealth does not lie in wealth itself but in people's attitude toward it. Tyndale says it thus: "[R]iches is the gift of God, given to man to maintain the degrees of the world, and therefore not evil; yes and some must be poor and some rich, if we shall have an order in this world." See W. Tyndale, *Expositions and Notes on Sundry Portions of the Holy Scriptures* (1532), H. Walter (Ed.), Parker Society, 1849, vol. XLIV, p. 18.
75 The name "livingless" underscores the precariousness of his life. In addition, Lupton characterizes him as lustful (1147–1148), a gambler (1151–1152), an example of simony (1142) whose ignorance of the Scriptures and corruption reach comic proportions.
76 *The Longer Thou Livest* was likely written around 1559, although it was entered into the record in April 1569. The indirect reference to the Statute of Artificers of 1563 (1032–1034), however, suggests an early date near the beginning of the decade. The play can be inserted within the homiletic tradition, as it portrays the spiritual pilgrimage of its protagonist, Moros, even though he fails to achieve any state of maturity or conversion. In the three stages of his life which are described – youth (71–1005), adulthood (1201–1684), and old age (1743–1890) – Moros fails to evolve beyond his stupidity, though he does progress in terms of his shamelessness and his

lack of respect toward God and his fellow men.

77 The denunciation of Mary's reign reaches its zenith with the appearance of the character People, the symbol of the English populace under the Catholic yoke. As in some of the pamphlets produced during the reign of Mary I, the Catholic government is considered to be divine punishment for the nation's sins: "Humbly we commit all to his judgement,/ We have offended him and his holy laws;/ Therefore, are we worthy of this punishment" (1740–1742).

78 See, for instance, *Jacob and Esau*, in Edward VI's reign.

79 *Sanctus bell* was the bell that was sounded with the singing of *Sanctus* during Mass. For the reformists, this was yet another proof of Catholic idolatry and superstition, since the sound of the bell marked the moment at which the faithful were to kneel. See Benbow in his edition of the work, p. 10, n. 164.

80 The madness of Moros (which may derive from the Latin *moror*, to be mad) is portrayed according to the iconographic tradition. Ripa states, for example, on the iconology of Madness that anyone who deviates from such actions concerned with the government, the family and the republic, and instead gives himself to gambling and childish occupations must be called mad (*Iconología*, vol. II, pp. 28–29). The character in the play ignores the virtues' words, consistently interrupting them with comments such as "Gay gear", "good stuff", "very well" and "fin-ado", in a clearly comic tone (see the quote on page 21 of that text). He pays no attention to Discipline's message, interpreting it as simply a game. His humorous commentary throughout the course of his instruction would certainly have provoked laughter from the audience, thus extending the character's irresponsibility to the spectators themselves. Additionally, the *Oxford English Dictionary* associates this word with amorality, specifically in the phrase "morose delectation": "The habit of dwelling with enjoyment upon evil thoughts".

81 *All for Money* picks up the same idea. The pardon that Laurence Livingless receives plainly shows the strength which Catholicism in England still enjoyed and the support it supposedly received from those within the circles of power, mostly at the local level. In effect, several studies of Catholicism in the areas of Lancashire, Cheshire and Sussex confirm that, despite the measures taken against Catholics since the middle 1560s, they still held considerable authority in parliament, in local corporations, in the commissions of the peace and in the rural administration. See Walsham, *Church Papists*, p. 83; Haigh, *Reformation and Resistance in Tudor Lancashire*, Cambridge, Cambridge University Press, 1975, pp. 284–285; and Robert Burrow Manning, *Religion and Society in Elizabethan Sussex: A Study of the Enforcement of the Religious Settlement, 1558–1603*, Leicester, Leicester University Press, 1969, pp. xv, xvi, 81, 241 and ff. It was also common for converted Catholics who held official posts to publicly criticize those who openly defended their faith, though they later secretly supported them. The judicial corruption which Lupton denounces is thus part of a long controversy which reveals the complexity of the process of conversion that Elizabeth expected from the Catholic community, still deeply rooted within the bosom of English society.

82 See Luke 10:38–42. With the interpretation of this passage, reformists denied the medieval opposition between active life and contemplative life, which the two sisters represented (*Enough is as Good*, p. 113); Martha does not listen to Jesus Christ and "[she] is troubled about many thynges", while Mary elects to "[hear] the Word of God".
83 The play had its debut that same year.
84 See Howard B. Nortland, *Drama in Early Tudor Britain 1485–1585*, Lincoln, University of Nebraska Press, 1995, p. 150.
85 These lines precisely define the audience as that of the universities or the Inns of Court, citizens whose education allowed them to advance. Since 1555, Gascoigne was a member of Gray's Inn, where there is a record of his staging three of his plays. The hypothesis that *The Glass of Government* might have been performed there is, therefore, plausible.
86 Erasmo, *Obras escogidas*, Madrid, Aguilar, 1964, pp. 1211–1212, 1214–1215.
87 These measures were accompanied by the imposition of Protestant communion, classes for those children with scant knowledge of the catechism of the Anglican Church (in these cases, the parents were also fined) and an increase in vigilance over private tutors. See Beales, *Education under Penalty*, pp. 36–38.
88 Ibid., pp. 52–57.
89 These characters are similar to those of classical comedy. Eccho (as already indicated in the *dramatis personae*) is identified with the parasite (*parasitus*); Lamia with the courtesan (*meretrix*); Dick Drummer, because of his boisterous and violent character, could be nearer to the boastful soldier (*miles gloriosus*). Pandarina is an aging prostitute (*meretrix*) who offers her services as procuress and instructor to her niece, Lamia.
90 The allegory that the work possibly posits (i.e., the return of Protestantism after the dark years of Mary I) also satisfies this optimistic vision that is communicated to the English people.
91 See the anonymous work *The Tribulations of Mary Magdelene* (1559?) and *The Play of Patient Grissell* (ca. 1560), by John Phillip.
92 According to Clifford Davinson, the fundamental change produced in the portrayal of the character lies in presenting her as an example of penitence and virtue, not as someone worthy of veneration. See his book *Iconoclasm vs. Art and Drama*, Michigan, Western Michigan University, 1989, pp. 105–106.
93 Jesus and Malicious Judgement participate in both plots, creating a link between the other characters.
94 This vision already appears in the Golden Legend: "Magdelene was very rich; but as riches and pleasures usually go hand-in-hand, as she was revealing in her beauty and her high economic status, she was giving herself over more and more to the satisfaction of her whims and her carnal appetites, so much so that when people spoke of her, would refer to her as 'the sinner' as if she had no other name" (translation by BD). Santiago de la Voragine, *La Leyenda Dorada*, Madrid, Alianza Forma, 1982, vol. I, p. 375.
95 The supper scene in the house of Simon the Pharisee is a clear example of

this. Mary Magdalene's humility and contrition finally wins out over the religious leader's arrogance (1679–1962).
96 See, for example, *Youth* (Anon, 1565), *Lusty Juventus* (Wever, 1550), *Nice Wanton* (Anon, 1560) and *The Disobedient Child* (Ingelend, 1570).
97 Robert Potter, *The English Morality Play*, p. 107. According to Mark Benbow, before 1536, Thomas Cromwell had urged parents to be strict in the education of their children so that they might receive honest employment; otherwise, they would encourage crime and social disorder. The commentary is found in his edition of the works of William Wager, which we have already examined (p. xi).
98 See Ripa, *Iconología*, vol. II, pp. 395, 263. The same idea appears in Alciatus's emblem VI, *Ficta Religio*.
99 In this, a woman appears "wearing a very dark-colored tunic, in tatters, appearing very sad and crying copious tears" (translated by BD). See Ripa, *Iconología*, vol. II, p. 191.
100 Woman "with downcast gaze" and who is "dressed in sackcloth, while she treads on valuable garments" (translated by BD). Ibid., vol. I, p. 499.
101 In the play, Perverse Doctrine and Ignorance decide to expel New Custom from the country (New Custom is a youthful figure who preaches the need for the official Church to again take up the foundations of the Primitive Church.) To achieve their purpose, they conspire with Hipocrisie, Crueltie and Avarice, who will attempt to discredit the young preacher's work. New Custom, who later reveals his true name to be Primitive Constitution, not only is not banished, but, with the help of Light of the Gospel, converts Perverse Doctrine to the reformist faith.
102 Perverse Doctrine's repentance at the end of the play is presented as the result of his being taught Calvinist principles.
103 The character's name, New Custom, further complicates interpretation, since both the Catholic and Protestant sectors appropriated the tradition of the Church. The newness implied in this character can only carry meanings that, if not negative, are at least ambiguous.

CHAPTER FOUR Elizabeth I (1580–1603): Gloriana and the Victory of Protestantism

1 The first was begun by William Allen in 1568.
2 See Peter Holmes, *Resistance and Compromise. The Political Thought of the Elizabethan Catholics*, Cambridge, Cambridge University Press, 1982, p. 42. The new missionaries continued William Allen's work of reforming and reconciling the "church papists" with the Church in Rome; hence they had to be especially discouraged from attending Protestant services. See Walsham, *Church Papists*, p. 62.
3 *Letters and Memorials of Father Robert Persons*, L. Hicks (Ed.), Catholic Record Society, vol. IXL, London, Whitehead, 1942, p. 38.
4 William Allen, *An Apology or True Declaration of the Institution and Endeavours of the Two English Colleges, the One in Rome, the Other Now Resident in Rhemes, against Certaine Sinister Informations Given up against the Same*, Reims, 1581, p. 51. Criticism of Protestant thought as

seditious was part of English Catholic tradition dating back to the writings of Sir Thomas More himself. The equating of heresy with rebellion, as well as the constant defense of tradition, order and stability associated with the Church of Rome, appears during the reigns of Edward VI, Mary Tudor and Elizabeth I. See Holmes, *Resistance and Compromise*, pp. 68–78.

5. These ideas were seen in many plays. Among them are the works of Persons, *A Brief Discourse Containing Certain Reasons why Catholics Refuse to Go to Church* (1580), *A Brief Censure upon two Books* (1581), *An Epistle of the Persecution of Catholics in England* (1582) and the first Catholic New Testament published in English, by Gregory Martin in Reims in 1582, with annotations that contained the ideas of obedience to the Crown preached by Allen and Persons. See A. C. Southern, *Elizabethan Recusant Prose*, London, Sands, 1950, pp. 231–262, and Holmes, *Resistance and Compromise*, pp. 38–41.

6. Some of the arguments used to impugn the papal document's validity were that it had been published in Rome rather than in England, and that it could be annulled for not having accomplished its goal, which was to help and improve the situation of English Catholics. Ibid., p. 43.

7. This document, to which Holmes gave no title whatsoever, is in Lambeth Library (Manuscript Source) 565, fol. 53.

8. See Dovai (Manuscript Source) 484, fols 423–424; Bodleian (Manuscript Source) Rawlinson D 1351, fols 13–14.

9. The Parliament of 1581 approved a law that punished with death those Catholic priests who celebrated Mass; it imposed stiff fines on all those who failed to attend Protestant services and, with the fourth offense, seized the goods and property of the accused. There were also provisions for punishment of Catholic lawyers and tutors (see M. Questier, *Conversion, Politics and Religion in England, 1580–1625*, Cambridge, Cambridge University Press, 1996, pp. 103–104; John E. Neale, *Elizabeth and her Parliaments*, London, Cape, 1953, pp. 385 and ff). That same year, a new law was imposed "against seditious words and rumours uttered against the Queen's most excellent Majesty," which harshened the relevant punishments and provided for punishment by death for the second offense (Ibid., p. 393). This law, especially directed against Catholic priests and their lay helpers, resulted in the first executions. See McGrath, *Papists and Puritans*, pp. 176–177.

10. Albert J. Loomie, *The Spanish Elizabethans: The English Exiles at the Court of Philip II*, London, Burns & Oates, 1963, pp. 14–51.

11. Since the late 1570s, numerous English Catholics had emigrated to France from England and the Low Countries. In 1578, the seminary at Douai was moved to Reims, where it developed important ties with the Guise family and other leaders of the Catholic League. English and French Catholics thus influenced each other in the development of their political ideas. See Holmes, *Resistance and Compromise*, p. 130 and H. J. M. Salmon, *The French Religious Wars in English Political Thought*, Oxford, Clarendon Press, 1959, chapter 2.

12. See W. Allen, *The Copy of a Letter . . . Concerning the Yielding up of the City of Daventry*, Antwerp, 1587, pp. 13–23.

13 See Williamson, *The Tudor Age*, pp. 359–360.
14 See McGrath, *Papists and Puritans*, pp. 194–195
15 Hicks, *An Elizabethan Problem. Some of the Careers of the Two Exile-Adventurers*, New York, Fordham University Press, 1964, p. 147.
16 R. Southwell, *An Epistle of Comfort to the Reverend Priest and to the Honourable Worshipful and Other of the Lay Sort Restrained in Durance for the Catholic Faith*, Margaret Vaugh (Ed.), London, Burns & Oates, 1966, sig. A7.
17 Williamson, *The Tudor Age*, p. 359.
18 The work seems to have had multiple authors. However. *The Short Title Catalogue* credits Richard Crompton as author; the copies of the manuscript which Cecil had prepared for printing were corrected by the Queen herself. There may have been a third collaborator, Francis Alford. Walshingham directed and coordinated several translations of the text into Latin, German and French in that same year (1587). It would soon be included in Holinshed's chronicles and in the first volume of *Somers Tracts* (London, 1750). See Kinney, *Elizabethan Backgrounds*, pp. 216–217. Kinney includes this text in which various speeches of members of the Council are recorded, as well as those of Parliament and, especially, declarations made by the Queen (pp. 219–236).
19 The text is found in the aforementioned work by Kinney, *Elizabethan Backgrounds*.
20 Metaphors relating to the family strengthen this idea: "And those countries [England and the Low Countries] have bene by common language of long time resembled and termed as man and wife" (p. 201). The mutuality and, especially, naturalness of the relationship between them (the result of dynastic and commercial associations, along with geographical proximity) are stressed: "that the *naturall* people and subjects of either side, should shewe *mutuall* favours and dueties one to the other, and should safely, *freely* and securely commerce together in every their countries, and so hath the same *mutuall and naturall* concourse and commerce bene without interruption continued in many ages" (p. 199) (my emphasis).
21 William of Orange had adopted this same strategy in a pamphlet that was published in London in 1573, directed at Philip II and entitled *A Supplication to the Kinges Maiestie of Spayne*, in which he blamed the Duke of Alba for the atrocities which had taken place in the Low Countries and for deceiving his king in this regard (sig. A3r-v).
22 See A. Loomie, *Spain and the Early Stuarts, 1585–1655*, New York, Fordham University, 1996, p. 391.
23 This took place on 8 August. For more detailed information, the broad bibliography on the conflict may be consulted. Titles which stand out are: *England and the Spanish Armada: The Necessary Quarrel* (New Haven, Yale University Press, 2005) by James McDermott; *Armada* (Stroud, Tempus, 2000; 1988) by Patrick Williams and Duff Hart-Davis, respectively; *La Armada española en la monarquía de Philip II y la defensa del Mediterráneo* (Madrid, Tempo, 1995) by Enrique García Hernán; *Brags and Boasts: Propaganda in the Years of the Armada* (Stroud, Sutton, 1995) by Bertrand Whiteheard; *Los sucesos de Flandes in 1588 en relación con la*

empresa de Inglaterra (Madrid, Naval, 1990) by Gonzalo Parente; *Las Armadas de Philip II* (Madrid, San Martín, 1989) by Ricardo Cerezo Martínez; *Los barcos españoles del siglo XVI y la Gran Armada de 1588* (Madrid, San Martín, 1988) by José Luis Casado Soto; *The Experience of the War in 1588* (Oxford, Oxford University Press, 1988) by Felipe Fernández Armesto; *La Gran Armada* (Madrid, Alianza, 1988) by Colin Martin and Geoffrey Parker; *The Enterprise of England: The Spanish Armada* (New York, St Martin's Press, 1988) by J. R. S. Whiting; *The Spanish Armada: La Invencible y la empresa de Inglaterra* (Madrid, Nerea, 1988) and *La Armada Invencible* (Madrid, Anaya, 1987), both by Carlos Gómez-Centurión; *La Armada Invencible: las verdaderas causas de un desastre naval* (Barcelona, Argos Vergara, 1982) by David Howarth; *The Spanish Armada* (New York, Thomas Y. Crowell, 1968) by Michael Arthur Lewis; *The Defeat of the Spanish Armada* (London, Penguin Books, 1962) and *The Armada* (Boston, Houghton Mifflin, 1959), both by Garret Mattingly.

24 Thomas Tymme, *A Preparation against the Prognosticated Dangers of this Yeare*, London, 1588, sigs B4v- B5r.

25 Anonymous, *An Exhortacion to all English Subiects to Ione for the Defence of Queene Elizabeth and their Native Country*, London, 1588, p. 2.

26 The image is inspired by Alciatus's emblem XLIII, *Spes Proxima* (Hope is near). Reformists and counter-reformists used it as a symbol of the Christian Church, particularly when this was the target of dissensions and heresies.

27 See examples in T. I., *A Ioyful Song of the Royall Receiving of the Queenes Most Excellent Maiestie into her Highness Campe at Tilsburie in Essex*, London, 1588, p. 1; A. Marten, *An Exhortation to Stirre up the Mindes of all her Maiesties Faithfull Subiects, to Defend their Country in this Dangerous Time, from the Invasion of the Enemies*, London, 1588, sigs E2r-E3v; T. Deloney, *The Queenes Visiting of the Campe at Tilsburie with her Entertainment There to the Tune of Wilsons Wide*, London, 1588, p. 1; and James Aske, *Elizabetha Triumphans. Conteyning the Damned Practizes, that the Divelish Popes of Rome Have Used Ever Sithence her Higness First Comming to the Crowne, by Moving her Wicked and Treaterous Subiects to Rebellion and Conspiracies, Thereby to Bereave her Maiestie Both of her Lawfull Seate, and Happy Life*, London, 1588, sig. C4v.

28 M. Kyffin, *The Blessedness of Brytain as a Celebration of the Queenes Holyday. Wherein is Briefly Discoursed the Most Happy Regiment of her Higness*, London, 1588, sig. D1r.

29 See other examples in Marten, *An Exhortation*, sigs A2v, E4v and *An Exhortacion to all English Subiects*, p. 3. The Spanish camp, however, utilized the same discourse to justify its position. The Jesuit Ribadeneira writes, shortly before the battle: "we go to a not too difficult enterprise, because the Lord God, whose cause and most holy religion we will defend, will go before us and, with such a captain, we have nothing to fear" (Translated by BD). Quoted in the work by Carlos Gómez Centurión, *La invencible y la empresa de Inglaterra*, pp. 67–70.

30 The pamphlets by Kyffin, *The Blessedness of Brytain* (sigs A4r, B1r, B3v, C2v) and Tymme, *A Preparation* (sigs A2v, A3r) are the most representative.
31 Reference to her virginity is made on many occasions (Ibid., p. 1; Aske, *Elizabetha Triumphans*, sig. B1r), which Helen Hackett interprets as a symbol of England's own inviolability (*Virgin Mother Maiden Queen*, p. 127). Elizabeth and her people remain uncorrupted before the foreign menace. England's (and the Queen's) borders were impenetrable.
32 Hackett, *Virgin Mother, Maiden Queen*, pp. 76–77.
33 Ripa, *Iconología*, vol. I, p. 393.
34 The court poet Edmund Spenser makes use of similar metaphors in *The Faerie Queene* (1590, 1596) to describe Gloriana -"As morning Sunne her beames dispredden cleare,/ And in her face faire peace, and mercy doth appeare" (II, ii, 40) – Mercilla – "As the bright sunne . . . / Towards the western brim begins to draw,/ Gins to abate the brightness of his beme,/ And fervour of his flames somewhat adaw" (V, ix, 35) – and Una: "The blazing brightness of her beauties beame,/ And glorious light of her sunshyny face . . . / My ragged rimes are all too rude and base,/ Her heavenly lineaments for to enhance" (I, xii, 23).
35 This ballad is comprised of a single sheet; for this reason there is no page number cited in the quotes.
36 Spenser's portrayal of Gloriana (Elizabeth) is one of the most representative examples: "That men beholding so great excellence,/ And rare perfection in mortalitie,/ Do her adore with sacred reverence,/ As th'Idole of her makers great magnificence" (II, ii, 41).
37 The very name which history gives it as "Invincible" is, in fact, evidence of the way a biased interpretation of Providence had become natural.
38 See the back cover of the book by Michael O'Connell, *Mirror and Veil. The Historical Dimension of Spenser's Faerie Queene*, Chapel Hill, The University of North Carolina Press, 1977.
39 See Jennifer Woodward's analysis of this sphinx's significance during the first years of the reign of James I. Her article "Images of a Dead Queen. Historical Record of the Mourning Ceremony for Queen Elizabeth I of England" – *History Today*, 1997, 47:11, 18–23 – can be found at www.Findarticles.com/cf_0/m/373/n11_v47/19987419/print.jhtml.
40 There were two clearly defined factions within the Catholic community: the pro-Scottish, which supported Mary Stuart, and then James VI after her death; and the pro-Spanish, who preferred Philip II, and were led by Allen, Persons, and the community in exile. See Questier, *Conversion*, pp. 51–53.
41 In 1579, they founded a seminary in Rome, which initiated the second stage of the missionary movement begun in Douai in 1574. It was joined by other similar colleges in Valladolid (1589) and in Seville (1593), in addition to a refuge for English merchants and students in Sanlúcar de Barrameda (1592). See Pritchard, *Catholic Loyalism in Elizabethan England*.
42 For further information, see Holmes, *Resistance and Compromise*, pp. 186–205 and John Bossy, *The English Catholic Community 1570–1850*, New York, Oxford University Press, 1976, pp. 35–38, 207–208.
43 See Pritchard, *Catholic Loyalism*, pp. 78–117.

44 They met secretly in private homes for the purpose of commenting on Scriptures and discussing problems of common interest. In addition, they were in contact with sympathizers in Scotland and the Low Countries, which demonstrates their desire to reform the hierarchical structure of the Church of England in alliance with the European centers of radical Protestantism. See McGrath, *Papists and Puritans*, pp. 205–212.
45 Ibid., pp. 213–243.
46 Ibid., pp. 249–251.
47 Ibid., pp. 301–337.
48 Hackett, *Virgin Mother, Maiden Queen*, p. 180.
49 Only one text has been found that deals extensively with the argument between tradition and Scripture, a recurring theme in the anti-Catholic texts of other times. This is *A Comparison between the Auncient Fayth of the Romans and the Romish Religion* (1595) by Francis Bunny.
50 Among others, Spain and Rome, who viewed their growing power with scepticism.
51 Thomas Bell, *The Anatomie of the Popish Tirannie*, London, 1603, p. 2.
52 The same author broadens this accusation by comparing them to chameleons: "they are creatures which varie their colours like the Camelion, according to the object" (p. 54).
53 The Jesuit seminaries on the continent taught the casuistic treatises in depth, since they were a useful way to prepare young priests for their mission in England. The Jesuit leaders of these institutions also produced numerous casuistic manuals which they used to train their disciples. See Holmes, *Resistance and Compromise*, p. 100.
54 L. Lewkenor, *The Estate of English Fugitives*, London, 1596, p. 90.
55 P. de Ribadeneira, *Tratado de la religión y virtudes que debe tener el príncipe cristiano para gobernar y conservar sus estados. Contra lo que Nicolás Maquiavelo y los políticos de este tiempo enseñan*, Madrid, Pedro Madrigal, 1595. The edition which has been used is that of the *Biblioteca de Autores Españoles* [Library of Spanish Authors], p. 60 (Translated by BD).
56 See the anonymous text, *The Downefall of the Iesuits*, London, s.n., pp. 17–18.
57 R. Persons, *A Treatise Tending to Mitigation tovvardes Catholike-subiectes in England Wherin is Declared that it is not Impossible for Subiects of Different Religion (Especially Catholiks and Protestantes) to Live Together in Dutifull Obedience and Subiections, under the Government of his Maiesty of Great Britany*, Saint-Omer, 1607, p. 547
58 See J. Lacouture, *Jesuitas I. Los Conquistadores*, Barcelona, Paidós, 1991, pp. 229–264.
59 See other examples on pages 9 and 46 of the same work.
60 R. Southwell, *A Humble Supplication to her Maiestie* (1600), R. C. Bald (Ed.), Cambridge, Cambridge University Press, 1953, pp. 8–9.
61 R. Persons, *Elizabethae Angliae Reginae*, Lyon, 1592, p. 164.
62 J. Gerard, *The Autobiography of an Elizabethan*, P. Caraman (Ed.), London, New York, Longmans, Green, 1951, p. 33.
63 See Bossy, *The English Catholic Community*, pp. 221–225.

64 See A. Arnauld, *The Arrainement of the Whole Societie of Iesuites in France*, London, 1594, p. 9, and Bell, *The Anatomie*, p. 34.
65 Lewis Lewkenor accuses the Society of separating children from their parents in *The Estate of English Fugitives*, p. 76.
66 Catholic women, in general, made possible the survival of Catholicism in many of the houses of the nobility, since their husbands outwardly adapted to the nation's religious laws, while they continued to practice the Catholic faith within the family nucleus, which included children and servants. This is the reason for the fear of the Jesuit, as a new authority figure who could supplant the head of the family. See Walsham, *Church Papists*, pp. 79–81.
67 Juan de Mariana, *Del rey y de la institución de la dignidad real*, Madrid, Mundo Latino, 1930, p. 109 (Translated by BD).
68 Arnauld stresses the Jesuits' defense of the supremacy of the pope, who "has power to put downe the Kinges and princes of the earth, alleaging for his reason, certain tirannous attemtats and enterprises" (p. 8). Pedro de Ribadeneira makes the Jesuit position on the matter quite clear: "In order to understand the obligation which princes have to turn to religion, it is enough to witness the oath that emperors and kings take at their coronation and *that they take possession of their kingdoms by the hand of the prelate and ecclesiastical minister* . . . This is why they are crowned in churches and why Mass is held, why they are placed before the altar, and in some locales why they are dressed in priest's robes, and why the bishops hand them the scepter and crown and take their oath and place curses upon those who would break it: *so that they know that it is God who grants them that royal dignity, that their hand is given in marriage to the Church, so that they love, serve, defend, and support its holy religion*" (Translated by BD; my emphasis). Quoted in "La Monarquía Católica." *Antología de textos de Philip II y los españoles*, Rafael Carrasco and Alain Milhou (Eds.), Paris, Editions Du Temps, 1998, p. 30.
69 Barrière served in Guise's Catholic army; motivated by religious zeal, he attempted to assassinate Henry IV. A member of the King's retinue managed to stop him. Before he was executed, he confessed that he had been urged to commit the crime by a Capuchin from Lyon, by the priest Aubry and the Jesuit Varade. See www.ucm.es/info/museoafc/ loscriminales/ magnicidios/enrique%204 html.
70 See the many examples in Bell, *The Anatomie*, pp. 37–39, 41, 87.
71 This idea was intensified with the Armada in 1588, when English Protestants in general blamed the pope for being the true inspirer of the attack. See examples in the anonymous pamphlet *An Oration Militarie to all Naturall Englishmen. Whether Protestants or, Otherwise in Religion Affected, so Move Resolution in These Dangerous Times*, London, 1588, sig. A4r and Aske, *Elizabetha Triumphans*, sigs B2r, C3v. Sixtus V nevertheless felt himself obligated against his will to support the Spanish campaign after the death of Mary Queen of Scots. Even so, "he continued to show himself very reticent with regard to the Spanish plans, lamenting delays and contributing to the creation in Rome of an atmosphere of pessimism and mistrust". Following the defeat, the Pontiff repeated his prior accusations against Philip II: "The King of Spain, as temporal sover-

Notes to p. 120

eign, seeks above all to preserve and extend his dominions ... Defense of the Catholic religion, which is the principal objective of the Pope, is but a pretext for the King of Spain" (Instructions of Sixtus V to Cardinal Caetani, legate in France, translated by BD). See Gómez-Centurión, *La invencible y la empresa de Inglaterra*, pp. 49, 84. The view held by English reformists of the relationship between Spain and Rome was thus a long way from reality.

72 R. Greene, *The Spanish Masquerado*, London, 1589, sigs B2v-B3r.
73 See the two anonymous texts *An Oration Militarie*, sig. B1v, and *A True and Perfect Description of a Straunge Monster Borne in Rome in 1585*, London, 1590, pp. 9–10 and W. Orange, *The Apology or Defence of the Most Noble Prince William, by the Grace of God, Prince of Orange ... against the Proclamation and Edict, Published by the King of Spaine, by which he Proscribeth the Said Lorde, wherby shall Appeare the Slaunders and False Accusations, Conteyned in the Said Proscription*, Delft, 1581, sigs F2r, F4r.
74 See the anonymous pamphlet, *A Treatise Paraenetical, that is to Say: an Exhortation, wherin is Shewed by Good and Evident Reasons Infallible Arguments, Most True and Certaine Histories and Notable Examples: the Right Way & True Meanes to Resist the Violence of the Castilian King: to Breake the Course of his Deseignes: to Beat Downe his Pride, and to Ruinate his Puissance*, London, 1598, pp. 17, 21–22, 94, 1102; H. W. *A Pageant of Spanish Humours wherin are Naturally Described and Lively Portrayed the Kinds and Quallities of a Signior of Spain*, London, 1599, sigs B1r, B2v; and G. B., *A Fig for the Spaniard*, London, 1591, sigs A4v-B1r.
75 Ibid; sig. C2r; *An Oration Militarie*, sig. B1r; *A Treatise Paraenetical*, pp. 23–24; and Lewkenor, *The Estate of the English Fugitives*, pp. 127–128.
76 Chilmead (Trad.), *Thomas Campanella an Italian Friar and Second Machiavel. His Advice to the King of Spain for Attaining the Universal Monarchy of the World*, London, 1660, p. 155. The translator calculates that the work was written around 1599 or 1600, seventy years before this translation, which is presented in the form of a warning to the English people of the dangerous nature of the forces of foreign Catholicism.
77 Although few references have been found regarding this, it seems that Protestant authors identified the Spanish empire with Castile.
78 This image contrasts with the pacific image of Philip II that was circulated in Spain: "If he were inclined to war, he would show a lively, bellicose spirit, with animosity toward peace; he would like to ride on horseback; he would speedily resolve important matters; in short, he would not fear hardships. In Philip, one sees the complete opposite, from which one may infer that by nature and inclination, he loves quietude; others, although by nature inclined to peace, would allow themselves to be dragged to war by the longing for honors and glory, while to HRH this is repugnant, as has been said, because of his temperament and inclination" (Translated by BD). "Relación de Antonio Tiépolo al regreso de su embajada cerca del rey católico en 1567" in L. P. Gachard, *Carlos V y Felipe II a través de sus contemporáneos*, Madrid, Atlas, pp. 115–116.

79 See also R. Ashley, *A Comparison of the English and Spanish Nations Composed by a French Gentleman*, London, 1589, pp. 21, 23.
80 Robert Wilson, *The Three Lords and Three Ladies of London* (1590), J. S. Farmer (Ed.), The Tudor facsimile Texts, Edinburgh, 1912, pp. 4–5.
81 In addition, this figure was a symbol of impiety and incest in Renaissance iconography. See Ripa, *Iconología*, vol. I, p. 510.
82 See also *A True and Perfect Description*, pp. 17–18, and Ashley, *A Comparison*, p. 36.
83 G. Mattingly, *The Defeat of the Spanish Armada*, Boston, Houghton Mifflin, 1959, p. 121. The Spanish ships had extremely high forecastles, which limited their manoeuverability. It was a mixed fleet, with ships of varying quality and all the inconveniences that that brought with it. On 21 June, after they had sailed from Lisbon on 18 May, a storm had done away with two-thirds of the vessels even before they reached Galicia. The ships were overloaded, hygienic conditions for the crew were entirely absent, the ships' stores of provisions were rotting, and drinking water was becoming scarce. Still far from the English coast, the Armada progressively weakened. See D. Howarth, *La Armada invencible: las verdaderas causas de un desastre naval*, Barcelona, Argos Vergara, 1981, pp. 61, 63, 67, 69, 73–75.
84 See Mattingly, *The Defeat of the Spanish Armada*, pp. 216–217. The Duke of Parma, who was to await Medina Sidonia's arrival in the English Channel with reinforcements from the Low Countries, remained sceptical of the enterprise's prospect. A year before the ships sailed, he told Philip II: "with all diligence I see the time is so short and the days pass so quickly, and so few of the precautions are made that must be, and all because of the late arrival and scarcity of money provisions, and these so short, as Your Majesty knows, that I am nearly discouraged, although I do not lift my hand from the task, but as I have said before, I do what I can to knock down the many difficulties with which I am confronted in attempting to defeat them, as in part has been done, although not all that should be done nor all that I would wish" (translated by BD). *Archivo General de Simancas*. Estado, 592, fols 109–112. Quoted in Parente, *Los sucesos de Flandes en 1588 en relación con la empresa de Inglaterra*, p. 89.
85 See Ripa, *Iconología*, vol. I, pp. 112, 271–272; vol. II, pp. 5, 92.
86 See other examples in Ashley, *A Comparison*, p. 21; Wilson, *The Three Lords*, pp. 4–5 Pride was also considered to be the cause of another vice sometimes associated with the Spanish: laziness (Greene, *The Spanish Masquerado*, sig. C1v), as Patricia Shaw gleans from the words of Lord Roos: "But, by nature, he loves to have nothing to do, and would rather depend on divine Providence than put himself to work. I observe that he feels special antipathy toward commerce and agriculture, and his pride prevents him from being a peasant, since he hopes to make a greater fortune by going to the University, to the Court, or to the Indies, and he says that his king has more means to improve his position without spending a cent than do all the kings of Christendom" (translated by BD). See P. Shaw, *España vista por los ingleses del siglo XVII*, Madrid, Sociedad General Española de Librerías, 1981, p. 155.
87 The accusations of parsimony of which the Spanish were frequently victims

(Wilson, *The Three Lords*, p. 40) contradict the charges of greed and love of pomp that were also attributed to them, revealing the paradoxes and contradictions in this type of discourse. Their sobriety, in fact, was one of the qualities which the English admired about the Spanish, in contrast to the flippancy of the French. See Shaw, *España vista por los ingleses*, p. 135.

88 See examples of this in *Midas* (1592) and *The Spanish Tragedy* (1586–1587).

89 For more information, see R. R. Kelley, "Elizabethan Political Thought", *The Varieties of British Political Thought*, J. G. A. Pocock (Ed.), Cambridge, Cambridge University Press, 1993, 47–79, p. 70.

90 Leonard Wright, *The Hunting of Antichrist*, London, 1589, p. 1.

91 This supports the traditional reformist idea of the continuity between the Primitive Church and the Anglican Church. In addition, this criticism of Catholicism allows it to be linked with other groups that were considered sectarian within Anglican discourse, as they inhibited religious uniformity. Willet points out the importance of fighting against these groups – "Brownists, Anabaptists, Papists" – which, according to the author, made peace in the Kingdom difficult. See his work *A Catholicon or Remedie against the Pseudocatholike Religion*, London, 1602, p. 128. The fact that Protestant authorities equated the Catholic menace with that posed by Puritanism or by separatist groups indicates an advance in the policies of the Elizabethan government, which kept itself in the exact middle between all these currents. This explains the abandonment of religious polemic or of the ideological struggles that could only slow down the process of conformity. See other examples of attacks on nonconformist groups in F. Bunny, *A Comparison between the Aunciert Fayth of the Romans and the Romish Religion*, London, 1595, p. 4 and Wright, *The Hunting of the Antichrist*, pp. 20, 26.

92 Kelley, "Elizabethan Political Thought", p. 72.

93 W. Chauncie, *The Rooting of the Romishe Supremacie*, London, 1580, pp. 117–129.

94 Strong, *The Cult of Elizabeth*, pp. 114–120.

95 Strong, *The Tudor and Stuart Monarchy*, pp. 17–53, 164–185.

96 Latin poets identified the figure of Astraea with Virgo, the astrological sign for August, and related the myth of Virgo-Astraea to Rome's imperial mission. Virgil thus includes in book VI of the *Aeneid* the prophecy of the return of the Golden Age under Caesar Augustus, an idea that Emperor Constantine would attempt to fulfill centuries later by mixing it with Christian tradition. For Constantine, the Golden Age was Christianity itself, which would come to all those inclined to accept it. This theme was elaborated during the Middle Ages and the Renaissance by authors such as St. Augustin, Dante, A. F. Doni and Cola di Rienzo. For more details, see Yates, *Astraea*, pp. 29–39.

97 D.F.R., *An Answer to the Untruthes Published in Spaine in Glorie of their Supposed Victorie against our English Navie*, London, 1589.

98 Rafael Portillo, "Desde los orígenes hasta Marlowe", *Historia crítica del teatro inglés*, Pilar Hidalgo et al. (Eds.), Alcoy, Marfil, 9–59, p. 46.

99 There is no doubt, however, about the date of publication and its entry into

the record: 4 October 1591. See C. Leech & T. W. Craik (Eds.), *The Revels History of Drama in English 1576–1613*, vol. III, London, New York, Routledge, 1998, p. 60.
100 Hackett, *Virgin Mother, Maiden Queen*, p. 174.
101 See David Bevington's edition of *Endymion, the Man in the Moon*, Manchester, Manchester University Press, 1996, p. 32. This is the edition which has been used to analyse this work. According to Bevington, this was a defense of the Earl of Oxford (whose secretary he had been) and other Catholic noblemen of the court at a time when, following Babington's conspiracy (1586) and the death of Mary Queen of Scots, the loyalty of the monarch's Catholic subjects was being questioned.
102 This feast commemorates the presentation of Jesus in the Temple and the purification of his mother, Mary.
103 See Bevington's edition, p. 10.
104 The figure of the moon carried these same connotations of immortality. See Hackett, *Virgin Mother, Maiden Queen*, pp. 176–177.
105 According to Ripa, the Ancients represented Ingratitude as "the figure of Acteon devoured by his own dogs". Loyalty appears dressed in white as a symbol of purity and innocence that in this case is sullied by the true intentions (violent and dishonest) of the character Treachery, hence his bloodstained hands. In contrast, the figure of Envy in Lyly's work is identical to that which Ripa describes. See Ripa, *Iconología*, vol. I, pp. 341–343, 525; vol. II, p. 14.
106 See more examples in V. iv. 67–74, 59–80.
107 See another example in II. i. 60–64.
108 Perhaps his position was influenced by his proximity to certain Catholic circles of the nobility: the Earl of Oxford (who sponsored the dramatist until 1588), Lord Henry Howard, and Arundel, among others. In addition, one of the author's uncles had served under Cardinal Pole, Archbishop of Canterbury during the reign of Mary I. Although Lyly's orthodox Anglicanism was apparent in the controversy surrounding the Marprelate pamphlets, his target was not so much Catholicism as it was the Puritans. See Bevington's edition, pp. 36–37.
109 See Bevington's edition, p. 180.
110 See Hackett, *Virgin Mother, Maiden Queen*, pp. 163–197.
111 It was soon in print and entered in the register on 4 October 1591. See Leech, *The Revels History*, p. 63.
112 Midas's scourge – that everything he touched turned to gold – and the curse of the donkey's ears.
113 A. Golding (Ed. & Trad.), *The XV Bookes of P. Ovidius Naso, Entituled Metamorphosis. A Worke Verie Pleasant and Delectable*, London, 1575, sig. A4. Quoted in S. Hilliard, "Lyly's Midas as an Allegory of Tyranny", *Studies in English Literature 1500–1900*, 1972, 22:2, 243–258, p. 245.
114 Ripa, *Iconología*, vol. I, p. 504.
115 Annaliese Connolly gives an interesting analysis of the work as a criticism of the imperialist desires and attitudes of the English sovereign, and presents Midas (Philip II) as the imperial figure that Elizabeth cannot equal. Consult her article "'O Unquenchable Thirst of Gold': Lyly's Midas and

the English Quest for Empire", *Early Modern Literary Studies*, 2002, 8:2, 4.1–36. Available on the web at http://purl.oclc.org/emls/08-2/con-ngold.html.

116 His description of the sovereign is a reference to the public image of Elizabeth I: "Their King is such a one as dazzleth the clearest eyes with majesty, daunteth the valiantest hearts with courage, and for virtue filleth all the world with wonder. If beauty go beyond sight, confidence above valor, and virtue exceed miracle, what is to be thought but that Midas goeth to undermine that by simplicity of man, that is fastened to a rock by the providence of the gods?" (p. 225). Her majesty and virtue stress her legitimacy as sovereign and God's representative; her valour and courage preclude any possible criticism of feminine weakness, and place her on a plane with all other (male) monarchs; finally, her beauty emphasizes her nature as a woman and her youth, and attempts to neutralize (or rather to conceal) the inevitable worry over the Queen's advanced age.

117 By blaming those near the king for his own poor decisions, the monarchical institution is kept intact. The indirect reference to the two bodies of the King thus permits respect for and defense of the monarchy (the political body) independently of the human frailties of the natural body.

118 A. R. Braunmuller et al. (Eds.), *The Cambridge Companion to English Renaissance Drama*, Cambridge, Cambridge University Press, 1990, p. 177.

119 See his edition of Marlowe's complete plays (Harmondsworth, Penguin, 1969), p. 235. References are made to this edition.

120 Ibid., p. 235.

121 Leech, *The Revels History*, p. 101.

122 Steane indicates as a principal source for the play the pamphlet authored by Ernest Varamund, *A True and Plaine Report of the Furious Outrages of France* (1573, 1574). See p. 235 of his edition.

123 According to George Watson, Machiavelli's writings were known as early as the 1570s among educated circles in England. French and Latin versions of his works circulated throughout England, and in fact various editions in Italian were published between 1584 and 1588 with false places of publication – Rome, Palermo, Piacenza – probably with the intention of promoting anti-Catholic sentiment during the times of the Armada and of Mary Queen of Scots. See his article "Machiavel and Machiavelli", *The Swane Review*, 1976, 84:4, 630–648, pp. 636–637.

124 See his work *Christopher Marlowe and the Renaissance Tragedy*, Westport, Connecticut, London, Greenwood Press, 1995, p. 81.

125 Up to this point, much of the criticism leveled against Spaniards included the Italians as well, especially in pamphlet literature. Innocent Gentillet, an important Huguenot pamphleteer, accuses them of being liars and disloyal, emphasizing their ambition and lustfulness. See I. Gentillet, *A Discours upon the Meanes of Vvel Governing and Maintaining in Good Peace, A Kingdome, or Other Principalitie*, London, 1602, sig. B1v. Henry Estienne highlights their cunning and secretive nature and makes them the target of all manner of moral accusations: "[The Florentines] doe enuy, disdayne and mortally hate all such as eyther in vertue, nobili-

tie or any other good qualitie, doe exceed them, but most especially, all those to whom in any respect they are bounde or beholdyng, notwithstandyng than in outward apparence they will seme affable unto all men . . . They are also more particularly noted of a certayne prodigalitie of other mens goods . . . In most filthy and beastly whordomes and lechery they doe excell: Depe dissimulation is naturally rooted in them: and in the execution of all kinde of treasons they be most readye." See his work *A Marvaylous Discourse upon the Lyfe, Deedes, and Behaviours of Katherine de Medicis, Queene Mother: Wherin are Displayed the Meanes which She Hath Practised to Atteyne unto the Usurping of the Kingedome of France, and to the Bringing of the Estate of the Same unto Utter Ruine and Destruction*, London, 1575, pp. 6, 9–10. R. Ascham was probably the author who was most explicit in the presentation of this stereotype, which characterizes what he calls the "inglese italianato": "For sinne, by lust and vanitie, hath and doth breed up every where, common contempt of Gods word, private contention in many families, open factions in every Citie and so, makyng them selves bonde, to vanitie and vice at home, they are content to beare the yoke of servyng straungers abroad." See Ascham, *The Scholemaster or Plaine and Perfite Way of Teachyng Children, to Understand, Write and Speake, the Latin Tong but Specially Purposed for the Private Bryngyng up of Youth in Ientlemen and Noble Mens Houses, and Commodious also for all such, as Have Forgot the Latin Tonge*, London, 1570, p. 24.

126 Also, the figure of the atheist was closely linked to the Italian stereotype. See examples in Estienne, *A Marvaylous Discourse*, p. 9 and Gentillet, *A Discours*, sigs B1r-v, H2v.

127 *Discursos sobre la primera década de Tito Livio*, Madrid, Alianza Editorial, 2000, pp. 68–69 (translated by BD).

128 The Catholic Church had included Machiavelli's writings in its index of Prohibited Books between 1559 and 1562. As Cutinelli-Rendina points out, according to many Catholic authors, Machiavelli had offered the Protestants more than one argument against the Pope. See the *Introduzione a Machiavelli*, Roma, Bari, Laterza, 1999, p. 143. Machiavelli becomes, then, a political instrument that both groups employed to discredit the other; such is the case of R. Ascham, who in 1564 (the year in which he wrote his *Scholemaster*), established a clear parallel between the Church of Rome and these atheist tendencies when he refers to the "Italianate Englishmen": "Yet though in Italie they may freely be of no Religion . . . neverthelesse returning home into England they must countenance the posession of the one or the other, howsoever inwardlie, they laugh to scorne both [Catholicism and Protestantism] . . . yet commonlie they allie themselves with the worst Papistes, to whom they be wedded, and do well agree togither in three proper opinions: In open contempte of Goddes worde: in a secret securitie of sinne: and in a bloodie desire to have all taken away by sword or burning, that be not of their faction" (p. 29).

129 See P. W. White, *Marlowe. History and Sexuality. New Critical Essays on Christopher Marlowe*, New York, AMS Press, 1998, pp. 19–20.

130 The seditious character of the figure of Guise was already popular in

pamphlet literature: "The Guysians by vow and profession ancient enimies to the blood royall of France ... do by their last propositions studie to bring al the estates of this realme out of tast with their duetie, whereto nature and the Law of God doth bind them, and under the kings support to oppresse the Princes of the blood, and by the subiects revolt to trippe away the kings legge". See *The Countre-Guyse: Wherein is Deciphered the Pretended Title of the Guyses, and the First Entrie of the Saide Family into Fraunce, with their Ambitious Aspiring and Pernitious Practices for the Obtaining of the French Crowne*, London, 1589, sigs I3v-I4r. See other examples in *An History Briefly Contayninge that Whiche Hath Happened sens the Departure of the House of Guise ... from the Court Being at S. Germains untill this Present*, London, 1562, sigs A8v, V1v, C5v-D4r; *The Destruction and Sacke Cruelty Commited by the Duke of Guyse and his Company, in the Towne of Wassy, the Fyrst of Marche, in the Yeare M.D.LXII*, London; David, Advocate of Paris, *A Summe of the Guisyan Ambassage to the Bishop of Rome*, London, 1579, sigs A2v-A4r; P. Mornay, *A Necessary Discours Concerning the Right Which the House of Guyse Pretendeth to the Crowne of France*, London, 1586, sigs A2r-v; and M. Hurault, *A Discourse upon the Present Estate of France. Togither with a Copie of the Kinges Letters Patents, Declaring his Mind after his Departure out of Paris. Whereunto is Added the Copie of Two Letters Written by the Duke of Guize*, London, 1592, sigs B1r-B2v, B4r.

131 Recall the character Sir Laurence Livinglesse in *All For Money* (1578) by Thomas Lupton.
132 Catherine de' Medici's ambition and cruelty were a commonplace in pamphlet literature. See Estienne, *A Marvaylous Discourse*, pp. 43, 50, 61, 80, 103, 113, 159, 178–179, 181; Tharua Phanit S., *A Letter Written by a French Gentleman to a Friend of his at Rome Conteyning a True Report of the Late Treaty between the Queene Mother of France and the King of Navarre*, London, 1587, sig. A3r, C3r and M. Hurault, *A Discourse*, sigs C4v-D1v.
133 R. Bushnell, *Tragedies of Tyrants. Political Thought and Theatre in the English Renaissance*, Ithaca, London, Cornell University press, 1990, pp. 66–67.
134 Numerous pamphlets in fact blamed Catherine for her children's failed political decisions. See Tharua, *A Letter*, p. 23; Hurault, *A Discourse*, pp. 16, 25, 26 and Estienne, *A Mervaylous Discourse*, pp. 59, 80.
135 See Bushnell, *Tragedies of Tyrants*, p. 130.
136 The same criticism is seen in some of the pamphlets analysed. See *The Countre-Guyse*, sig. I4r and Hurault, *A Discourse*, sigs A2v-A3v.
137 *El Príncipe*, Madrid, Espasa Calpe, 1996, pp. 120–121 (translated by BD).
138 The pamphlet literature sometimes resorts to similar means in order to preserve the monarchy from this type of criticism. See Tharua, *A Letter*, p. 13, Hurault, *A Discourse*, pp. 18, 50–51.
139 See D. Grantley & P. Roberts, *Christopher Marlowe and English Renaissance Culture*, Aldershot, Ashgate, 1999, pp. 80–87.
140 The portrayal of Navarre emphasizes his legitimacy, his commitment to the truth, and his continuous support by Providence, which finally leads him

to the Throne of France (xiv, 29–52; xvi, 1–15; xviii, 1–19). His role and appearances onstage are far smaller than those of his opponent, which would relegate him to a secondary plane, and one that would probably scarcely capture the audience's attention. His promise to avenge the death of Henry III (xxv, 109) complicates the perception of the character; like his predecessor, he ends up with a clear intention of disobeying the country's laws.

141 For more information, see Leech, *The Revels History*, p. 83; D. F. Rowan, "The Staging of The Spanish Tragedy", *The Elizabethan Theatre*, G. R. Hibbard (Ed.), London, 1975, pp. 112–123; and J. R. Mulryne's edition of Kyd's work (London, New Mermainds, 2000), p. xxxi. The date of the play's composition is variously listed as between 1582 and 1592, when it was premièred by Lord Strange's Men (p. xiv). The play was printed in 1592, 1592, 1599, 1602 and 1603, in addition to at least nine times more, prior to 1633 (p. xxxi).

142 As Mulryne indicates, during the 1580s Portugal was considered to be merely another of Spain's possessions. Philip II had inherited the Portuguese crown in 1580, which, in view of the Spanish Empire's growing maritime power, caused grave concern in other European countries. Their reaction was to support the claims to the throne of Don Antonio, the illegitimate son of the Duke of Braganza. The Dutch, France and England funded his attempts at rebellion against Philip. Nevertheless, the Portuguese people did not support him, so these plans resulted in a fiasco. See his article "Nationality and Language in Thomas Kyd's *The Spanish Tragedy*", *Travel and Drama in Shakespeare's Time*, 1996, Jean Pierre Maquerlot & M. Willens (Eds.), Cambridge, Cambridge University Press, 87–105, pp. 102–103.

143 For more information on this topic, see *The Elizabethan Image of Italy* (Washington, Folger Shakespeare Library, 1964) by John Lievsay; *The Paradise of Travellers: The Italian Influence on Englishmen in the Seventeenth Century* (London, G. Allen & Unwin, 1964) by Arthur Lytton Sells; *The English Face of Machiavelli* (London, Routledge, 1964) by Felix Raab and *Machiavelli and the Elizabethans* (Folcroft, PA, Folcroft Library Editions, 1973) by Mario Praz.

144 W. Rankins, *The English Ape, the Italian Imitation, the Footsteppes of Fraunce. Wherein is Explained . . . the Secret Found of Many Hollow Hearts*, London, 1588, pp. 2–3.

145 The Portuguese general falsely accused by Viluppo of the death of Balthazar during the war with Spain.

146 This is what Alexandro does when he is condemned to death. His patience and faith in God is rewarded by the news that arrives from Spain (III, i, 35–46, 57–68).

147 See the article by James T. Henke, "Politics and Politicians in The Spanish Tragedy", *Studies in Philology*, 1981, 78:4, 353–369, p. 361.

148 These reveal the identities of Horatio's murderers and appear at decisive moments in the play, when the old man asks for God's help in finding those guilty (III, ii, 24–52; III, vii, 19–73).

149 In view of her inability to avenge Horatio's death herself – since such a

"duty" belonged to the father, not to the mother – Isabella destroys the garden and the tree where her son died. Shortly afterwards she commits suicide, foreshadowing Hieronimo's tragic end.
150 These same Machiavellian tendencies are seen in Viluppo, who manages to deceive the Portuguese Viceroy in favor of his own economic interests. Pedingrano, a symbol of disloyalty and amorality, lacks his predecessor's cunning and merely becomes Lorenzo's puppet.
151 W. Maltby, *La Leyenda Negra. Desarrollo del sentimiento antihispánico 1558–1660*, Méjico, Fondo de cultura económica, 1982, pp. 68–69.
152 Other scenes of torture, executions and rape appear in D1r-D3v, E1r-v, E3v and F1r-F3v.
153 Maltby, *La Leyenda Negra*, p. 67.
154 See other examples in sigs C2r and F1v.
155 See Braunmuller, *The Cambridge Companion*, p. 176.
156 Leech, *The Revels History*, p. 85.
157 Margot Heinemann describes the influence of commercial theatre on the formation of "a secular public opinion far beyond the limits of the recognized 'political nation', the natural rulers as represented at court, in Parliament and in central and local governments". This novel situation alarmed successive governments, who attempted to preserve the authority of the elite ruler with the invaluable help of censorship (Braunmuller, *The Cambridge Companion*, p. 167). In moments of political crisis (such as the final years of Elizabeth's reign), these methods reemerged, which explains the various strategies employed by the authors to avoid them.
158 Born around 1378, he was accused of heresy, took part in suppressing the Welsh revolt led by Owen Glendower, and supported the Duke of Burgundy (1411). Charged with aiding Lollard preachers in 1413, he was excommunicated and burned at the stake in 1417. See www.encyclopedia.com/html.0.oldcastl.asp and www.gospelcom.net/chi/archivef/09/daily-90-23-2001.html.
159 The portrayal of this character is strengthened by the deep anticlerical sentiment that predominates in the play. The most ready example is the character of Sir John, an old priest, miserly and lustful, who appears in the boarding house scene to which Oldcastle escapes on one occasion. See sigs C4r-D1r, F3r-G1v, I3r and K4r.
160 The statement seems to refer to the medieval constitutionalism still present in Elizabeth's policies. This concept emphasized the relationship between the king, the parliament, and the common law courts, which limited the absolute power of the monarch. According to this theory, the king's authority depended on the consent of the people, which pact was established during the coronation ceremony. Thus the people held the power to depose a monarch who failed to rule accordingly, not holding up his end of this agreement. See Kelley, "Elizabethan Political Thought", pp. 51–52 and Holmes, *Resistance and Compromise*, pp. 147–148.
161 He also appears as the figure of the father-protector, who is concerned for his subjects; he decides to go to Westminster in disguise in order to test the people's disposition (sigs F2r-F3v). This image of the populist monarch recalls that of Elizabeth, whose parallelism with the King's character is

controversial, given the accusations of irresponsibility that were leveled at him before.

162 Iudge's denunciations evoke the words of Henry VIII, who complained in 1546 of the easy access to Scripture that the common people continued to have and of their readiness to enter into theological disputes: "The worde of God is disputed rymed, song, and iangeled in every Alehouse and Taverne". See McEachern, *Religion and Culture*, p. 63. The play thus establishes an indirect parallel between the unrest that such political and religious involvement of the common people provoked within Elizabeth's government and in that of Henry VIII and his collaborators. Through a comparison of Elizabeth's policies with those of the last years of her father's reign, she is criticized for distancing herself from groups who demanded more profound changes.

163 Leech, *The Revels History*, pp. 42, 44–45.
164 Braunmuller, *The Cambridge Companion*, p. 423.
165 Strong, *The Cult of Elizabeth*, pp. 148–149.
166 The names of the characters, for example, carry clearly pejorative connotations. Lucre is defined in the *Oxford English Dictionary* as "gain, profit, pecuniary advantage. Now only with unfavourable implication: gain viewed as a low motive for action"; Pomp is identified with "ostentatious display . . . specious or boastful show; vain glory; esp. in phr. 'pomp and pride'"; finally, Policy also carries a negative meaning in some cases, when it is associated with "political cunning, craftiness, dissimulation". Their names relate the characters to elements particular to the Spanish or Catholic stereotype by questioning their supposed virtuous nature.

EPILOGUE Nostalgia for Elizabeth and Anti-Catholic Discourse

1 Freud, Sigmund, *Psicología de las masas. Obras Completas*, James Strachey (Ed.), Paraguay, Amorrotu Editores, 1995, vol. XVIII, 65–136, pp. 79–80 (Translation by BD).
2 Ibid; pp. 110, 115.
3 Quoted in Joseph V. R. Tanner (Ed.), *Constitutional Documents of the Reign of James I*, Ad. 1603–1625, Cambridge, Cambridge University Press, 1930, p. 220.
4 After 1610, persecution of the Catholic community notably diminished, as the number of Catholic subjects executed demonstrates: between 1607 and 1610, eight; between 1611 and 1618, nine; and between 1619 and 1625, zero. See J. P. Kenyon, *Stuart England*, London, Penguin Books, 1985, p. 72.
5 Ibid; p. 60.
6 Brewer, *Letters and Papers*, vol. I, pp. 96–98. Quoted in C. Perry, "The Citizen Politics of Nostalgia: Queen Elizabeth in Early Jacobean London", *Journal of Medieval and Renaissance Studies*, 1993, 23, 89–111, p. 89.
7 See Woodward, "Images of a Dead Queen", p. 5, and Kenyon, *Stuart England*, p. 77.
8 See his article "The Citizen Politics of Nostalgia", p. 90. John Watkins supports the same idea in his work *Representing Elizabeth in Stuart*

England. Literature, History, Sovereignty, Cambridge, Cambridge University Press, 2002.
9   Quoted in W. Notestein et al. (Eds), *Common Debates 1621*, New Haven, Yale University Press, 1935, vol. II, p. 8.
10 Curiously, in the first stage of her government, Elizabeth I had taken on the same role as Europe's mediator, and had followed a similar policy regarding religious dissidents; many of her subjects who now denounced James's conciliatory posture were exercising a selective memory with regard to the beginnings of the previous reign.
11 There would be no substantial opposition in the matter until the image of Spain and Catholicism began to be forged in the context of Romantic orientalism.
12 For a detailed study of this conspiracy, see *Faith and Treason: The Story of the Gunpowder Plot* (New York, Doubleday, 1996) by Antonia Fraser; *Gunpowder Plot: Faith in Rebellion* (Strout, A. Sulton, 1994) by Alan Haynes; *Investigating the Gunpowder Plot* (New York, Manchester, Manchester University Press, 1991) by Mark Nicholls; *Gunpowder, Treason and Plot* (New York, St. Martin's Press, 1977) by C. Northcote Parkinson; *Intended Treason, what Really Happened in the Gunpowder Plot* (South Brunswick, A. S. Barnes, 1971) by Paul Durst; *Guy Fawkes: The Real Story of the Gunpowder Plot?* (London Hart Davis, 1969) by Francis Edwards, and *Henry Garnett (1555–1606) and the Gunpowder Plot* (London, Longmans, 1964) by Philip Caraman.
13 Son of Sir William Catesby, an important leader of the Catholic community during Elizabeth's reign. He was imprisoned in 1581 for harbouring Edmund Campion, head of the Society of Jesus in England.
14 Descendent of the Earls of Northumberland who had intervened in various plots against Elizabeth I.
15 Garnett concealed Catesby's intentions as a confessional secret, as a letter to the king dated 4 April 1606 (after Garnett was sentenced to death) indicates: "Also I acknowledge that I was bound to reveal all knowledge that I had of this or any other treason out of the Sacrament of Confession. And whereas partly upon hope of prevention, partly for I would not betray my friend, I did not reveal the general knowledge of Mr. Catesby's intention which I had by him. I do acknowledge myself highly guilty and to have offended God, the King's Majesty and estate, and humbly ask of all forgiveness." Quoted in E. Taunton, *The History of the Jesuits in England 1580–1773*, London, Methuen & Co, 1901, p. 317.
16 Nevertheless, the pope had his suspicions, as is seen in a letter addressed to Garnett that the Jesuit Aquaviva wrote in his name on 25 June 1605. In it he makes known his opposition to any revolt: "We have heard, although clearly and very secretly, what I am persuaded your reverence knows, that the Catholics are planning something for their liberty; but as such an attempt, especially at this time, will bring not only many and grave inconveniences to religion, but will call into question the whole body of Catholics our Holy Father orders me to write to your Reverence in his name that you should use all your influence with these noblemen and gentlemen, especially with the Archpriest, that nothing of the sort should be discussed or carried

out on account of the above-mentioned causes, especially because of the orders of His Holiness". Ibid., pp. 291–292.

17 Persons wrote to the pope in September 1605, asking that he tell him of the conspiracies of the English Catholics. He received no reply. Once the plan was discovered, he did not attempt to exculpate the Jesuits involved in it, but worked instead to distance the rest of the Catholic community from any responsibility for the plot. Ibid., pp. 300, 331.

18 Watkins, *Representing Elizabeth*, p. 26. For more information on commemorations of the Armada and the Gunpowder Plot, see the work by David Cressy, *Bonfires and Bells: National Memory and the Protestant Calendar in Elizabethan and Stuart England*, London, Weidenfeld and Nicolson, 1989.

19 Nicholls, *Investigating Gunpowder Plot*, p. 47.

20 James I, *His Maiesties Speach in this Last Session of Parliament*, London, 1605, sigs C2r-C3r.

21 The work enters the register on 20 April 1607. See Leech, *The Revels History*, p. 89.

22 Both texts enjoyed great popularity, as the multiple editions that were made of them demonstrates. The first part was edited eight times: in 1605, 1606, 1608, 1610, 1613, 1623, 1632 and 1639; the second part a total of four times: 1606, 1609, 1623 and 1633. See the edition of both of Heywood's works published by AMS Press (New York) in 1935, I, p. 14; II, p. viii. The appeal to the queen's memory and to the tradition of Protestant victimhood continued to fill theatres up until the civil war.

23 The dramatist dedicates his work to Prince Henry, the patron of the company (Prince Henry's Men) that performed it in the Fortune Theatre. From the beginning, his patronage indicates its anti-Spanish, Protestant tone, since, after their disappointment with James's policies, many English Protestants centred their attention on the figure of the heir to the throne, who appeared to be closer to the Protestant cause than his father.

24 *The Whore of Babylon* describes the Catholic conspiracies against Elizabeth throughout her reign, and *If you Know Not Me* focuses on the obstacles which she had to overcome during the reign of Mary I.

25 Elizabeth personifies innocence (*The Whore*, sig. I3r; *If You Know* I, sigs B4r, C1v), wisdom (*The Whore*, sig. B4r; *If You Know* II, sig. F1r), purity and virginity (*The Whore*, sigs B4r, C1r, I3r, C4v), commitment to the truth (*The Whore*, sig. A3v, *If You Know* I, sigs C1v, D1r), bravery (*The Whore*, sig. C4v; *If You Know* II, sig. K1r), beauty, virtue and perfection (*If You Know* I, sigs B4r, F3v).

26 See examples in *The Whore*, sigs B4r, G3v, and in *If You Know* I, sigs B1v, B4f-v, C4r, F2r-F3r. In fact, Foxe's text is the principal source of the dramatic action in the first part of Heywood's work. It reproduces in its entirety an episode from the 1589 edition of *Actes and Monuments* in which is described "The miracolous preservation of Lady Elizabeth, now our most gratious queen of England" (pp. 268–278). The parallels between the two writings are almost exact, although *If You Know not Me* stresses, in addition to her pathos, the legitimate and populist character of the queen. Such emphasis was necessary in order to produce an attractive and powerful

persona onstage, though it probably also developed in response to an awakening fascination with the deceased queen.

27. The influence of the moral allegory is even more obvious in these dumb shows, which made up a key dramatic element in anti-Catholic theatre. In *The Spanish Tragedy*, these shows are inserted throughout the play and foretell that which is about to happen onstage; this is the most direct forerunner to Dekker. Additionally, Thomas Heywood includes a dumb show in the first part of his play, in which Philip II's intercession on Elizabeth's behalf before Mary I is dramatized (sig. D1v).

28. In it the figure of Truth appears, deep in sleep, while her father (Time) attempts to wake her. At their side, a court of bishops, cardinals and monks chant in Latin. Suddenly Truth awakens and, taking note of her circumstance, flees along with Time, later returning "cloathed in a robe spotted with Starres"; this opens the eyes of the Royal Council, who then disappear with her, leaving the rest of the retinue onstage. Shortly afterward, Titania enters together with members of the Council. Time and Truth present a book to her, which she kisses, to the joy of those surrounding her, who draw their swords in obeisance.

29. See Daly, *The English Emblem Tradition*, p. 93.

30. See Ripa, *Iconología*, vol. II, pp. 360–361; 391–393.

31. Heywood repeats this scene at the conclusion of *If You Know Not Me*, again to convey the play's Protestant intent.

32. In fact, Titania is described as "the Faerie Queene" (sig. A4v).

33. Hackett, *Virgin Mother, Maiden Queen*, p. 141.

34. The work carries a clear admonitory sense that applies to contemporary reality: English citizens who support the enemy would be fashioning their own destruction, since these enemies "imploy them/ As Bees while they have stings, & bring things laden/ With hony, hive them, when they are droanes, destroy them" (sig. E4v).

35. Another dumb show opens the second part of the play, disclosing the Catholic faction's strategies.

36. While in *The Whore of Babylon* the character of the King of Spain is seen as responsible for all the attempts on the Queen's life, in *If You Know not Me*, Philip II's character is more positive, acting as mediator between Mary I and Princess Elizabeth (sig. B3v). His wish for peace and harmony between the two nations alludes to the treaty of 1604 and to his own goodwill, which also appears as a guarantor of honour and justice. He is portrayed in this way in the scene depicting a compatriot's punishment for having murdered an English nobleman. The character of the other Spaniard – false, vain, cowardly and traitorous – conforms to the Spanish stereotype. Even so, criticizing the monarch was dangerous, so Dekker resorts to abstract and allegorical characters, while Heywood altogether avoids direct confrontation.

37. Quoted in Kenyon, *Stuart England*, p. 64. Perry also analyses this possible association in his article "The Citizen Politics of Nostalgia", pp. 103–104.

38. Jonathan Goldberg contrasts the image of reciprocity between subjects and sovereign conveyed during Elizabeth's entry to London with that of James and its emphasis on hierarchy and the authority of the monarch.

39　See several examples in *The Whore*, sig. B4v.
40　See *If You Know* I, sigs B2v-B4r, C2v-C3v, D3r-D4v, E2v. Elizabeth shows herself to be attentive to the poor (sigs D3v, D4v), which stresses the connection that many reformist authors – led by Foxe – forged between Protestantism and the lower classes. Elizabeth is the vehicle for such identification. Her motherly love for the people is symbolized by a dove (*The Whore*, sig. C3r), which refers to Alciatus's emblem CXCIV, *Amor Filiorum* (Love of one's children), in which the bird plucks all its own feathers in order to keep its chicks warm, though it risks dying of cold. Her capacity for sacrifice is a reference to her image as martyr and mother of the nation, often used during critical times. Also, this idea explains her politics regarding the Low Countries – "[FIDELI:] [The Netherlands pray] That you would be their mother, and their nurse,/ Their Guardian and their governour" (sig. D4r) – which is an implied criticism of James I, who, according to his detractors, seemed to have forgotten his commitment to other Protestant countries after signing the peace with Spain.
41　See B. Coward, *The Stuart Age*, London, New York, Longman, 1980, p. 96.
42　Nevertheless, Mary was not the object of harsh criticism; instead, she is portrayed as the victim of the influence of Winchester, the play's true antagonist. In this way the monarchy's image is preserved, though the necessity of protecting oneself against the advice of bad counsellors is stressed.
43　Even so – as John Watkins points out – during the time of her rule, Elizabeth had been characterized in a rather different way, as her incessant disputes with parliament and her readiness to invoke the royal prerogative demonstrate. Her supposed constitutionalist tendencies thus form part of the mythology that was generated about her from the late sixteenth century. For a more detailed analysis of this phenomenon, see Watkins, *Representing Elizabeth*, p. 36.
44　There was a rumour that he had attempted to poison her. Both plays depict this episode: *If You Know* II, sigs H3v-I1v and *The Whore*, sigs D2r-v, F3v-F4r.
45　The identification of Elizabeth and Protestantism with loyalty to the monarchy (*If You Know* I, sig. C1r), as well as the association of Catholicism with seditious acts (sigs D2v-D3r), support this.
46　See Hackett, *Virgin Mother, Maiden Queen*, p. 174.
47　Thomas H. Cain, *Praise in the Faerie Queene*, Lincoln, Nebraska, University of Nebraska Press, 1978, p. 145.
48　This figure had inherited the chivalric character of the Tudors, and openly demonstrated his antipathy for Rome and Spain, which gave rise to a new mythology surrounding him as a successor to the popular Elizabeth. For more information on the iconographic image that was created around the prince, see S. Krantz, "Thomas Dekker's Political Commentary in *The Whore of Babylon*", pp. 276, 279 and Roy Strong, *Henry, Prince of Wales and England's Lost Renaissance* (London, Pimlico, 2000) and *The Cult of Elizabeth*, pp. 187-191.
49　The barely perceptible anti-Catholic discourse, which only appears in the scenes with Parry and with the Armada, is used to praise the Queen's virtu-

ousness and the courage of her soldiers; it is not a political or religious denunciation, but merely a bridge to the first part of the play, in which the construction of this discourse has a prominent role. It could also be a commercial ploy aimed at London audiences, ever susceptible to anti-Catholic rhetoric. In fact, it seems that this ending was added to a play that, in principle, had been commissioned to celebrate Sir Thomas Gresham.

50 Thus the dramatist evokes the same concerns that many plays from the first stage of the Elizabethan era had portrayed regarding the progressive transformation of English society because of money. While in those plays – *All for Money* (1559–1577) and *Enough is as Good as a Feast* (1559–1570) are clear examples – the figure of the monarch did not appear, in *If You Know* II, the character of the queen alludes to a new appreciation of profitable enterprise: the development of England's empire.

51 In fact, this had already happened in Elizabethan times, when pirates and entrepreneurs such as Drake or Raleigh were thought of as authentic popular heroes.

Recommended Reading

ASTON, MARGARET 1988: *England's Iconoclasts. Laws against Images*. Oxford: Clarendon Press.
—— 1993: *The King's Bedpost. Reformation and Iconography in Tudor or Group Portrait*. Cambridge: Cambridge University Press.
BEALES, A. C. F. 1963: *Education under Penalty. English Catholic Education from the Reformation to the Fall of James II 1547–1689*. London: The Athlone Press.
BETTERIDGE, TOM 2004: *Literature and Politics in the English Reformation*. Manchester: Manchester University Press.
BOSSY, JOHN 1976: *The English Catholic Community 1570–1850*. New York: Oxford University Press.
CHRISTIANSON, PAUL 1978: *Reformers and Babylon: English Apocalyptic Visions from the Reformation to the Eve of the Civil War*. Toronto: University of Toronto Press.
CLANCY, T. H. 1964: *Papist Pamphleteers*. Chicago: Loyola University Press.
COLLINSON, PATRICK 1982: *The Elizabethan Puritan Movement*. London, New York: Methuen.
CORTHELL, R.F.E. ET AL. 2007: *Catholic Culture in Early Modern England*. Notre Dame Ind.: The University of Notre Dame Press.
CRAWFORD, PATRICIA 1993: *Women and Religion in England, 1500–1720*. London, New York: Routledge.
CROSS, CLAIRE 1976: *Church and the People 1450–1660. The Triumph of the Laity in the English Church*. Atlantic Highlands, NJ: Humanities Press Inc.
DAVINSON, CLIFFORD ET AL. 1989: *Iconoclasm vs Art and Drama*. Michigan: Western Michigan University. Medieval Institute Publications.
—— 2002: *History, Religion and Violence: Cultural Contexts for Medieval and Renaissance English Drama*. Burlington: Ashgate.
DICKENS, A. G. 1964: *The English Reformation*. Oxford: Clarendon Press.
DIEHL, HUSTON 1997: *Staging Reform, Reforming the Stage. Protestantism and Popular Theatre in Early Modern England*. Ithaca, London: Cornell University Press.
DILLON, ANNE 2002: *The Construction of Martyrdom in the English Catholic Community, 1535–1603*. Aldershot: Ashgate.
DOLAN, FRANCES E. 1999: *Whores of Babylon. Catholicism, Gender and Seventeenth Century Print Culture*. Ithaca, London: Cornell University Press.
DORAN, SUSAN & CHRISTOPHER DURSTON 2002: *Princes, Pastors and People: The Church and Religion in England, 1500–1689*. London: Routledge.

Recommended Reading

DUFFY, EAMON 1992: *The Stripping of the Altars: Traditional Religion in England, 1400–1580.* New Haven: Yale University Press.
DURSTON, CHRISTOPHER & JACQUELINE EALES (Eds.) 2003: *The Culture of English Puritanism, 1560–1700.* New York: Palgrave Macmillan.
GARRET, CRISTINA H. 1938: *The Marian Exiles: A Study in the Origins of Elizabethan Puritanism.* Cambridge: Cambridge University Press.
GREEN, IAN 2000: *Print and Protestantism in Early Modern England.* Oxford: Oxford University Press.
HACKETT, HELEN 1995: *Virgin Mother, Maiden Queen. Elizabeth I and the Cult of the Virgin Mary.* London: Macmillan Press.
HAIGH, CHRISTOPHER 1987: *The English Reformation Revised.* New York, Cambridge: Cambridge University Press.
—— 1993: *English Reformations: Religion, Politics and Society under the Tudors.* Oxford: Clarendon Press.
HIGHLEY, CHRISTOPHER 2008: *Catholics Writing the Nation in Early Modern Britain and Ireland.* Oxford: Oxford University Press.
HILL, CHRISTOPHER 1971: *Antichrist in Seventeenth Century England.* London: Verso.
HOLMES, PETER 1982: *Resistance and Compromise. The Political Thought of the Elizabethan Catholics.* Cambridge: Cambridge University Press.
HÖPFL, HARRO 2004: *Jesuit Political Thought: The Society of Jesus and the State, c. 1540–1640.* Cambridge: Cambridge University Press.
HOULISTON, VICTOR 2007: *Catholic Resistance in Elizabethan England: Robert Person's Jesuit Polemic, 1580–1610.* Aldershot: Ashgate.
HSIA, R. PO-CHIA 2005: *The World of Catholic Renewal, 1540–1770.* Cambridge: Cambridge University Press.
KING, JOHN 1982: *English Reformation Literature. The Tudor Origins of the Protestant Tradition.* Princeton: Princeton University Press.
—— 1989: *Tudor Royal Iconography: Literature and Art in an Age of Religious Crisis.* Princeton: Princeton University Press.
KILROY, GERARD 2005: *Edmund Campion: Memory and Transcription.* Aldershot: Ashgate.
LAKE, PETER & MICHAEL QUESTIER (Eds.) 2002: *The Antichrist's Lewd Hat: Protestants, Papists and Players in Post-Reformation England.* New Haven & London: Yale University Press.
—— 2000: *Conformity and Orthodoxy in the English Church, c. 1560–1660.* Suffolk: Boydell & Brewer.
LANDER, JESSE M. 2009: *Inventing Polemic: Religion, Print and Literary Culture in Early Modern England.* Cambridge: Cambridge University Press
LOOMIE, ALBERT J. 1973/ 1978: *Spain and the Jacobean Catholics 1603–1624.* Vols. I–II. Norfolk: Catholic Record Society.
—— 1996: *Spain and the Early Stuart, 1585–1655.* New York: Fordham University.
LORIMER, PETER 1895: *John Knox and The Church of England.* Edinburgh.
MALTBY, WILLIAM 1982: *La Leyenda Negra. Desarrollo del sentimiento antihispánico 1558–1660.* Méjico: Fondo de Cultura Económica.
MAROTTI, ARTHUR ET AL. (Eds.) 1997: *Texts and Cultural Change in Early Modern England.* New York: St. Martin's Press.

―― 1999: *Catholicism and Anti-Catholicism in Early Modern English Texts.* London: MacMillan.
MARSHALL, SHERRIN 1989: *Women in Reformation and Counter-Reformation Europe: Public and Private Worlds.* Bloomington: Indiana University Press.
MATHESON, PETER 1998: *The Rhetoric of the Reformation.* Edinburgh: T & T Clark.
―― 2000: *The Imaginative World of the Reformation.* Edinburgh: T & T Clark.
MCEACHERN, CLARIE & DEBORA SHUGER. (Eds.) 1997: *Religion and Culture in Renaissance England.* Cambridge: Cambridge University Press.
MCGRATH, PATRICK 1967: *Papists and Puritans under Elizabeth I.* London: Blandford Press.
MEYER, A. O. 1967: *England and the Catholic Church under Elizabeth.* London: Routledge & K. Paul.
MILTON, ANTHONY 1995: *Catholic and Reformed: The Roman and Protestant Churches in English Protestant Thought 1600–1640.* Cambridge: Cambridge University Press.
PATRIDES, C. A. & JOSEPH WITTREICH (Eds.) 1984: *The Apocalypse in English Renaissance Thought and Literature. Patterns, Antecedents and Repercussions.* Ithaca, New York: Cornell University Press.
PILARZ, SCOTT R. 2004: *Robert Southwell, and the Mission of Literature, 1561–1595. Writing Reconciliation.* Aldershot: Ashgate.
PRITCHARD, ARNOLD 1979: *Catholic Loyalism in Elizabethan England.* Chapel Hill: The University of North Carolina Press.
QUESTIER, MICHAEL 1996: *Conversion, Politics and Religion in England, 1580–1625.* Cambridge: Cambridge University Press.
ROSE, ELLIOT 1975: *Cases of Conscience: Alternatives Open to Recusants and Puritans under Elizabeth I and James I.* London, New York, Cambridge: Cambridge University Press.
ROWLANDS, MARIE B. 1985: "Recusant Women, 1560–1640". *Women in English Society, 1500–1800.* Mary Prior (Ed.). London. Methuen. 149–180.
RUPP, GORDON 1969: *Patterns of Reformation.* Philadelphia: Fortress Press.
SALMON, H. J. M. 1959: *The French Religious Wars in English Political Thought.* Oxford: Clarendon Press.
SHAGAN, ETHAN P. 2008: *Popular Politics and the English Reformation.* Cambridge: Cambridge University Press.
SHAW, PATRICIA 1981: *España vista por los ingleses del siglo XVII.* Madrid: Socidad General Española de Librerías, S.A.
SHELL, ALLISON 1999: *Catholicism, Controversy and the English Literary Imagination, 1558–1660.* Cambridge. Cambridge University Press.
STREETE, ADRIAN 2009: *Protestantism and Drama in Early Modern England.* Cambridge: Cambridge University Press.
STRONG, ROY 1977: *The Cult of Elizabeth: Elizabethan Portraiture and Pageantry.* London: Thames & Hudson.
―― 1995: *The Tudor and Stuart Monarchy: Pageantry, Painting, Iconography.* Woodbridge: The Boydell Press.
VALBUENA, OLGA 2003: *Subjects to the King's Divorce: Equivocation,*

Recommended Reading

Infidelity, and Resistance in Early Modern English Literature. Bloomington: Indiana University Press.

WALSHAM, ALEXANDRA 1993: *Church Papists. Catholicism, Conformity and Confessional Polemic in Early Modern England.* New York: The Boydell Press.

—— 1999: *Providence in Early Modern England.* Oxford: Oxford University Press.

WARNER, MARINA 1985: *Alone of All Her Sex: The Myth and the Cult of the Virgin Mary.* London: Pan-Picador.

WARNICKE, RETHA M. 1983: *Women of the English Renaissance and Reformation.* Westport: Greenwood Press.

WATKINS, JOHN 2002: *Representing Elizabeth in Stuart England. Literature, History, Sovereignty.* Cambridge: Cambridge University Press.

WEIR, ALISON 1996: *Children of England. The Heirs of King Henry VIII.* London: Pimlico.

WHITEHEAD, BERTRAND T. 1994: *Brags and Boasts: Propaganda in the Years of the Armada.* Stroud: Sutton.

WHITE, PAUL W. 1993: *Theatre and Reformation. Protestantism, Patronage, and Playing in Tudor England.* Cambridge: Cambridge University Press.

YATES, FRANCES A. 1975: *Astraea. The Imperial Theme in the Sixteenth Century.* London, Boston: Routledge, Kegan Paul.

Index

Alba, Duke of, 72, 148, 196 (n. 21)
Albion Knight (1565), 21–22, 29–32
Allen, William
　An Apology or True Declaration of the Institution and Endeavours of the Two English Colleges, the One in Rome, the Other Now Resident in Rhemes, against Certain Sinister Informations Given up against the Same (1581), 101, 194 (n. 4)
　The Copy of a Letter . . . Concerning the Yielding up of the City of Daventry (1587), 195 (n. 12)
An Answer to the Untruthes Published and Printed in Spain in Glorie of their Supposed Victorie against our English Navie (1589), 126, 203 (n. 97)
Anti-Catholic drama at court, 127–134, 179 (n. 85), 190 (n. 58)
Anticlericalism, 18–20, 59–60, 75–76, 81–82, 168–169, 209 (n. 159)
An Apologie or Defence against the Calumnacion of Certayne Men, which Preferring Wylful Wyll and Carnal Reason before the Playn Trueth of Gods Gospel (Do Slaunder those Men, which for the Better Servinge of God with a more Pure Conscience, according to his Holy Word) Have Abandonned theyr Lives and Vocation, Abydinge as Exiles in Poore Estate oute of theyr Natyve Countrye (1555), 45–46
Arnauld, A., and *The Arrainement of the Whole Societie of Iesuites in France* (1594), 118–119, 200 (n. 64, 68)
Ascham, Robert, and *The Scholemaster* (1570), 141–142, 205 (n. 125), 206 (n. 128)
Ashley, R., *A Comparison of the English and Spanish Nations Composed by a French Gentleman* (1589), 121–122, 202 (n. 79, 82, 86)
Aske, James, and *Elizabetha Triumphans* (1588), 111, 197 (n. 27), 198 (n. 31)

Bale, John
　The Image of Both Churches (1541), 27, 64
　King Johan (1539), 20–21, 24–29, 174 (n. 40, 41, 42, 44), 175 (n. 51), 176 (n. 56, 58), 177 (n. 61, 64)
　The Three Laws (1538), 20, 21, 22, 24–29, 174 (n. 39, 41, 44), 176 (n. 60), 177 (n. 65)
Becon, Thomas, *An Answer to a Certaine Godly Mannes Lettres Desiring his Frendes Iudgement whether it be Lawful for a Christian Man to Be Present at the Popishe Masse, and other Supersticious Services* (1557), 182 (n. 29)
Bell, Thomas, *The Anatomie of the Popish Tirannie* (1603), 116, 118, 199 (n. 51), 200 (n. 64)
Boleyn, Anne, 14
Bonner, Edmund, Bishop, 17, 38, 45, 49, 50, 150
The Books of Kings, and the Tudor Monarchy, 23
The Book of Revelation
　The Woman Clothed with the Sun, the Protestant Church as, 63–64, 186 (n. 16)
　Elizabeth I as, 63, 110
　The Whore of Babylon, Rome as, 20, 63–64, 160–165, 186 (n. 16), 189 (n. 44)
Bullinger, H., *Confutation of the Popes Bull against Elizabeth Queen of England* (1579), 189 (n. 52), 190 (n. 55)
Bunny, Francis, *A Comparison between the Aunciept Fayth of the Romans and the Romish Religion* (1595), 199 (n. 49), 203 (n. 91)

Calvinism, 70–71, 97–99
　Doctrine of Reprobation, *see* Reprobation
Charles V, 8, 13, 39, 180 (n. 6)
Catherine of Aragon, 7–9, 11–12, 14
Catherine De Medici, 135, 137–139, 205 (n. 125)

Index

Catholicism
    and Absolutism, 163, 164, 167
    and Atheism, 136–138, 146
    anti-Catholic discourse as a theatrical device, 82–83, 99, 137, 168–169. 214 (n. 49)
    anti-Catholic discourse as a vehicle for attacks against the crown, 22–23, 74–75, 93–94, 98–99, 163, 164, 168
    the Catholic stereotype, 19–22, 24–25, 64–65, 74–75, 85–86, 96–97, 130–131, 132, 145, 150, 161–162, 168–169, 189 (n. 44)
Catholics, English
    accusations of treason and disloyalty to the Crown, 24, 64–65, 71–72, 73–77, 88–89, 103–104, 119, 159–160, 162–163, 167–168, 204 (n. 101), 214 (n. 45)
    and other European Catholic groups, 72, 102–103, 108
    and the pope, 71–72, 75–76, 108
    and foreign Catholic powers, 28–29, 108
    and education, 89, 195 (n. 11), 198 (n. 41)
    conversions to Protestantism, 86, 101, 200 (n. 66), 192 (n. 81)
    internal divisions among, 69, 113, 198 (n. 40)
    missions, *see* Society of Jesus
    recusants, 69–72, 186 (n. 15), 198 (n. 41)
    repression of, 72, 89, 103–104, 131, 210 (n. 4)
    tolerance towards, 69, 74, 86, 158, 159–160, 186 (n. 15)
Cecil, Robert
    The Copie of a Letter to the Earle of Leycester (1587), 104–106
    A Declaration of the Causes to Give Aide in the Lowe Countries (1584), 106–108
Censorship
    of political and doctrinal pamphlets, 77, 114, 188 (n. 43)
    of political and doctrinal plays, 77, 152, 179 (n. 84), 209 (n. 157)
Chauncie, W., *The Rooting out of the Romishe Supremacie* (1580). 124, 203 (n. 93)
Chilmead (Trad.), *Thomas Campanella an Italian Friar and Second Machiavel* (1660), 120. 201 (n. 76)
A Commission Sent to the Bloudy Butcher Bishop of London, 49
Councils, of the Church
    Council of Trent (1545–1563), 69, 75

    Superiority of the councils over the pope, 13–14
The Contre-Guyse (1589), 138, 206 (n. 130), 207 (n. 136)
Cranmer, Thomas, 14, 17, 25, 183 (n. 41)
    Martyrdom, 43–45
    A Confutation of that Popishe and Antichristian Doctryne which Mainteineth the Ministry on Receiving of Sacrament under one Kind (1557), 182 (n. 29, 31)
Cromwell, Thomas 16, 19, 24–25, 37, 194 (n. 97)
Dekker, Thomas, *The Whore of Babylon* (1607), 159–163, 164–165, 212–214 (n. 21, 22, 23, 24, 25, 26, 27, 28, 32, 34, 35, 36, 39)
Deloney, T., *The Queenes Visiting of the Campe at Tilsburie with her Entertainment There to the Tune of Wilsons Wilde* (1588), 110, 111–112, 197 (n. 27)
The Destruction and Sacke Crueltie Commited by the Duke of Guyse and his Company, in the Towne of Wassy, the Fyrst of Marche, in the year; M.D.L.X.I.I. (1562), 206 (n. 130)
The Downefall of the Iesuits, 116–117, 199 (n. 56)

Edward VI
    Coronation, 16
    First Book of Common Prayer (1549, 1550), 17
    as symbol of English Protestantism, 17–18, Plate 1
Elizabeth I
    Attacks upon and criticisms of, 71, 94, 97, 98–99, 103, 131–132, 133–134, 138–139, 151–152, 158–159, 164–165
    Catholic plots against
        Babington and Parry 103, 164, 204 (n. 101), 214 (n. 49)
        Ridolfi, 72
        Throckmorton, 103
    Controversy over her taste for ceremony and ritual, 186 (n. 15)
    Coronation ceremonies, 62–68
    Cult of Elizabeth, 112–113, 123, 124–126. 128, 131–132, 157, 158–159, 162–163
    Excommunication (1570), 71–72, 75–76, 88, 194
    Foreign Policy
        towards France, 70, 89, 126

Index

towards the Low Countries, 70, 89, 106–108, 146–149, 214 (n. 40)
towards Scotland, 70–72, 126
towards Spain, and war, 99, 100, 106–113, 119–123, 126, 132–133, 136, 160, 165, 200 (n. 71)
Iconography
Astraea, 115, 125, 203 (n. 96)
Constantine, 76, 123, Plate 3
Deborah, 67
Gloriana, 112–114, 198 (n. 34, 46)
Populism, 63, 111–112, 163–164, 214 (n. 40)
Providentialism, 104–106, 126, 155–156
successor to Charles V, 112, 123
symbol of English Protestantism, 64–65, 90–92, 104–106, 129–130, 157–158, 161–167, 214 (n. 40)
as victim, 104–106, 133–134, 161, 214 (n. 40)
Legitimacy, 62, 67–68
Prisoner of Mary I, 40
Nostalgia for, 157–159
Succession problem, 113, 114, 131–132, 140, 149
Erasmus, and Erasmian Humanism, 15, 78, 84, 87, 88, 90
Estienne, Henry, *A Mervaylous Discourse upon the Lyfe, Deedes, and Behaviours of Katherine de Medicis, Queene Mother, wherin are Displayed the Meanes which She had Practised to Atteyne unto the Usurping of the Kingedome of France, and to the Bringing of the Estate of the Same unto Utter Ruine and Destruction* (1575) 205 (n. 125), 206 (n. 126), 207 (n. 132)
An Exhortacion to all English Subiects to Ioine for the Defence of Queene Elizabeth and their Native Country (1588), 109, 110, 197 (n. 25, 29)

Foxe, John, *Actes and Monuments* (1563), 43, 76, 161, 180 (n. 10), 181 (n. 16)
on Bishop Bonner, 183 (n. 38)
on Elizabeth I, 76–77, 212 (n.26)
on Lady Jane Grey, 182 (n. 35)
on the martyrdom of Latimer, Ridley and Cranmer, 43–45
on the Entry of Mary I and Philip II into London, 180 (n. 10)
on Philip II, 42, 183 (n. 42)
A Fig for the Spaniard (1591), 121
Fulke, William, *An Answer of a True Christian to a Counterfeit Catholike* (1577), 189 (n. 44)

Gardiner, Stephen, Bishop, 17, 38, 45, 49–50, 150
Garnett, Henry, 159, 211 (n. 15)
Gascoigne, George
The Glass of Government (1575), 78, 87–90
The Spoyle of Antwerpe Faithfully Reported by a True Englishman who was Present at the Same (1576), 146
Gentillet, I., *A Discours upon the Meanes of Vuel Governing and Maintaining in Good Peace, a Kingdome, or Other Principalitie* (1602), 205 (n. 125)
Greene, R., *The Spanish Masquerado* (1589), 119–120, 201 (n. 72)
Gresham, Sir Thomas, 165, 214 (n. 49)
Grey, Lady Jane
Imprisonment and execution, 39
as Protestant martyr, 48, 182 (n. 35)
Queen of England, 38
Guise, House of, French Catholic family, and Duke of Guise, 70, 106, 135–141
Guise, Marie de, Queen-Regent of Scotland, 184 (n. 46)
Gwalther, Rudolph, *Antichrist* (1556), 50–51, 183 (n. 41)

Henry VIII
Act of Dissolution of monastic orders, 16, 19
Act of Supremacy (1534), 7, 15, 19
Defensor Fidei, 8
Divorce, 8–15
Theological arguments for the divorce: *A Glass of the Truth* (1532) and *Articles Devisid* (1533), 9–15
Dispensations of 1503 and 1528, 11
Trials before Papal Court (1529, 1530), 12
Statute in Restraint of Appeals (to Rome), 14
Privilegium Angliae, 12
Royal iconoclasm, 16
Henry Stuart, Prince, symbol of English Protestantism, 165, 212 (n. 23), 214 (n. 48)
Heywood, Thomas
If You Know not Me You Know Nobody (I, 1605, II, 1606), 159, 160, 163, 165–167, 212 (n. 24, 25, 26), 213 (n. 31, 36), 214 (n. 40, 44, 45), 215 (n. 50)
An History Briefly Contayninge that whiche Hath Happened sens the Departure of the House of Guise... from the Court Being at St.

222

Index

Germaines, until this Present (1562), 206 (n. 130)
Hooper, John, *Whether Christian Faith Maye Be Kepte in Secret in the Heart, without Confession thereof Openly* (1555), 46–47, 182 (n. 28)
Huguenots, 70–71, 89, 134–135, 140, 205 (n. 125), 206 (n. 130)
The Hunting and Finding out of the Romish Fox (1543), 22–24, 174 (n. 41), 175 (n. 45, 50)
Hurault, M., *A Discourse upon the Present Estate of France* (1592), 138, 206 (n. 130), 207 (n. 134, 136, 138)

Impacient Poverty (1547), 32–33
Imperial theory, 12–13, 15, 29, 76–77, 100, 111–113, 114, 123–126, 132–133, 152, 154, 155–156, 161, 163, 165–167
Ioful Song of the Royall Receiving of the Queenes Most Excellent Maiestie into her Higness Campe at Tilsburie in Essex (1588), 197 (n. 27)

James I
  Absolutism, 163–164
  Attacks upon and criticisms of, 158, 159, 160, 163, 164–167
  Gunpowder Plot, 159–160
  Peace with Spain, 158, 159–160
  Religious policy, 158–160, 161, 164, 165

Knox, John, 53, 65, 70, 184 (n. 46), 187 (n. 19)
  The First Blast of the Trumpet against the Monstruous Regiment of Women (1558), 53–55, 65
Kyd, Thomas, *The Spanish Tragedy*, 127, 134, 141–146, 203 (n. 88), 208–209 (n. 141–150), 213 (n. 27)
Kyffin, M., *The Blessedness of Brytain as a Celebration of the Queenes Holyday* (1588), 109, 111, 197 (n. 28), 198 (n. 30)

A Larum for London (1602), 127, 134, 146–149
Latimer, John, 179 (n. 2)
  Martyrdom of, 43
Lewkenor, L., *The Estate of the English Fugitives* (1596), 116, 125, 199 (n. 54), 200 (n. 65)
The Life of Sir John Oldcastle (1600), 127, 134, 149–152, 209–210 (n. 158–163)
Lollards and Lollardism, 18–19, 20, 24, 29, 150, 152

Low Countries
  Commercial rivalry with England, 59–60
  Revolt against Spain, 70, 106–108, 146–149, 196 (n. 20)
Lupton, Thomas, *All for Money* (1559–1570), 78, 79–83, 192 (n. 81), 215 (n. 50)
Luther, Martin, 7–8
  Conflict with Henry VIII, 8
  De Captivate Babylonia (1520), 8
Lyly, John
  Endymion, the Man in the Moon (1591), 127–132
  Midas (1592), 128, 132–134, 203 (n. 88)
Lynne, Walter, *The Beginning and Endyng of all Popery* (1548), 20, 174 (n. 38)

Machiavelli, Niccolò, and Machiavellianism, 52, 115–117, 135, 136, 137, 140–146, 189 (n. 52), 206 (n. 128)
Marlowe, Christopher, *The Massacre at Paris* (1594?), 127, 134–140
Marten, A., *An Exhortation to Stirre up the Mindes of all her Maiesties Faithfull Subiects, to Defend their Country in this Dangerous Time, from the Invasion of the Enemies* (1588), 110, 197 (n. 27, 29)
Mary I
  Attacks upon and criticisms of, 45–49, 52–55, 83, 91, 139, 163, 192 (n. 77), 212 (n. 24)
  Marriage to Philip II, 39–40, 52, 58–60, 180 (n. 5, 6)
  Pregnancy, 48
  Religious persecution, 43–45, 83, 212 (n. 22, 24)
  Restoration of Catholicism, 38–39, 43
  Royal Entry into London, 40–42
Mary Queen of Scots
  Abdication and flight to England, 71
  Accusations of treason, 72, 103, 104–106, 164, 205 (n. 123)
  Attacks upon and criticisms of, 53–55, 139
  Dynastic rights to the throne of England, 70–71
  Execution, 104–106, 131, 204 (n. 101)
  Queen of France and Scotland, 70–71
  Symbol of Catholicism in England, 72, 90, 103–106
Melanchthon, Philip
  Of the Two Wonderful Popish Monsters to Wyt, of a Popish Asse which was Found at Rome in the River of Tyber, and of a Monkish

Calfe, Calved at Friberge in Misne (1579), 75–76, 189–190 (n. 52, 53, 54)
A Faithful Admonition of a Certeyne True Pastor and Prophete Sent unto the Germanes (1554), 48, 51, 182 (n. 31)
Mornay, P., *A Necessary Discours Concerning the Right which the House of Guyse Pretendeth to the Crowne of France* (1586), 206 (n. 130)

Naogeorg, T., *The Popish Kingdome, or Reigne of Antichrist* (1570), 189–190 (n. 52, 53)
Netherlands, *see* Low Countries
New Custom (1573), 78–79, 97–99, 189 (n. 44)
Northumberland, Duke of, 17, 38–39, 56, 185 (n. 55)
Norton, Thomas, *A Warning against the Dangerous Practices of Papistes* (1569), 74, 189 (n. 45)

Old, John, *A Short Description of Antichrist unto the Nobilitie of England* (1555), 43, 50, 181 (n. 22)
Orange, William of, 103, 106, 147, 196 (n. 21)
The Apology or Defence of the Most Noble Prince William, by the Grace of God, Prince of Orange against the Proclamation and Edict, Published by the King of Spain, by which he Proscribeth the Said Lorde, wherby shall Appeare the Slaunders and False Accusations, Conteyned in the Said Proscription (1581), 120, 121, 122, 201 (n. 73)
A Supplication to the Kinges Maiestie of Spayne (1573), 196 (n. 21)
An Oration Militarie to all Natural Englishmen. Whether Protestants, or Otherwise in Religion Affected, so Move Resolution in these Dangerous Times (1588), 200–201 (n. 71, 73, 75)

A Pageant of Spanish Humours wherin are Naturally Described and Lively Portrayed the Kinds and Quallities of a Signior of Spain (1599), 121, 122, 201 (n. 74)
Pamphlet literature, and its influence, 2–4
   Anonymity, 2
   Printing and distribution, 2–4
   Relation to dramatic literature, 3

Persons, Robert, 101, 116–118, 160, 212 (n. 17)
A Brief Censure upon Two Books (1581), 195 (n. 5)
A Briefe Discourse Containing Certain Reasons why Catholics Refuse to Go to Church (1580), 195 (n. 5)
"Confessio Fidei" (1580), 101, 194 (n. 3)
Elizabethae (1592), 118, 199 (n. 61)
A Treatise Tending to the Mitigation tovvardes Catholike-subiectes in England Wherin is Declared that it is not Impossible for Subiects of Different Religion (Especially Catholiks and Protestantes) to Live Together in Dutifull Obedience and Subiections, under the Government of his Maiesty of Great Britany (1607), 116–117, 119 (n. 57)
Phanit, Tharua, *A Letter Written by a French Gentleman to a Friend of his at Rome Conteynyng a True Report of the Late Treaty between the Queene Mother of France ad the King of Navarre* (1587), 207 (n. 132, 134, 138)
Philip II, King of Spain
   and the Low Countries, 70, 106–108, 146–149
   Attacks upon and criticisms of, 52, 119–120, 133, 183 (n. 42), 200 (n. 71), 201 (n. 78)
   English prejudices towards, 41–42, 51–52, 58, 60, 185 (n. 59)
   Marriage to Mary I, 39–40, 52, 58–60, 180 (n. 5, 6)
   Mediator between Elizabeth and Mary I, 213 (n. 36)
   Opposition to religious persecution, 52
   Relations with the papacy, 52, 108, 120–121, 200 (n. 71)
Phillips, John, *A Frendly Larum or Faithful Warnynge to the True Hearted Subiectes of England Discovering the Actes, and Malicious Myndes of those Obstinate and Rebellious Papistes that Hope (as they Terme it) to Have their Golden Day* (1569), 73–74
Popes, and the papacy
   Defence of papal supremacy, 103, 200 (n. 68)
   Excommunication of Elizabeth I and attitudes towards her government, 71–72, 73–77, 108
   and Gunpowder Plot, 160, 211–212 (n. 16, 17)
   Relations with Spain, Charles V and

Index

Philip II, 8, 52, 108, 120–121, 200 (n. 71)
Types of anti-papal discourse
  Abuse of the Confessional, 28–29, 119
  Aggression and abuse of power, 9, 12–14, 25–26, 50, 115, 125, 161, 173 (n. 20, 23), 176 (n. 60), 200 (n. 71), 206 (n. 128)
  Ambition, cruelty and tyranny, 20, 24–28, 75–77, 119, 173 (n. 33), 200 (n. 68)
  as the cause of disputes between Christian monarchs and peoples, 13–14, 28, 75–77, 118–119, 120, 200 (n. 68)
  Deception, corruption and idolatry, 14, 19–21, 22, 64, 84–86, 136, 174 (n. 42), 176 (n. 56)
  Deviation from Divine Law and the word of God, 14, 19–21, 64–66, 84–85, 124, 183 (n. 41)
  Pride, 75–76
Protestantism, English
  Discourse of victimhood, 45–47, 66, 83–84, 99, 100, 149–152, 161
  Education, 86–91, 92–93, 96–99, 194 (n. 97)
  English Protestants in exile, 39, 45–48
  Iconoclasm, 16, 75, 97
  Providencialism, 109–113
  Restorer of the Word of God, image of, 66
  as chosen people (New Israel), image of, 67, 83
  True Church, image of, 64–68
Puritanism, English, 73, 97–99, 113–114
  Accusations of sedition, 114
  Attacks from the Church of England, 100, 114
  Attacks upon the Church of England, 68–69, 97–99, 113–114, 194 (n. 101, 102, 103)
  Relations with other European Calvinist groups, 199 (n. 44)

Rankins, William, *The English Ape* (1588), 141, 208 (n. 144)
Reprobation, doctrine of, 84, 87, 88, 90
Ridley, Nicholas, 38, 179 (n. 2)
  Martyrdom, 43–45
  Certen Godly, Learned and Comfortable Conferences (1556), 182 (n. 27, 33)

Scotland
  Conflict over French influence, 70–71
  Religious revolts, 71

Scottish influence at court of James I, 158–159
Society of Jesus
  and civil disobedience, 101–103, 113
  and other Catholic groups, 113, 115, 117–118
  and the papacy, 101–102, 119, 162, 199 (n. 50), 200 (n. 68)
  and regicide, 14, 102–104, 118–119
  and Spain, 101–102, 119, 162
  Casuistry, 116–117, 199 (n. 53)
  Colleges in Europe, 72, 102, 113, 198 (n. 41), 199 (n. 53)
  'Equivocation', 116–119
  Missions to England, 72, 101–103, 113, 117–118, 199 (n. 53), 200 (n. 66)
  Stereotype of the Jesuit, 115–119, 189 (n. 52),
Spain
  Relation to Italian and Machiavellian stereotypes, 52, 136, 141–142
  Relations with the papacy, 39, 51–52, 77, 100, 108, 119–120, 161–163, 168–169
  Spanish Armada, 100, 108–113, 120–122, 123, 125, 126, 132–134, 160, 165, 167, 196 (n. 23), 197 (n. 24, 25, 27, 28, 29), 198 (n. 37), 200 (n. 71), 202 (n. 83, 84, 86)
  Stereotype of Spaniards, 51, 106–108, 119–123, 132–134, 141–146, 153–155, 162, 168–169, 183 (n. 42), 202 (n. 87)
The Serpent of Division, Whych hath Ever Bene Yet the Chefest Undoer of any Region or Citie (1559), 189 (n. 50)
Skinner, Vincent, *A Discovery and Playne Declaration of Sundry Subtill Practices of the Holy Inquisition of Spayne* (1569), 189 (n. 49)
Somerset, Duke of, 17
Southwell, Robert, 104, 117
  An Epistle of Comfort to the Reverend Priest and to the Honourable Worshipful and Other of the Lay Sort Restrained in Durance for the Catholic Faith (1587), 104, 196 (n. 16)
  A Humble Supplication to her Maiestie, 117, 199 (n. 60)
Spenser, Edmund, *The Fairie Queene* (1590, 1596), 162, 165, 198 (n. 34), 214 (n. 47)
A Summe of the Guisyan Ambassage to the Bishop of Rome (1579), 206 (n. 130)

Theory of the Two Churches, 27–29
Traheron, B., *A Warning to England to*

Index

Repente and to Turne to God from Idolatrie and Poperi (1558), 47, 48, 49, 182 (n. 30)

A Treatise Paraenetical, that is to Say: an Exhortation, wherin is Shewed by Good and Evident Reasons Infallible Arguments, most True and Certaine Histories and Notable Examples; the Right Way & True Meanes to Resist the Violence of the Castilian King (1598), 120, 121, 122, 201 (n. 74)

A Treatise Wherin Christ and his Teachinges are Compared with the Pope and his Doinges (1534), 174 (n. 41)

A True and Perfect Description of a Straunge Monster Borne in Rome in 1585 (1590), 120, 121, 122, 201 (n. 73)

Turner, William, *The Hunting of the Fox and the Wolfe* (1568), 49, 50, 183 (n. 36)

Tymme, Thomas, *A Preparation against the Prognosticated Dangers of this Yeare* (1588), 109, 110, 197 (n. 24), 198 (n. 30)

Udall, Nicholas
  Iacob and Esau (1550–1557?), 34–37, 178 (n. 78)
  Respublica (1553), 56–58, 184–185 (n. 51–57)

Varamund, Ernest, *A True and Plaine Report of the Furious Outrages of France* (1573–1574), 205 (n. 122)

Wager, Lewis, *The Life and Repentaunce of Marie Magdelene* (1558), 78, 79, 90–97

Wager, William
  Enough is as Good as a Feast (1559–1570), 75, 78, 79–87, 189 (n. 44, 52), 190 (n. 65), 191 (n. 70, 71, 74), 215 (n. 50)
  The Longest Thou Livest the More Fool Thou Are (1559), 78, 79, 83–86, 190 (n. 60), 191 (n. 76), 192 (n. 80)

Welth and Helth (1553–1555?), 56, 58–60, 185 (n. 58, 59)

Willet, A., *A Catholicon or Remedie against the Pseudocatholike Religion* (1602), 203 (n. 91)

Wilson, Robert, *The Three Lords and Three Ladies of London*, 127, 152–155, 202 (n. 80, 87), 210 (n. 166)

Wolsey, Cardinal Thomas, 7, 12

Wright, Leonard, *The Hunting of Antichrist* (1589), 123, 203 (n. 91)

Wyatt, Sir Thomas, rebellion led by, 39–40, 180 (n. 8)

Xenophobia, 51, 81, 141–142, 146, 153–155, 205 (n. 125)